Portable Edition | Book 5   Fifth Edition

ART HISTORY

A View of the World: Part Two

MARILYN STOKSTAD

Judith Harris Murphy Distinguished Professor of Art History Emerita
The University of Kansas

MICHAEL W. COTHREN

Scheuer Family Professor of Humanities
Department of Art, Swarthmore College

PEARSON

Boston   Columbus   Indianapolis   New York   San Francisco   Upper Saddle River
Amsterdam   Cape Town   Dubai   London   Madrid   Milan   Munich   Paris   Montréal   Toronto
Delhi   Mexico City   São Paulo   Sydney   Hong Kong   Seoul   Singapore   Taipei   Tokyo

Editorial Director: Craig Campanella
Editor in Chief: Sarah Touborg
Senior Sponsoring Editor: Helen Ronan
Editorial Assistant: Victoria Engros
Vice-President, Director of Marketing: Brandy Dawson
Executive Marketing Manager: Kate Mitchell
Marketing Assistant: Paige Patunas
Managing Editor: Melissa Feimer
Project Managers: Barbara Cappuccio and Marlene Gassler
Senior Operations Supervisor: Mary Fischer
Operations Specialist: Diane Peirano
Media Director: Brian Hyland
Senior Media Editor: David Alick
Media Project Manager: Rich Barnes
Pearson Imaging Center: Corin Skidds
Printer/Binder: Courier / Kendallville
Cover Printer: Lehigh-Phoenix Color / Hagerstown

This book was designed by
Laurence King Publishing Ltd, London
www.laurenceking.com

Editorial Manager: Kara Hattersley-Smith
Senior Editor: Clare Double
Production Manager: Simon Walsh
Page Design: Nick Newton
Cover Design: Jo Fernandes
Picture Researcher: Evi Peroulaki
Copy Editor: Jennifer Speake
Indexer: Vicki Robinson

Cover image: *Jahangir and Prince Khurram Feasted by Nur Jahan*, Mughal period, 1617. Paint and gold on paper, 9¹⁵⁄₁₆″ × 5⅝″ (25.2 × 14.3 cm). Freer Gallery of Art, Smithsonian Institution, Washington, DC.

Credits and acknowledgments borrowed from other sources and reproduced, with permission, in this textbook appear on the appropriate page within text or on the credit pages in the back of this book.

Library of Congress Cataloging-in-Publication Data
Stokstad, Marilyn
   Art history / Marilyn Stokstad, Judith Harris Murphy Distinguished
Professor of Art History Emerita, The University of Kansas, Michael W.
Cothren, Scheuer Family Professor of Humanities, Department of Art,
Swarthmore College. -- Fifth edition.
      pages cm
   Includes bibliographical references and index.
   ISBN-13: 978-0-205-87347-0 (hardcover)
   ISBN-10: 0-205-87347-2 (hardcover)
1. Art--History--Textbooks. I. Cothren, Michael Watt. II. Title.
N5300.S923 2013
709--dc23
                         2012027450

10 9 8 7 6 5 4 3 2 1

Prentice Hall
is an imprint of

PEARSON

www.pearsonhighered.com

ISBN 10:   0-205-87380-4
ISBN 13: 978-0-205-87380-7

Contents

Give Your Students Choices

ORDERING OPTIONS

Pearson arts titles are available in the following formats to give you and your students more choices—and more ways to save.

MyArtsLab with eText: the Pearson eText lets students access their textbook anytime, anywhere, and any way they want, including listening online or downloading to an iPad.

MyArtsLab with eText Combined: 0-205-88736-8
MyArtsLab with eText Volume I: 0-205-94839-1
MyArtsLab with eText Volume II: 0-205-94846-4

Build your own Pearson Custom e-course material. Pearson offers the first eBook-building platform that empowers educators with the freedom to search, choose, and seamlessly integrate multimedia. *Contact your Pearson representative to get started.*

The **Books à la Carte edition** offers a convenient, three-hole-punched, loose-leaf version of the traditional text at a discounted price—allowing students to take only what they need to class. Books à la Carte editions are available both with and without access to MyArtsLab.

Books à la Carte edition Volume I: 0-205-93840-X
Books à la Carte edition Volume I plus MyArtsLab: 0-205-93847-7
Books à la Carte edition Volume II: 0-205-93844-2
Books à la Carte edition Volume II plus MyArtsLab: 0-205-93846-9

The **CourseSmart eTextbook** offers the same content as the printed text in a convenient online format—with highlighting, online search, and printing capabilities. **www.coursesmart.com**

Art History **Portable edition** has all of the same content as the comprehensive text in six slim volumes. If your survey course is Western, the Portable Edition is available in value-package combinations to suit Western-focused courses (Books 1, 2, 4, and 6). Portable Edition volumes are also available individually for period or region specific courses.

Book 1 – Ancient Art (Chapters 1–6): 978-0-205-87376-0
Book 2 – Medieval Art (Chapters 7–9, 15–18): 978-0-205-87377-7
Book 3 – A View of the World, Part One (Chapters 9–14): 978-0-205-87378-4
Book 4 – Fourteenth to Seventeenth Century Art (Chapters 18–23): 978-0-205-87379-1
Book 5 – A View of the World, Part Two (Chapters 24–29): 978-0-205-87380-7
Book 6 – Eighteenth to Twenty-first Century Art (Chapters 30–33): 978-0-205-87756-0

INSTRUCTOR RESOURCES

All of our instructor resources are found on MyArtsLab and are available to faculty who adopt *Art History*. These resources include:

PowerPoints featuring nearly every image in the book, with captions and without captions.

Teaching with MyArtsLab PowerPoints help instructors make their lectures come alive. These slides allow instructors to display the very best rich media from MyArtsLab in the classroom—quickly and easily.

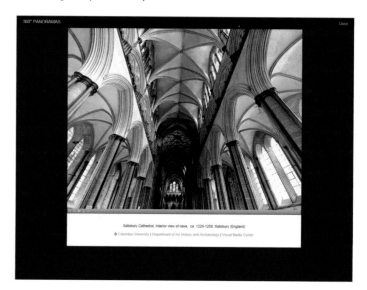

Instructor's Manual and Test Item File
This is an invaluable professional resource and reference for new and experienced faculty.

The Class Preparation Tool collects these and other presentation resources in one convenient online destination.

Use Notes

The various features of this book reinforce each other, helping the reader to become comfortable with terminology and concepts that are specific to art history.

Starter Kit and Introduction The Starter Kit is a highly concise primer of basic concepts and tools. The Introduction explores the way they are used to come to an understanding of the history of art.

Captions There are two kinds of captions in this book: short and long. Short captions identify information specific to the work of art or architecture illustrated:

> artist (when known)
> title or descriptive name of work
> date
> original location (if moved to a museum or other site)
> material or materials a work is made of
> size (height before width) in feet and inches, with meters and
>   centimeters in parentheses
> present location

The order of these elements varies, depending on the type of work illustrated. Dimensions are not given for architecture, for most wall paintings, or for most architectural sculpture. Some captions have one or more lines of small print below the identification section of the caption that gives museum or collection information. This is rarely required reading; its inclusion is often a requirement for gaining permission to reproduce the work.

Longer, discursive captions contain information that complements the narrative of the main text.

Definitions of Terms You will encounter the basic terms of art history in three places:

> **In the Text,** where words appearing in boldface type are defined, or glossed, at their first use.
>
> **In Boxed Features,** on technique and other subjects, where labeled drawings and diagrams visually reinforce the use of terms.
>
> **In the Glossary,** at the end of the volume (p. 905), which contains all the words in boldface type in the text and boxes.

Maps At the beginning of each chapter you will find a map with all the places mentioned in the chapter.

Boxes Special material that complements, enhances, explains, or extends the narrative text is set off in six types of tinted boxes.

Art and Its Contexts and A Broader Look boxes expand on selected works or issues related to the text. A Closer Look boxes use leader-line captions to focus attention on specific aspects of important works. Elements of Architecture boxes clarify specifically architectural features, often explaining engineering principles or building technology. Technique boxes outline the techniques and processes by which certain types of art are created. Recovering the Past boxes highlight the work of archaeologists who uncover and conservators who assure the preservation and clear presentation of art.

Bibliography The bibliography at the end of this book beginning on page 914 contains books in English, organized by general works and by chapter, that are basic to the study of art history today, as well as works cited in the text.

Learn About It Placed at the beginning of each chapter, this feature captures in bulleted form the key learning objectives, or outcomes, of the chapter. They point to what will have been accomplished upon its completion.

Think About It These critical thinking questions appear at the end of each chapter and help students assess their mastery of the learning objectives (Learn About It) by asking them to think through and apply what they have learned.

MyArtsLab prompts These notations are found throughout the chapter and are keyed to MyArtsLab resources that enrich and reinforce student learning.

Dates, Abbreviations, and Other Conventions This book uses the designations BCE and CE, abbreviations for "Before the Common Era" and "Common Era," instead of BC ("Before Christ") and AD ("Anno Domini," "the year of our Lord"). The first century BCE is the period from 99 BCE to 1 BCE; the first century CE is from the year 1 CE to 99 CE. Similarly, the second century CE is the period from 199 BCE to 100 BCE; the second century CE extends from 100 CE to 199 CE.

100's	99–1	1–99	100's
second century BCE	first century BCE	first century CE	second century CE

Circa ("about") is used with approximate dates, spelled out in the text and abbreviated to "c." in the captions. This indicates that an exact date is not yet verified.

An illustration is called a "figure," or "fig." Thus, figure 6–7 is the seventh numbered illustration in Chapter 6, and fig. Intro-3 is the third figure in the Introduction. There are two types of figures: photographs of artworks or of models, and line drawings. Drawings are used when a work cannot be photographed or when a diagram or simple drawing is the clearest way to illustrate an object or a place.

When introducing artists, we use the words *active* and *documented* with dates, in addition to "b." (for "born") and "d." (for "died"). "Active" means that an artist worked during the years given. "Documented" means that documents link the person to that date.

Accents are used for words in French, German, Italian, and Spanish only. With few exceptions, names of cultural institutions in Western European countries are given in the form used in that country.

Titles of Works of Art It was only over the last 500 years that paintings and works of sculpture created in Europe and North America were given formal titles, either by the artist or by critics and art historians. Such formal titles are printed in italics. In other traditions and cultures, a single title is not important or even recognized.

In this book we use formal descriptive titles of artworks where titles are not established. If a work is best known by its non-English title, such as Manet's *Le Déjeuner sur l'Herbe (The Luncheon on the Grass)*, the original language precedes the translation.

Starter Kit

Art history focuses on the visual arts—painting, drawing, sculpture, prints, photography, ceramics, metalwork, architecture, and more. This Starter Kit contains basic information and addresses concepts that underlie and support the study of art history. It provides a quick reference guide to the vocabulary used to classify and describe art objects. Understanding these terms is indispensable because you will encounter them again and again in reading, talking, and writing about art.

Let us begin with the basic properties of art. A work of art is a material object having both form and content. It is often described and categorized according to its *style* and *medium*.

FORM

Referring to purely visual aspects of art and architecture, the term *form* encompasses qualities of *line, shape, color, light, texture, space, mass, volume,* and *composition.* These qualities are known as *formal elements.* When art historians use the term *formal,* they mean "relating to form."

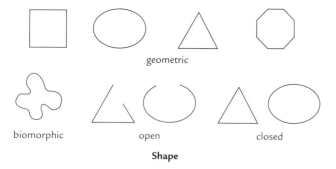

geometric

biomorphic   open   closed

Shape

Line and **shape** are attributes of form. Line is an element—usually drawn or painted—the length of which is so much greater than the width that we perceive it as having only length. Line can be actual, as when the line is visible, or it can be implied, as when the movement of the viewer's eyes over the surface of a work follows a path determined by the artist. Shape, on the other hand, is the two-dimensional, or flat, area defined by the borders of an enclosing *outline* or *contour.* Shape can be *geometric, biomorphic* (suggesting living things; sometimes called *organic*), *closed,* or *open.* The *outline* or *contour* of a three-dimensional object can also be perceived as line.

Color has several attributes. These include *hue, value,* and *saturation.*

Hue is what we think of when we hear the word *color,* and the terms are interchangeable. We perceive hues as the result of differing wavelengths of electromagnetic energy. The visible spectrum, which can be seen in a rainbow, runs from red through violet. When the ends of the spectrum are connected through the hue red-violet, the result may be diagrammed as a color wheel. The primary hues (numbered 1) are red, yellow, and blue. They are known as primaries because all other colors are made by combining these hues. Orange, green, and violet result from the mixture of two primaries and are known as secondary hues (numbered 2). Intermediate hues, or tertiaries (numbered 3), result from the mixture of a primary and a secondary. Complementary colors are the two colors directly opposite one

another on the color wheel, such as red and green. Red, orange, and yellow are regarded as warm colors and appear to advance toward us. Blue, green, and violet, which seem to recede, are called cool colors. Black and white are not considered colors but neutrals; in terms of light, black is understood as the absence of color and white as the mixture of all colors.

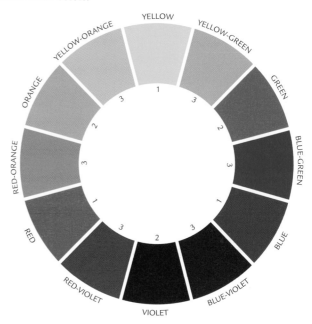

Value is the relative degree of lightness or darkness of a given color and is created by the amount of light reflected from an object's surface. A dark green has a deeper value than a light green, for example. In black-and-white reproductions of colored objects, you see only value, and some artworks—for example, a drawing made with black ink—possess only value, not hue or saturation.

Value scale from white to black.

+ WHITE   PURE HUE   + BLACK

Value variation in red.

Saturation, also sometimes referred to as *intensity*, is a color's quality of brightness or dullness. A color described as highly saturated looks vivid and pure; a hue of low saturation may look a little muddy or grayed.

PURE HUE   DULLED   PURE HUE

Intensity scale from bright to dull.

Texture, another attribute of form, is the tactile (or touch-perceived) quality of a surface. It is described by words such as *smooth*, *polished*, *rough*, *prickly*, *grainy*, or *oily*. Texture takes two forms: the texture of the actual surface of the work of art and the implied (illusionistically described) surface of objects represented in the work of art.

Space is what contains forms. It may be actual and three-dimensional, as it is with sculpture and architecture, or it may be fictional, represented illusionistically in two dimensions, as when artists represent recession into the distance on a flat surface—such as a wall or a canvas—by using various systems of perspective.

Mass and volume are properties of three-dimensional things. Mass is solid matter—whether sculpture or architecture—that takes up space. Volume is enclosed or defined space, and may be either solid or hollow. Like space, mass and volume may be illusionistically represented on a two-dimensional surface, such as in a painting or a photograph.

Composition is the organization, or arrangement, of forms in a work of art. Shapes and colors may be repeated or varied, balanced symmetrically or asymmetrically; they may be stable or dynamic. The possibilities are nearly endless and artistic choice depends both on the

time and place where the work was created as well as the objectives of individual artists. Pictorial depth (spatial recession) is a specialized aspect of composition in which the three-dimensional world is represented on a flat surface, or *picture plane*. The area "behind" the picture plane is called the *picture space* and conventionally contains three "zones": *foreground*, *middle ground*, and *background*.

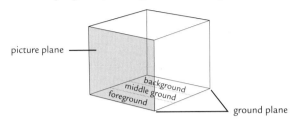

Various techniques for conveying a sense of pictorial depth have been devised by artists in different cultures and at different times. A number of them are diagrammed here. In some European art, the use of various systems of *perspective* has sought to create highly convincing illusions of recession into space. At other times and in other cultures, indications of recession are actually suppressed or avoided to emphasize surface rather than space.

TECHNIQUE | Pictorial Devices for Depicting Recession in Space

overlapping

In overlapping, partially covered elements are meant to be seen as located behind those covering them.

diminution

In diminution of scale, successively smaller elements are perceived as being progressively farther away than the largest ones.

vertical perspective

Vertical perspective stacks elements, with the higher ones intended to be perceived as deeper in space.

atmospheric perspective

Through atmospheric perspective, objects in the far distance (often in bluish-gray hues) have less clarity than nearer objects. The sky becomes paler as it approaches the horizon.

divergent perspective   intuitive perspective

In divergent or reverse perspective, forms widen slightly and imaginary lines called orthogonals diverge as they recede in space.

Intuitive perspective takes the opposite approach from divergent perspective. Forms become narrower and orthogonals converge the farther they are from the viewer, approximating the optical experience of spatial recession.

linear perspective

Linear perspective (also called scientific, mathematical, one-point and Renaissance perspective) is a rationalization or standardization of intuitive perspective that was developed in fifteenth-century Italy. It uses mathematical formulas to construct images in which all elements are shaped by, or arranged along, orthogonals that converge in one or more vanishing points on a horizon line.

CONTENT

Content includes *subject matter*, but not all works of art have subject matter. Many buildings, paintings, sculptures, and other art objects include no recognizable references to things in nature nor to any story or historical situation, focusing instead on lines, colors, masses, volumes, and other formal elements. However, all works of art—even those without recognizable subject matter—have content, or meaning, insofar as they seek to communicate ideas, convey feelings, or affirm the beliefs and values of their makers, their patrons, and usually the people who originally viewed or used them.

Content may derive from the social, political, religious, and economic *contexts* in which a work was created, the *intention* of the artist, and the *reception* of the work by beholders (the audience). Art historians, applying different methods of *interpretation*, often arrive at different conclusions regarding the content of a work of art, and single works of art can contain more than one meaning because they are occasionally directed at more than one audience.

The study of subject matter is called *iconography* (literally, "the writing of images") and includes the identification of *symbols* —images that take on meaning through association, resemblance, or convention.

STYLE

Expressed very broadly, *style* is the combination of form and composition that makes a work distinctive. *Stylistic analysis* is one of art history's most developed practices, because it is how art historians recognize the work of an individual artist or the characteristic manner of groups of artists working in a particular time or place. Some of the most commonly used terms to discuss *artistic styles* include *period style*, *regional style*, *representational style*, *abstract style*, *linear style*, and *painterly style*.

Period style refers to the common traits detectable in works of art and architecture from a particular historical era. It is good practice not to use the words "style" and "period" interchangeably. Style is the sum of many influences and characteristics, including the period of its creation. An example of proper usage is "an American house from the Colonial period built in the Georgian style."

Regional style refers to stylistic traits that persist in a geographic region. An art historian whose specialty is medieval art can recognize Spanish style through many successive medieval periods and can distinguish individual objects created in medieval Spain from other medieval objects that were created in, for example, Italy.

Representational styles are those that describe the appearance of recognizable subject matter in ways that make it seem lifelike.

Realism and **Naturalism** are terms that some people used interchangeably to characterize artists' attempts to represent the observable world in a manner that appears to describe its visual appearance accurately. When capitalized, Realism refers to a specific period style discussed in Chapter 31.

Idealization strives to create images of physical perfection according to the prevailing values or tastes of a culture. The artist may work in a representational style and idealize it to capture an underlying value or expressive effect.

Illusionism refers to a highly detailed style that seeks to create a convincing illusion of physical reality by describing its visual appearance meticulously.

Abstract styles depart from mimicking lifelike appearance to capture the essence of a form. An abstract artist may work from nature or from a memory image of nature's forms and colors, which are simplified, stylized, perfected, distorted, elaborated, or otherwise transformed to achieve a desired expressive effect.

Nonrepresentational (or Nonobjective) Art is a term often used for works of art that do not aim to produce recognizable natural imagery.

Expressionism refers to styles in which the artist exaggerates aspects of form to draw out the beholder's subjective response or to project the artist's own subjective feelings.

Linear describes both styles and techniques. In linear styles artists use line as the primary means of definition. But linear paintings can also incorporate *modeling*—creating an illusion of three-dimensional substance through shading, usually executed so that brushstrokes nearly disappear.

Painterly describes a style of representation in which vigorous, evident brushstrokes dominate, and outlines, shadows, and highlights are brushed in freely.

MEDIUM AND TECHNIQUE

Medium (plural, *media*) refers to the material or materials from which a work of art is made. Today, literally anything can be used to make a work of art, including not only traditional materials like paint, ink, and stone, but also rubbish, food, and the earth itself.

Technique is the process that transforms media into a work of art. Various techniques are explained throughout this book in Technique boxes. Two-dimensional media and techniques include painting, drawing, prints, and photography. Three-dimensional media and techniques are sculpture (for example, using stone, wood, clay or cast metal), architecture, and many small-scale arts (such as jewelry, containers, or vessels) in media such as ceramics, metal, or wood.

Painting includes wall painting and fresco, illumination (the decoration of books with paintings), panel painting (painting on wood panels), painting on canvas, and handscroll and hanging scroll painting. The paint in these examples is pigment mixed with a liquid vehicle, or binder. Some art historians also consider pictorial media such as mosaic and stained glass—where the pigment is arranged in solid form—as a type of painting.

Graphic arts are those that involve the application of lines and strokes to a two-dimensional surface or support, most often paper. Drawing is a graphic art, as are the various forms of printmaking. Drawings may be sketches (quick visual notes, often made in preparation for larger drawings or paintings); studies (more carefully drawn analyses of details or entire compositions); cartoons (full-scale drawings made in preparation for work in another medium, such as fresco, stained glass, or tapestry); or complete artworks in themselves. Drawings can be made with ink, charcoal, crayon, or pencil. Prints, unlike drawings, are made in multiple copies. The various forms of printmaking include woodcut, the intaglio processes (engraving, etching, drypoint), and lithography.

Photography (literally, "light writing") is a medium that involves the rendering of optical images on light-sensitive surfaces. Photographic images are typically recorded by a camera.

Sculpture is three-dimensional art that is *carved*, *modeled*, *cast*, or *assembled*. Carved sculpture is subtractive in the sense that the image is created by taking away material. Wood, stone, and ivory are common materials used to create carved sculptures. Modeled sculpture is considered additive, meaning that the object is built up from a material, such as clay, that is soft enough to be molded and shaped. Metal sculpture is usually cast or is assembled by welding or a similar means of permanent joining.

Sculpture is either free-standing (that is, surrounded by space) or in pictorial relief. Relief sculpture projects from the background surface of the same piece of material. High-relief sculpture projects far from its background; low-relief sculpture is only slightly raised; and sunken relief, found mainly in ancient Egyptian art, is carved into the surface, with the highest part of the relief being the flat surface.

Ephemeral arts include processions, ceremonies, or ritual dances (often with décor, costumes, or masks); performance art; earthworks; cinema and video art; and some forms of digital or computer art. All impose a temporal limitation—the artwork is viewable for a finite period of time and then disappears forever, is in a constant state of change, or must be replayed to be experienced again.

Architecture creates enclosures for human activity or habitation. It is three-dimensional, highly spatial, functional, and closely bound with developments in technology and materials. Since it is difficult to capture in a photograph, several types of schematic drawings are commonly used to enable the visualization of a building:

> **Plans** depict a structure's masses and voids, presenting a view from above of the building's footprint or as if it had been sliced horizontally at about waist height.

Plan: Philadelphia, Vanna Venturi House

Sections reveal the interior of a building as if it had been cut vertically from top to bottom.

Section: Rome, Sta. Costanza

Isometric drawings show buildings from oblique angles either seen from above ("bird's-eye view") to reveal their basic three-dimensional forms (often cut away so we can peek inside) or from below ("worm's-eye view") to represent the arrangement of interior spaces and the upward projection of structural elements.

Isometric cutaway from above: Ravenna, San Vitale

Isometric projection from below: Istanbul, Hagia Sophia

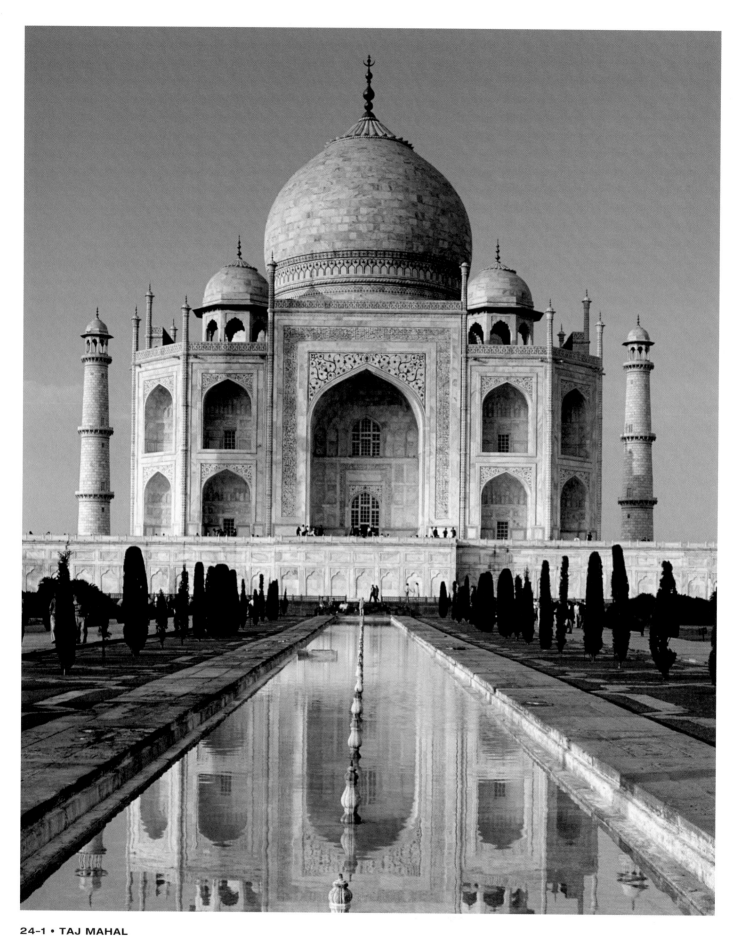

24-1 • TAJ MAHAL

Agra, India. Mughal period, reign of Shah Jahan, c. 1632–1648.

Watch an architectural simulation about the Taj Mahal on myartslab.com

Art of South and Southeast Asia after 1200

Upon entering the gateway that today serves as the entrance to the great Taj Mahal complex, the visitor beholds the majestic white marble structure that is one of the world's best-known monuments. Its reflection shimmers in the pools of the garden meant to evoke a vision of paradise as described in the Qur'an. The building's façades are delicately inlaid with inscriptions designed by India's foremost calligrapher of the time, Amanat Khan, and floral arabesques in semiprecious stones—carnelian, agate, coral, turquoise, garnet, lapis, and jasper. Above, its luminous, white marble dome reflects each shift in light, flushing rose at dawn, dissolving in its own brilliance in the noonday sun. This extraordinary building, originally and appropriately called the Illuminated Tomb and only from the nineteenth century known as the **TAJ MAHAL** (**FIG. 24–1**), was built between 1632 and 1648 by the Mughal ruler Shah Jahan as a mausoleum for his favorite wife, Mumtaz Mahal, who died in childbirth, and likely as a tomb for himself.

Inside, the Taj Mahal invokes the *hasht behisht* ("eight paradises"), with the eight small chambers that ring the interior—one at each corner and one behind each *iwan*, a vaulted opening with an arched portal, that is a typical feature of eastern Islamic architecture. In two stories (for a total of 16 chambers), the rooms ring the octagonal central area, which rises the full two stories to a domed ceiling that is lower than the outer dome. In this central chamber, surrounded by a finely carved octagonal openwork marble screen, are the exquisite inlaid **cenotaphs** (funerary monuments) of Shah Jahan and his wife, whose actual tombs lie in the crypt below.

The Taj Mahal complex includes much more than the white marble tomb. On one side is a mosque, while opposite and very similar in appearance is a building that may have served as a rest house. The enormous garden, both in front of the building and in its continuation on the opposite side of the Jamuna River, lends a lush setting consistent with Islamic notions of paradise. Both the side buildings and the two parts of the garden provide a sense of perfect symmetry to the entire complex.

A dynasty of Central Asian origin, the Mughals were the most successful of the many Islamic groups that established themselves in India beginning in the twelfth century. Under their patronage, Persian and Central Asian influences mingled with older traditions of the South Asian subcontinent, adding yet another dimension to the already ancient and complex artistic heritage of India.

LEARN ABOUT IT

24.1 Consider how an artwork's scale and the choice of media relates to its intended function and audience.

24.2 Understand how exogenous influences from trade and conquest affected the art of South and Southeast Asia and the way those influences were shaped locally.

24.3 Recognize that similar-looking works of art, like religious icons or traditional architectural forms, can function differently in different contexts.

24.4 Understand how a work of art like the Taj Mahal or a Khmer Buddha can have both a personal and public meaning.

((•— **Listen** to the chapter audio on myartslab.com

MAP 24–1 • SOUTH AND SOUTHEAST ASIA

Throughout its history, the kingdoms comprising the Indian subcontinent engaged—sometimes peacefully, sometimes militarily—with neighboring and more distant people, contributing significantly to the development of its art.

SOUTH ASIA AFTER 1200

By 1200, India was already among the world's oldest civilizations (see "Foundations of Indian Culture," page 774). The art that survives from its earlier periods is almost exclusively sacred, most of it inspired by the three principal religions: Buddhism, Hinduism, and Jainism. These three religions remained a primary focus for Indian art, even as dynasties arriving from the northwest began to establish the new religious culture of Islam.

CHANGES IN RELIGION AND ART

After many centuries of prominence, Buddhism began to decline as a cultural force in India after the eighth century. As patronage diminished, many Indian Buddhist monks sought out more supportive communities in Southeast Asia for whom Buddhism remained an important religion. At the start of the twelfth century, Kyanzittha, the Burmese king of Bagan, who was known to have hosted Indian monks, actually sent crews to Buddhist centers

in South Asia to repair the neglected monuments. By 1200, the remaining Buddhist enclaves in South Asia were concentrated in the northeast, in the region that had been ruled by the Pala dynasty (c. 750–1199). There, in great monastic universities that attracted monks from as far away as China, Korea, and Japan, a form of Buddhism known as Tantrism or Vajrayana was cultivated.

Over these same centuries, Hinduism quickly rose to new prominence, inspiring grand temples, sculpture, and poetry across the subcontinent. Jainism continued to prosper as its relatively small community of adherents grew in regional influence. And the new religion of Islam entered from the northwest, growing to have a profound influence on South Asian culture.

THE BODHISATTVA AVALOKITESHVARA The practices of Tantric Buddhism, which include techniques for visualizing deities, encourage the development of images with precise iconographic details such as the twelfth-century gilt-bronze sculpture

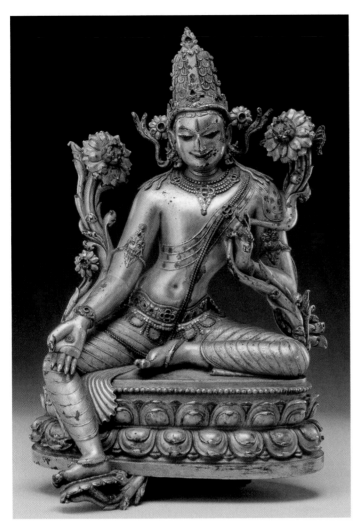

24-2 • THE BODHISATTVA AVALOKITESHVARA
From Kurkihar, Bihar. Pala dynasty, 12th century. Gilt-bronze, height 10″ (25.5 cm). Patna Museum, Patna.

of **THE BODHISATTVA AVALOKITESHVARA** in **FIGURE 24-2** from the site of Kurkihar in eastern India. Bodhisattvas are compassionate beings who are well advanced on the path to buddhahood (enlightenment) and who have vowed to help others achieve enlightenment. Avalokiteshvara, the bodhisattva of greatest compassion, who vowed to forgo buddhahood until all others become buddhas, became the most popular of these saintly beings in India and in East Asia.

Characteristic of bodhisattvas, Avalokiteshvara is distinguished in art by his princely garments, unlike a buddha, who wears monk's robes. Avalokiteshvara is specifically recognized by the lotus flower he holds and by the presence in his crown of his "parent" Buddha, in this case Amitabha, the Buddha of the Western Pure Land (a Buddhist paradise). Other marks of Avalokiteshvara's extraordinary status are the third eye (symbolizing his omniscience) and the wheel on his palm (an emblem of the Buddhist *dharma*). Avalokiteshvara is shown here in the relaxed pose known as the posture of "royal ease." One leg angles down; the other is drawn up onto the lotus seat.

With the fall of the Pala dynasty in the late twelfth century, the last centers of Buddhism in northern India collapsed, and most of the monks dispersed, mainly into Nepal and Tibet (**MAP 24-1**). From that time, they have remained the principal stronghold of Tantric Buddhist practice and its arts. The artistic style perfected under the Palas, however, came to influence international style throughout East and Southeast Asia.

LUNA VASAHI, MOUNT ABU The history of Jainism makes an interesting counterpoint to that of Buddhism. Although both are monastic traditions, the Jains never gained the widespread popularity of Buddhism but neither did they suffer a precipitous decline. The Jain religion traces its roots to a spiritual leader called Mahavira (c. 599–527 BCE), whom it regards as the last in a series of 24 saviors known as pathfinders (*tirthankaras*). Devotees seek through purification and moral action to become worthy of escaping the cycle of rebirth. Jain monks live a life of austerity, and even lay persons avoid killing any living creature. The Jain commitment to non-violence means that there are relatively few Jain kings in South Asian history, but this same commitment led many Jains to gravitate toward lucrative professions in banking and trade. It is from these ranks of merchants and ministers that some of the most important donors of Jain art come, as in the case of the Dilwara Temples erected on Mount Abu in Rajasthan, India. The modest exterior enclosure walls and relatively small size of the of the five Dilwara Temples do little to prepare the visitor for the lacelike splendor of the interior. Every inch of these spaces is filled with deeply cut relief carvings in white marble whose complicated details had to be produced through abrasion and rubbing rather than with a chisel. One of the most impressive of these temples, the Luna Vasahi, was dedicated to the 22nd Jain *tirthankara*, Neminatha, and was built in 1230 by two brothers, Tejpala and Vastupala, who served as ministers to the local ruler. They are known to have sponsored temples in at least two other locations. The structure has had to be repaired in places, the damage most likely caused by raids, but most of the delicate sculpture is still intact.

The main sanctuary is set in a courtyard surrounded by two columned arcades. These open to reveal the temple's most impressive architectural feature, the ornate dome that crowns the *mandapa* hall. This corbeled dome is made of concentric bands of sculpted stone capped with a meticulously carved pendant which hangs down from the apex. Surrounding this decorative element are images of 16 goddesses of wisdom, attached individually to the surface of the dome. This, in turn, is held aloft by eight pillars linked by undulating architraves (**FIG. 24-3**). Every surface is adorned with narrative scenes, animals, protective deities, and plant motifs. These riotous forms highlight the calm, unadorned image of the *tirthankara*, which looks out from the quietude of the sanctuary. The dramatic contrast speaks to the difference between the active world of constant rebirth and the steady peace of enlightenment.

The earliest civilization on the Indian subcontinent flourished toward the end of the third millennium BCE along the Indus River in present-day Pakistan. Remains of its expertly engineered brick cities have been uncovered, together with works of art that intriguingly suggest spiritual practices and reveal artistic traits known in later Indian culture.

The decline of the Indus civilization during the mid second millennium BCE coincides with the arrival from the northwest of a seminomadic people who spoke an Indo-European language and referred to themselves as Aryans. Over the next millennium they were influential in formulating the new civilization that gradually emerged. The most important Aryan contributions to this new civilization included the Sanskrit language and the sacred texts called the Vedas. The evolution of Vedic thought under the influence of indigenous Indian beliefs culminated in the mystical philosophical texts called the Upanishads, which took shape sometime after 800 BCE.

The Upanishads teach that the material world is illusory; only Brahman, the universal soul, is real and eternal. We—that is, our individual souls—are trapped in this illusion in a relentless cycle of birth, death, and rebirth. The ultimate goal of religious life is to liberate ourselves from this cycle and to unite our individual soul with Brahman.

Buddhism and Jainism are two of the many religions that developed in the wake of Upanishadic thought. Buddhism (see "Buddhism," page 301) is based on the teachings of Shakyamuni Buddha, who lived in central India about 500 BCE. Jainism was shaped slightly earlier by the followers of the spiritual leader Mahavira. Both religions acknowledged the cyclical nature of existence and taught a means of liberation from it, but they rejected the authority, rituals, and social strictures of Vedic religion. Whereas the Vedic religion was in the hands of a hereditary priestly class, Buddhist and Jain communities welcomed all members of society, which gave them great appeal. The Vedic tradition eventually evolved into the many sects now collectively known as Hinduism (see "Hinduism," page 309).

Through most of its history India was a mosaic of regional dynastic kingdoms, but from time to time empires emerged that unified large parts of the subcontinent. The first was that of the Maurya dynasty (c. 322–185 BCE), whose great king Ashoka patronized Buddhism. From this time Buddhist doctrines spread widely and its artistic traditions were established.

In the first century CE the Kushans, a Central Asian people, created an empire extending from present-day Afghanistan down into central India. Buddhism prospered under Kanishka, the most powerful Kushan king, and spread into Central Asia and to East Asia. At this time, under the new Kushan cultural and political climate, the image of the Buddha in art first appeared.

Later, under the Gupta dynasty (c. 320–550 CE) in northern India, Buddhist art and culture reached a high point. However, Gupta monarchs also patronized Hindu art, and from this time Hinduism grew to become the dominant Indian religious tradition, with its emphasis on the great gods Vishnu, Shiva, and the Goddess—all with multiple forms.

After the tenth century, numerous regional dynasties prevailed, some quite powerful and long-lasting. Hindu temples, in particular, developed monumental and complex forms that were rich in symbolism and ritual function, with each region of India producing its own variation.

24-3 • LUNA VASAHI, MANDAPA CEILING
Mount Abu, India. 1230.

TEMPLE AT MADURAI As Buddhism gradually declined, Hinduism grew in prominence. With the increasing popularity of Hindu sects came the rapid development of Hindu temples. Spurred by the ambitious building programs of wealthy rulers, well-formulated regional styles had evolved by about 900. The most spectacular structures of the era were monumental, with a complexity and grandeur of proportion rarely equaled even in later Indian art.

Emphasis on monumental temples gave way to the building of vast temple complexes and more moderately scaled, yet more richly ornamented, individual temples. These developments took place largely in the south of India, although some of the largest temples are in the north, for example, the Sun Temple at Konarak, built in the thirteenth century, and the Govind Deva Temple in Brindavan, built in the sixteenth century under the patronage of the Mughal emperor Akbar. The mightiest of the southern Indian kingdoms was Vijayanagar (c. 1336–1565), whose rulers successfully countered the potential incursions of neighboring dynasties, both Hindu and Muslim, for more than 200 years. Under the patronage of the Vijayanagar kings and their successors, the Nayaks, some of India's most spectacular Hindu architecture was created.

The enormous temple complex at Madurai, one of the capitals of the Nayaks, is an example of this fervent expression of Hindu faith. Founded around the thirteenth century, it is dedicated to the goddess Minakshi (the local name for Parvati, the consort of the god Shiva) and to Sundareshvara (the local name for Shiva himself). The temple complex stands in the center of the city and is the focus of Madurai life. At its heart are the two oldest shrines, one to Minakshi and the other to Sundareshvara. Successive additions over the centuries gradually expanded the complex around these small shrines and came to dominate the visual landscape. The most dramatic features of this and similar southern "temple cities" were the thousand-pillar halls, large ritual-bathing pools, and especially the entrance gateways (**gopuras**) that tower above the temple site and the surrounding city like modern skyscrapers (**FIG. 24–4**).

Gopuras proliferated as a temple city grew, necessitating new and bigger enclosing walls, and thus new gateways. Successive rulers, often seeking to outdo their predecessors, donated taller and taller *gopuras*. As a result, the tallest structures in temple cities are often at the periphery, rather than at the central temples, which are sometimes totally overwhelmed by the height of the surrounding structures. The temple complex at Madurai has 11 *gopuras*, the largest over 160 feet tall.

Formally, the *gopura* has its roots in the pyramidal tower characteristic of the seventh-century southern temple style. As the *gopura* evolved, it took on the graceful concave silhouette shown here. The exterior is embellished with thousands of sculpted figures, evoking a teeming world of gods and goddesses. Inside, stairs lead to the top for an extraordinary view.

QUTB MINAR Traders and merchants were probably the first to bring Islam to South Asia, but the backing of powerful

24-4 • OUTER GOPURA OF THE MINAKSHI-SUNDARESHVARA TEMPLE
Madurai, Tamil Nadu, south India. Nayak dynasty, mostly 13th to mid 17th century, with modern renovations.

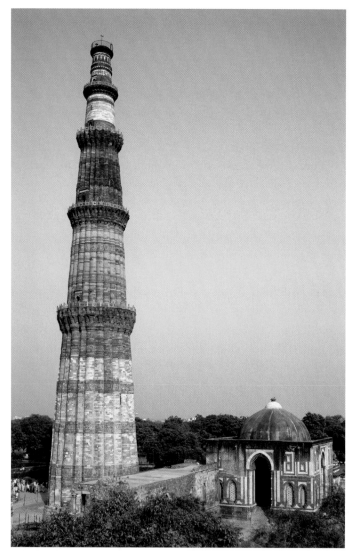

24-5 • QUTB MINAR
Quwwat ul-Islam Mosque, Mehrauli Archaeological Park, Delhi.
1211–1236.

Hindu religious structures from this location were reused in the construction of the mosque. By far the most visible element of this complex is the tower known as the **QUTB MINAR** (FIG. 24-5). This minaret was begun by Aibak and completed under his successor Iltutmish. It stands over 237 feet high and was among the tallest structures in South Asia at the time. It was constructed of sandstone in five segments, each of which is marked by the presence of a balcony that encircles the tower. The stories get smaller further up the tower and the final balcony rests on the top. Minarets are traditionally used to call Muslims to prayer, but this tower is too tall to serve that purpose easily and serves more clearly as an expression of power and political authority than as a functioning religious structure.

MUGHAL PERIOD

The Mughals, like many of the Delhi sultans, came from Central Asia. Muhammad Zahir-ud-Din, known as Babur ("Lion" or "Panther"), was the first Mughal emperor of India (r. 1526–30). He emphasized his Turkic heritage, though he had equally impressive Mongol ancestry. After some initial conquests in Central Asia, he amassed an empire stretching from Afghanistan to Delhi, which he conquered in 1526. Akbar (r. 1556–1605), the third ruler, extended Mughal control over most of north India, and under his two successors, Jahangir and Shah Jahan, northern India was generally unified by 1658. The Mughal Empire lasted until 1858, when the last Mughal emperor was deposed and exiled to Burma (Myanmar) by the British.

Mughal architects were heir to a 300-year-old tradition of Islamic building in India. The Delhi sultans who preceded them had great forts housing government and court buildings. Their architects had introduced two fundamental Islamic structures, the mosque and the tomb, along with construction based on the arch and the dome. (Earlier Indian architecture had been based primarily on post-and-lintel construction.) They had also drawn freely on Indian architecture, borrowing both decorative and structural elements to create a variety of hybrid styles, and had especially benefited from the centuries-old Indian virtuosity in stonecarving and masonry. The Mughals followed in this tradition, synthesizing Indian, Persian, and Central Asian elements for their forts, palaces, mosques, tombs, and cenotaphs (tombs or monuments to someone whose remains are actually somewhere else).

The third emperor, Akbar presided over a period of openness and expansion. His inclusive policies and tolerance toward religious difference did much to help solidify and stabilize his massive empire. A dynamic, humane, and just leader, Akbar enjoyed religious discourse and loved the arts, especially painting. He created an imperial atelier (workshop) of painters, which he placed under the direction of two artists from the Persian court. Learning from these two masters, the Indian painters of the atelier soon transformed Persian styles into the more vigorous, naturalistic styles that mark Mughal painting (see "Indian Painting on Paper," page 782).

political rulers, which helped to establish it across the region, did not occur until the eighth century, when Arab armies captured a small territory near the Indus River. Later, beginning around 1000, Turkic factions from Central Asia, relatively recent converts to Islam, began military campaigns into north India, at first purely for plunder, then seeking territorial control. From the thirteenth century various Turkic and Afghan dynasties ruled portions of the subcontinent from the northern city of Delhi. These sultanates, as they are known, constructed forts, mausoleums, monuments, and mosques.

The first Delhi Sultanate was founded in 1206 by Qutb-ud-din Aibak of the Slave dynasty, so named because Aibak had begun his life as a soldier-slave (*mamluk*) under the Ghorids. Although he did not reign long, he began construction of a large mosque adorned with a truly massive minaret. The mosque complex, called Quwwat ul-Islam (strength of Islam), was built over the citadel of Delhi's previous rulers and portions of the Jain and

FATEHPUR SIKRI Despite all this success Akbar was concerned about who would follow him on the throne. In desperation, he sought the advice of the Sufi mystic Shaikh Salim Chishti. This Muslim holy man foretold the birth of a prince, and when his prediction proved accurate, Akbar built a new capital near Chishti's home to commemorate and celebrate the event. Built primarily during Akbar's residence at the site from about 1572 to 1585, there are two major components to Fatehpur Sikri: a religious section including the Jami Mosque, which houses the tomb of Salim Chishti, and the administrative and residential section. Among the most extraordinary buildings in the administrative and residential section is the private audience hall or **DIWAN-I-KHAS** (**FIG. 24-6**). In the center of the hall is a tall pillar supporting a circular platform reached by four walkways. On this perch Akbar could sit in safety as he received his nobles and dispensed justice. The structure recalls, perhaps consciously, the pillars erected by Ashoka (see Chapter 10) to promulgate his law.

24-7 • AKBAR INSPECTING THE CONSTRUCTION OF FATEHPUR SIKRI

From the *Akbarnama*. c. 1590. Opaque watercolor on paper, 14¾" × 10" (37.5 × 25 cm). Victoria & Albert Museum, London. (I.S.2-1896 91/117)

Many of the painters in the Mughal imperial workshops are recorded in texts of the period. Based on those records and on signatures that occur on some paintings, the design of this work has been attributed to Tulsi Kalan (Tulsi the Elder), the painting to Bandi, and the portraits to Madhu Kalan (Madhu the Elder) or Madhu Khurd (Madhu the Younger).

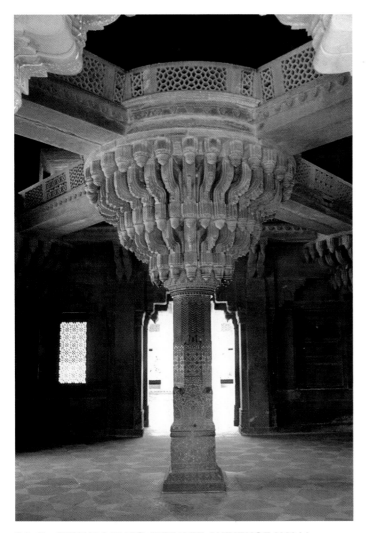

24-6 • DIWAN-I-KHAS (PRIVATE AUDIENCE HALL)
Fatehpur Sikri, India. 1570.

 View the Closer Look for the Diwan-i-Khas (private audience hall) on myartslab.com

Unlike most Mughal emperors, Akbar did not write his own biography; instead he entrusted its creation to his vizier Abul Fazl. This text, the *Akbarnama*, details the actions and accomplishments of the emperor including the events leading to the construction of Fatehpur Sikri. Paintings commissioned to illustrate this event round out our understanding of Mughal building techniques and reveal Akbar's personal interest in the progress. Among the most fascinating illustrations in this manuscript are those that record Akbar's supervision of the construction of Fatehpur Sikri. One painting (**FIG. 24-7**) documents his inspection of the stonemasons and other craftsmakers. Akbar's love of painting set a royal precedent that his successors enthusiastically continued.

At first glance this painting of two rulers embracing seems to tell of a close bond of friendship between the men (**FIG. 24–8**). The presence of a lion and lamb lying peacefully together, an ancient symbol of harmony, also appears to bolster this interpretation. Indeed, the fact that the men are framed by the sun and moon while standing on a map of the world might imply that these bonds of trust and peace extend even to their respective states. Yet nothing could be further from the truth.

This painting was created in a moment of high tension between Shah Abbas and the Mughal throne. The trouble centered on Kandahar in Afghanistan. The prosperous city had been given to Shah Abbas's ancestor by the Mughal emperor Humayun, but later, in the time of Akbar, the Mughals took back control of the city. Shah Abbas then waited for a chance to reclaim it, believing it was his right to do so. When the Mughals were distracted by a war in Iran, he seized the opportunity and recaptured Kandahar in a swift assault. He immediately made conciliatory gestures to Jahangir, who was furious but unable to spare the military force needed to retake the city.

Another look at the painting reveals new details. Jahangir is depicted much larger than Shah Abbas, who appears to bow deferentially to the Mughal emperor. Jahangir's head is centered in the halo and he stands on the predatory lion, whose body spans a vast territory, including Shah Abbas's own holdings in Afghanistan and Iran. These details invert the initial impression conveyed by the subject, revealing a new meaning. The painting is a strong reminder of Mughal power and a potent warning against further expansion, but couched in the diplomatic language of reconciliation.

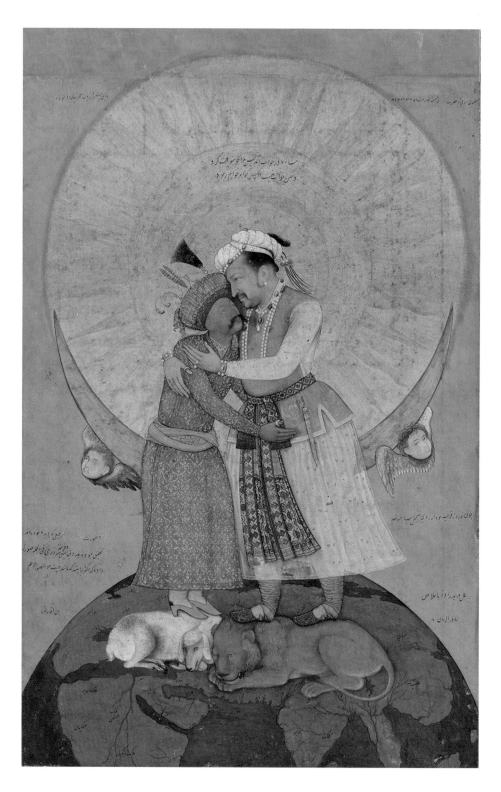

24-8 • Nadir al-Zaman (Abu'l Hasan) **JAHANGIR AND SHAH ABBAS** From the St. Petersburg Album. Mughal period, c. 1618. Opaque watercolor, gold and ink on paper, 9⅜″ × 6″ (23.8 × 15.4 cm). Freer Gallery of Art, Smithsonian Institution, Washington, DC. Purchase, F1945.9. Freer Gallery, Washington

24-9 • JAHANGIR AND PRINCE KHURRAM FEASTED BY NUR JAHAN

Mughal period, 1617. Paint and gold on paper, 9^{15}/$_{16}$" × 5^{5}/$_{8}$" (25.2 × 14.3 cm). Freer Gallery of Art, Smithsonian Institution, Washington, DC. Gift of Charles Lang Freer (F1907.258)

PAINTING IN THE COURT OF JAHANGIR Jahangir (r. 1605–1627), Akbar's son and successor, was a connoisseur of painting; he had his own workshop, which he established even before he became emperor. His focus on detail was much greater than that of his father. In his memoirs, he claimed:

> My liking for painting and my practice in judging it have arrived at such a point that when any work is brought before me, either of deceased artists or of those of the present day, without their names being told me I say on the spur of the moment that it is the work of such and such a man, and if there be a picture containing many portraits, and each face be the work of a different master, I can discover which face is the work of each of them. And if any other person has put in the eye and eyebrow of a face, I can perceive whose work the original face is and who has painted the eye and eyebrows.

Portraits become a major art under Jahangir. We can only speculate on the target audience for the portrait Jahangir commissioned of himself with the Safavid-dynasty Persian ruler, Shah Abbas. A painting of such small size could not be publicly displayed and was, therefore, certainly not intended for Jahangir's subjects. But because we know that paintings were commonly conveyed by embassies from one kingdom to another, it may have been intended as a gift for Shah Abbas, one with a message of clear strength and superiority cloaked in the diplomatic language of cordiality (see "Painting of Jahangir and Shah Abbas," opposite).

Despite the proliferation of portrait painting, depictions of court women occur rarely in Mughal art due in part to the restricted access male painters had to the women's quarters. An important exception to this was Jahangir's favorite wife, the Empress Nur Jahan, of whom a few images exist. As Jahangir grew older he succumbed to addiction and illness. During this period, in which he was largely incapacitated, Nur Jahan ran the empire on his behalf, carrying his seal and issuing decrees in his name. Although she ruled in Jahangir's name, the images of her at court and the imperial coins that bore her name suggest her role was no secret.

The idyllic scene depicted in **FIGURE 24-9** portrays Nur Jahan serving food and drink to Jahangir and his son by another wife, Prince Khurram. Seated on ornate carpets the royal family members sit near a fountain as court women bring food and wave fans. This deceptively harmonious tableau is qualified by the verses in Persian surrounding the painting. These refer to Jahangir's displeasure over Khurram's attempts to take the throne, an outcome that Nur Jahan also wished to forestall. After Jahangir died, however, and Nur Jahan was confined to her palace, Khurram managed to seize the throne, taking the royal name Shah Jahan.

THE TAJ MAHAL Shah Jahan (r. 1628–58) achieved a number of military and political victories but he is best known as the patron of what is perhaps the most famous of all Indian Islamic structures, the Taj Mahal. Built between 1631 and 1648 on the banks of the Jamuna River, it was commissioned as a mausoleum for Mumtaz Mahal, the wife of Shah Jahan, who is believed to have taken a major part in overseeing its design and construction. Shah Jahan's personal motivations add a poignancy to this structure, but it must also be recalled that this was the first major architectural undertaking of Shah Jahan's reign. That the Taj Mahal effectively evokes both personal loss and imperial authority is perhaps its most remarkable strength.

As visitors enter through a monumental, hall-like gate, the tomb rises before them across a spacious garden set with long reflecting pools (see FIG. 24-1). Measuring some 1,000 by 1,900 feet, the enclosure is unobtrusively divided into quadrants planted with trees and flowers, and framed by broad walkways and stone inlaid in geometric patterns. In Shah Jahan's time, fruit trees and

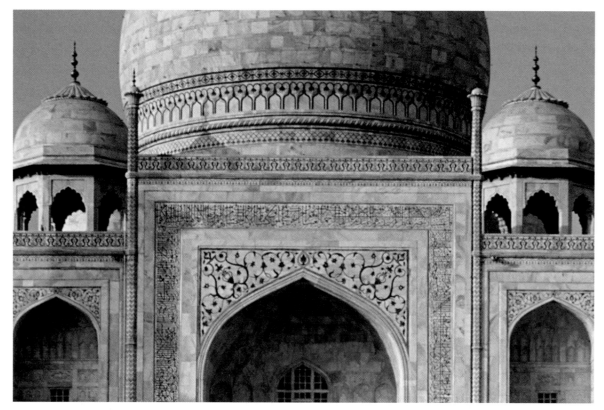

24-10 • TAJ MAHAL, DETAIL
Agra, India. Mughal period, reign of Shah Jahan, c. 1631–1648.

View the Closer Look for the Taj Mahal on myartslab.com

cypresses—symbolic of life and death, respectively—lined the walkways, and fountains played in the shallow pools. Collectively these features evoked paradise on earth.

Recent archaeology has revealed that the garden continues on the far bank of the Jamuna River. A garden filled with night-blooming plants and a large octagonal fountain provided a vantage point for viewing the Taj Mahal from across the river. Thus while the structure appears to visitors to be set at the end of a garden, it is in fact in the center of a four-part garden, a traditional Mughal tomb setting used for earlier tombs. The tomb is flanked by two smaller structures not visible in FIGURE 24–1, one a mosque and the other a hall designed to mirror it. Like the entrance hall, they are made mostly of red sandstone, rendering even more startling the full glory of the tomb's white marble, a material previously reserved for the tombs of saints and here implying an elevated religious stature for Shah Jahan and Mumtaz Mahal. The tomb is raised higher than these structures on its own marble platform emphasizing its importance. This aggrandizement of the tomb is further achieved by having the minarets flank the tomb rather than the mosque. The minarets' three levels correspond to those of the tomb, creating a bond between them. Crowning each minaret is a **chattri** (pavilion). Traditional embellishments of Indian palaces, *chattris* quickly passed into the vocabulary of Indian Islamic architecture, where they appear prominently. A lucid geometric symmetry pervades the tomb. It is basically square, but its **chamfered**

(sliced-off) corners create a subtle octagon. Measured to the base of the **finial** (the spire at the top), the tomb is almost exactly as tall as it is wide. Each façade is identical, with a central *iwan* flanked by two stories of smaller *iwans*. By creating voids in the façades, these *iwans* contribute to the building's sense of weightlessness. On the roof, four octagonal *chattris*, one at each corner, create a visual transition to the lofty, bulbous dome. Framed but not obscured by the *chattris*, the dome rises gracefully and is lifted higher by its drum than in earlier Mughal tombs, allowing the swelling curves and elegant lines of its surprisingly large form to emerge with perfect clarity.

The pristine surfaces of the Taj Mahal are embellished with utmost subtlety (**FIG. 24-10**). Even the sides of the platform on which the Taj Mahal stands are carved in relief with a **blind arcade** (decorative arches set into a wall) motif and carved relief panels of flowers. The portals are framed with verses from the Qur'an and inlaid in black marble, while the spandrels are decorated with floral arabesques inlaid in colored semiprecious stones, a technique known by its Italian name pietra dura. Not strong enough to detract from the overall purity of the white marble, the embellishments enliven the surfaces of this impressive yet delicate masterpiece.

RAJPUT PAINTING Outside the Mughal strongholds at Delhi and Agra, much of northern India was governed regionally by local princes, often descendants of the so-called Hindu Rajput warrior clans, who were allowed to keep their lands in return for allegiance to the Mughals. Like the Mughals, Rajput princes frequently supported painters at their courts, and in these settings a variety of strong, indigenous Indian painting styles were perpetuated. Rajput painting, more abstract than the Mughal style, included subjects like those treated by Mughal painters, royal portraits and court scenes, as well as indigenous subjects such as Hindu myths, love poetry, and Ragamala illustrations (illustrations of musical modes).

The Hindu devotional movement known as *bhakti*, which had done much to spread the faith in the south from around the seventh century, now experienced a revival in the north. As it had earlier in the south, *bhakti* inspired an outpouring of poetic literature, this time devoted especially to Krishna, the popular human incarnation of the god Vishnu. Most renowned is the *Gita*

Govinda, a cycle of rhapsodic poems about the love between God and humans expressed metaphorically through the love between the young Krishna and the cowherd Radha.

The illustration here (**FIG. 24-11**) is from a manuscript of the *Gita Govinda* probably produced in present-day Rajasthan about 1525–1550. The blue god Krishna sits in dalliance with a group of cowherd women. Standing with her maid and consumed with love for Krishna, Radha peers through the trees, overcome by jealousy. Her feelings are indicated by the cool blue color behind her, while the crimson red behind the Krishna grouping suggests passion. The bold patterns of curving stalks and flowering vines express both the exuberance of springtime, when the story unfolds, and the heightened emotional tensions of the scene. Birds, trees, and flowers are as brilliant as fireworks against the black, hilly landscape edged in an undulating white line. All the figures are of a single type, with plump faces in profile and oversized eyes. Yet the resilient line of

24-11 • KRISHNA AND THE GOPIS

From the *Gita Govinda*, Rajasthan, India. Mughal period, c. 1525–1550. Gouache on paper, 4⅞″ × 7½″ (12.3 × 19 cm). Prince of Wales Museum, Mumbai.

The lyrical poem *Gita Govinda*, by the poet-saint Jayadeva, was probably written in eastern India during the latter half of the twelfth century. The episode illustrated here occurs early in the relationship of Radha and Krishna, which in the poem is a metaphor for the connection between humans and God. The poem traces the progress of their love through separation, reconciliation, and fulfillment.

Before the fourteenth century most painting in India had been on walls or palm leaves. With the introduction of paper, about the same time in India as in Europe, Indian artists adopted painting techniques from Persia and over the ensuing centuries produced jewel-toned works on paper.

Painters usually began their training early. As young apprentices, they learned to make brushes and grind pigments. Brushes were made from the curved hairs of a squirrel's tail, arranged to taper from a thick base to a single hair at the tip. Paint came from pigments of vegetables and minerals—lapis lazuli to make blue, malachite for pale green—that were ground to a paste with water, then bound with a solution of gum from the acacia plant. Paper was made by crushing fibers of cotton and jute to a pulp, pouring the mixture onto a woven mat, drying it, and then burnishing with a smooth piece of agate, often achieving a glossy finish.

First, the painter applied a thin wash of a chalk-based white, which sealed the surface of the paper while allowing the underlying sketch to show through. Next, outlines were filled with thick washes of brilliant, opaque, unmodulated color. When the colors were dry, the painting was laid face down on a smooth marble surface and burnished with a rounded agate stone, rubbing first up and down, then side to side. The indirect pressure against the marble polished the pigments to a high luster. Then outlines, details, and modeling—depending on the style— were added with a fine brush.

Sometimes certain details were purposely left until last, such as the eyes, which were said to bring the painting to life. Gold and raised details were applied when the painting was nearly finished. Gold paint, made from pulverized, 24-carat gold leaf bound with acacia gum, was applied with a brush and burnished to a high shine. Raised details such as the pearls of a necklace were made with thick, white, chalk-based paint, with each pearl a single droplet hardened into a tiny raised mound.

---

the drawing gives them life, and the variety of textile patterns provides some individuality. The intensity of the color and resolute flatness of the scene engage the viewer in the drama.

24-12 • HOUR OF COWDUST
From Punjab Hills, India. Mughal period, Kangra School, c. 1790. Gouache on paper, 14^{15}⁄₁₆″ × 12^{9}⁄₁₆″ (36 × 31.9 cm). Museum of Fine Arts, Boston. Denman W. Ross Collection (22.683)

Quite a different mood pervades **HOUR OF COWDUST**, a work from the Kangra School in the Punjab Hills, foothills of the Himalayas north of Delhi (**FIG. 24-12**). Painted around 1790, some 250 years later than the *Gita Govinda* illustration, it shows the influence of Mughal naturalism on the later schools of Indian painting. The theme is again Krishna. Wearing his peacock crown, garland of flowers, and yellow garment—all traditional iconography of Krishna-Vishnu—he returns to the village with his fellow cowherds and their cattle. All eyes are upon him as he plays his flute, said to enchant all who hear it. Women with water jugs on their heads turn to look; others lean from windows to watch and call out to him. We are drawn into this charming village scene by the diagonal movements of the cows as they surge through the gate and into the courtyard beyond. Pastel houses and walls create a sense of space, and in the distance we glimpse other villagers going about their work or peacefully sitting in their houses. A rim of dark trees softens the horizon, and an atmospheric sky completes the aura of enchanted naturalism. Again, all the figures are similar in type, this time with a perfection of proportion and a gentle, lyrical movement that complement the idealism of the setting.

BRITISH COLONIAL PERIOD AND THE INDEPENDENCE MOVEMENT

By the time *Hour of Cowdust* was painted, India's regional rulers, both Hindu and Muslim, had reasserted themselves, and the vast Mughal Empire had shrunk to a small area around Delhi. At the same time, however, a new power, Britain, was making itself felt, inaugurating a markedly different period in Indian history.

First under the mercantile interests of the British East India Company in the seventeenth and eighteenth centuries, and then under the direct control of the British government as a part of the British Empire in the nineteenth century, India was brought forcefully into contact with the West and its culture. The political

24-13 • Frederick Stevens **VICTORIA TERMINUS**
Mumbai, India. 1887.

concerns of the British Empire extended even to the arts. Over the course of the nineteenth century, the great cities of India, such as Calcutta (present-day Kolkata), Madras (Chennai), and Bombay (Mumbai), took on a European aspect as British architects built in the revivalist styles favored in England.

VICTORIA TERMINUS, MUMBAI The British insistence on utilizing European styles of architecture was at its most strident in the early years of colonial rule. Even after South Asia transitioned to direct control by the British Crown in 1858, a period known as the Raj, British architects were keen on emphasizing difference. Nowhere is this more visible than at the **VICTORIA TERMINUS** (now Chhatrapati Shivaji Terminus) in Mumbai (**FIG. 24-13**). This massive train station built in a Gothic Revival style was designed by architect Frederick William Stevens and opened in 1887, the year of Queen Victoria's Golden Jubilee. The building makes a few concessions to its South Asian setting, as with the inclusion of turretlike domes, but it is overwhelmingly a self-conscious statement of British imperial power. This pairing of cathedral architecture and train station celebrates ideas of British technology and authority. In place of the saints that might normally decorate a cathedral,

personifications of Progress, Commerce, Agriculture, and Science adorn the exterior. Originally, this structure was crowned by an image of Queen Victoria, which has subsequently been removed.

GATEWAY OF INDIA, MUMBAI Over time, the British reduced their insistence on promoting difference through their choice of architectural forms and began to appreciate aspects of indigenous style. Completed in 1924, the **GATEWAY OF INDIA** was built to welcome King George V on his visit to India (**FIG. 24-14**). The British constructed the monument in the form of a European triumphal arch, while embellishing it with architec-

24-14 • George Wittet
GATEWAY OF INDIA
Mumbai, India. 1924.

tural features drawn heavily from South Asian precedents. Stone screens, ornate brackets, pointed arches, and floral decorations were taken directly from earlier architectural practices in the subcontinent. This hybrid style, known as the Indo-Saracenic style, borrows techniques from the Hindu and Muslim architectural traditions of South Asia and became the preferred architectural style for British governmental buildings and elite private estates by the late nineteenth century, a few examples of which were built in England and in other parts of the empire. India won its independence in 1947 and the last British troops in South Asia departed through this gate a year later in 1948.

MOTHER INDIA Far prior to Britain's consolidation of imperial power in New Delhi a new spirit asserting Indian independence and pan-Asiatic solidarity was awakening. For example, working near Calcutta (Kolkata), the painter Abanindranath Tagore (1871–1951)—nephew of the poet Rabindranath Tagore (1861–1941), who went on to win the Nobel Prize for Literature in 1913—deliberately rejected the medium of oil painting and the academic realism of Western art. Like the Nihonga artists of Japan (see FIG. 26–18) with whom he was in contact, Tagore strove to create a style that reflected his ethnic origins. In **BHARAT MATA** (Mother India) he invents a nationalistic icon by using Hindu

Prior to the fourteenth century China dominated the international trade in ceramics, but with the rise of the Ming dynasty, China began to look inward, limiting and regulating most forms of international trade. The resulting scarcity of Chinese trade ceramics, sometimes called the "Ming gap," was an opportunity for the merchants and artists of Southeast Asia. Both the Burmese and Thai kingdoms produced ceramics, often inspired by stonewares and porcelains from China. Sukhothai potters, for example, made green-glazed and brown-glazed wares at the renowned kilns of Sawankhalok. But it was the potters of Vietnam who were most successful in meeting the international demand for porcelains. So many ceramics were exported from Vietnam that most of what remained to be found by archaeologists were the broken or discarded leftovers.

This changed with the excavation of a sunken ship laden with ceramics for export found 22 miles off the coast of Hoi An. This wreck brought to light over 250,000 ceramic works made by Vietnamese potters of the late fifteenth to early sixteenth century (**FIG. 24–16**). Painted in underglaze cobalt blue and further embellished with overglaze enamels, these wares were shipped throughout Southeast Asia and beyond, as far east as Japan and as far west as England and the Netherlands.

24–16 • GROUP OF VIETNAMESE CERAMICS FROM THE HOI AN HOARD
Late 15th to early 16th century. Porcelain with underglaze blue decoration; barbed-rim dishes: (left) diameter 14″ (35.1 cm); (right) diameter 13¼″ (34.7 cm). Phoenix Art Museum, Arizona. (2000.105–109)

symbols while also drawing upon the format and techniques of Mughal and Rajput painting (**FIG. 24–15**).

SOUTHEAST ASIA AFTER 1200

India's Buddhist and Hindu traditions found acceptance in Southeast Asia (discussed in Chapter 10), and were instrumental in validating newly rising kingdoms. These religions, Buddhism in particular, quickly found wide acceptance among the populace. Starting in the twelfth century, Islam, carried by Arab and Chinese traders, began to gain influence in the region as well. Religious ideas, however, were not the only sort of foreign influence at work in Southeast Asia. Throughout this time trade expanded and, as demand for Southeast Asian goods rose abroad, colonial powers saw the region as an attractive target (see "Southeast Asian Ceramics," above). European, East Asian, and American economic and military interests had profound consequences on regional history, culture, and society.

BUDDHIST ART AND KINGSHIP

As Buddhism declined in the land of its origin, it continued to thrive in Southeast Asia, where it was shaped and developed in new ways. As it gained adherents among the population it, at times, became vital for rulers to align themselves with Buddhist ideas. Yet, in each case the individual incentives for espousing Buddhist ideas were as varied as the artistic forms they employed.

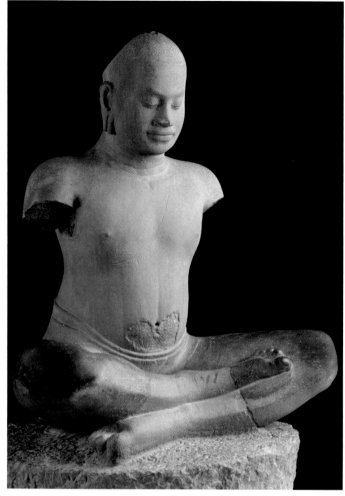

24-17 • SEATED BUDDHA
From Angkor Thom. Reign of Jayavarman VII, late 12th–early 13th century. Sandstone, 4′6″ (1.4 m). National Museum of Cambodia, Phnom Penh.

SEATED BUDDHA When Khmer king Jayavarman VII took his place on the throne of Angkor in 1181, it marked the end of a long struggle against internal rebellions and foreign invaders. Under his reign, he raised up the kingdom of Angkor in a final efflorescence, building more than any of his royal predecessors. In an unusual move, he elected to associate himself with the Buddha, rather than with a Hindu deity and in so doing adapted Buddhist ideas to the Khmer concept of the god-king or, in his case, the buddha-king (*buddharaja*). Before undertaking construction of his massive temple-mountain complex at Angkor Thom, he sought legitimacy for his claims of Buddhist authority by dedicating large temples to each of his parents in the guise of bodhisattvas. This process was taken to a logical conclusion by associating himself directly with the Buddha (as well as with the bodhisattva Lokeshvara).

Although Jayavarman VII's artists and architects produced a staggering number of spectacular sculptures and grand temples, few are as sublime as a simple sandstone Buddha image in the collection of the National Museum of Cambodia in Phnom Penh (**FIG. 24-17**). A few similar images exist and in each example the seated

Buddha displays similar physiognomic features. The consistency in these facial features has led scholars to believe that these works are in fact portraits of Jayavarman VII himself, seated serenely in the guise of the Buddha. Just as his ancestors had conceptually linked themselves with Hindu deities, Jayavarman VII represented himself as a Buddha with downturned meditative eyes, distended earlobes, hair pulled back into a topknot, and dressed in a simple garment. The authority of the king and Buddha are here expressed in a single understated, almost humble, image.

SHWEDAGON STUPA, MYANMAR In northern Burma, from the eleventh to the thirteenth century, rulers raised innumerable religious monuments—temples, monasteries, and stupas—in the Bagan Plain, following the scriptures of Theravada Buddhism. To the south arose the port city of Yangon (formerly known as Rangoon, called Dagon in antiquity). Established by Mon rulers before the eleventh century, Yangon is the site of the **SHWED-AGON STUPA** (**FIG. 24-18**), which enshrines relics of the four past Buddhas, including hair from Shakyamuni. The modern structures of Shwedagon ("Golden Dagon") rise from an ancient Mon core that was rebuilt and enlarged in the fourteenth century.

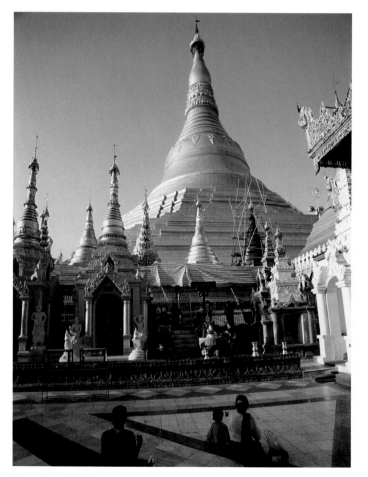

24-18 • SHWEDAGON STUPA (PAGODA)
Yangon, Myanmar. 15th century; construction at the site dates from at least the 14th century, with continuous replastering and redecoration to the present.

A CLOSER LOOK | The Sukhothai Buddha

From Wat Mahathat, now in Wat Benchamabophit, Bangkok, Thailand.
Bronze, 7'22" (2.2 m). Sukhothai period, 14th–15th century.

The graceful Buddhas of the Sukhothai period were at times further enhanced by a second Sukhothai innovation, images of the walking Buddha. Sukhothai Buddhas reveal not just the surface of the Buddha's form, but also suggest aspects of his character and life. Smooth skin is indicative of royal upbringing; long arms and broad shoulders mark someone born into a linage of warriors; and by not depicting his genitals the artists allude to his celibacy as an ascetic. Consider the following descriptions taken from Buddhist texts in relation to this example.

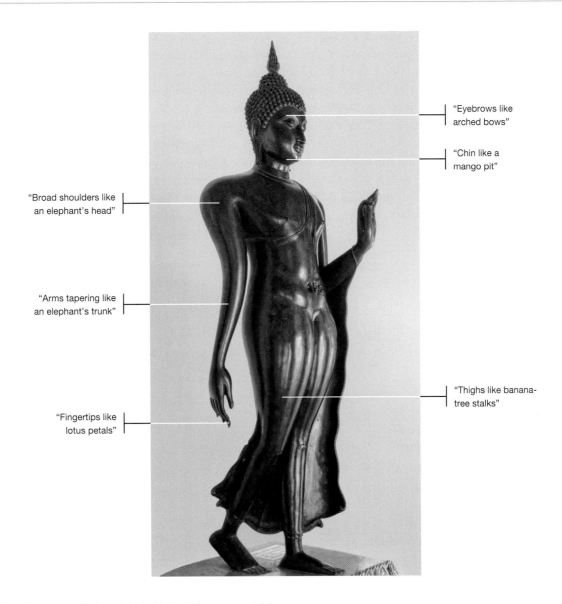

"Eyebrows like arched bows"

"Chin like a mango pit"

"Broad shoulders like an elephant's head"

"Arms tapering like an elephant's trunk"

"Thighs like banana-tree stalks"

"Fingertips like lotus petals"

View the Closer Look for the Sukhothai Buddha on myartslab.com

In subsequent decades it underwent continual restoration and enhancement at the hands of pious Burmese kings and queens. The site continues to be a focus for lavish devotion and generosity. The bell-shaped spire is capped by a umbrellalike ornament (*hti*) adorned with a large diamond and the sides of the terraces are covered in sheets of gold plate. While most of this wealth was donated by royalty, over the centuries people from all walks of life have offered gold for its construction and maintenance. Images of the Buddha, and sometimes his footprints alone, provide focal points for devotion.

TEMPLE OF THE EMERALD BUDDHA, THAILAND The Dvaravati culture remained regionally dominant until Khmer invasions in the tenth century. During this turmoil a new ethnic group, the Thai, entered the scene from the north, gradually gaining control and adopting Buddhism, as well as some aspects of Hinduism, from the Mon. The first Thai kingdom, Sukhothai, was established in 1238 and flourished under the guidance of kings like the renowned Ram Khamhaeng, before falling to rival Thai states.

The Sukhothai period is praised as a formative time of innovation and creativity in Thai art. Among their creations, the artists of this period championed an elegant new style of Buddha image. With attenuated heads adorned with spirelike flames and draping, almost boneless, limbs, the Buddha images of this period are immediately recognizable. The otherworldly qualities of the Sukhothai Buddhas have led art historians to explore possible explanations for their distinctive features. One strong possibility is that they are, quite literally, poetry given tangible form (see "A Closer Look," page 787). The artists may have been working from descriptions found in the Indian Buddhist texts, which use evocative similes to describe the Buddha's beautiful appearance.

Despite its cultural importance, the kingdom of Sukhothai did not last long, giving way to a succession of dynasties. The capital was eventually moved south to Bangkok and under the rule of the Chakri king Rama I, construction began there on a grand new temple to house the Thais' most sacred Buddha image.

The Emerald Buddha ("emerald" refers to its color; it is actually made of jadeite) is featured in legends that place its creation in India under the direction of major Buddhist figures and trace its travels through great Buddhist nations of the past. These stories, although not grounded in historical evidence, suggest that the image has a special link to the world's foremost Buddhist kings, among whose lineage the Thai king is the most recent. The king himself ritually changes the image's golden garments three times a year. In one of these costumes the Emerald Buddha is dressed as a king, further strengthening the association between the Buddha and the state.

The temple complex that houses this sacred image is suitably spectacular (**FIG. 24–19**). The enclosure covers over 200 acres and contains hundreds of buildings, most of which are crowned by high pointed roofs tiled in vibrant orange and green. These colorful rooftops shade the walls and pillars whose surfaces are inset with intricate patterns of glass, gold leaf, and tile that shimmer in

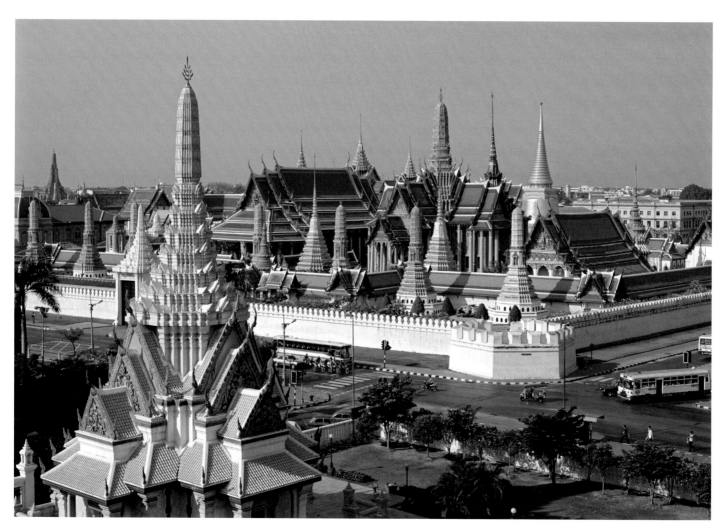

24-19 • TEMPLE OF THE EMERALD BUDDHA (WAT PHRA KAEW)
Grand Palace Complex, Bangkok, Thailand. 1782, and greatly expanded in later centuries.

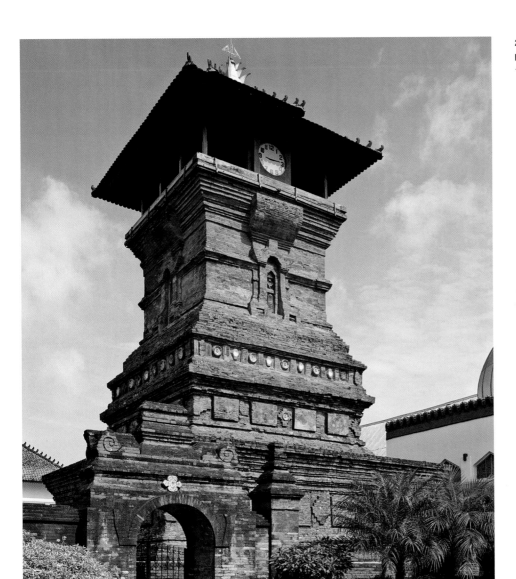

dedicated to one of Java's nine great saints. Although the mosque itself has been renovated, most of the towerlike **MINARET** still survives from the earliest phase of construction in 1549 (**FIG. 24-20**). Its brickwork and decorative niches are reminiscent of earlier Hindu shrine towers but this structure served to call Muslims to worship five times daily. In a traditional Javanese fashion, this was done with a large drum (*bedug*) along with the sung prayers typical in other parts of the world. The lower bands of the tower are decorated with inset porcelain plates imported from China, which add color to the exterior. The various indigenous and international influences that helped shape this tower speak to the remarkably cosmopolitan nature of sixteenth-century Java.

the intense sunlight. Although the core of this complex dates to 1782, it has been greatly expanded in later centuries and remains an important Thai religious and political center.

ISLAMIC ART IN SOUTHEAST ASIA

Muslim merchants played a major role in overseas trade and they frequently spent months at port waiting for the trade winds to change. Over time their faith, Islam, was accepted by local populations living in Malaysia and the island of Sumatra (Indonesia) around the Straits of Malacca. From there it spread across island Southeast Asia. Indonesia is today the world's most populous Muslim country.

KUDUS MOSQUE, INDONESIA Islamic monuments in Indonesia, like the earlier Hindu and Buddhist ones, draw from a rich and diverse repertoire of styles and motifs. One of the earliest examples of Islamic architecture in Java is the Kudus mosque,

THE MODERN PERIOD

Marked by both inspirational expressions of peaceful resistance and bloody warfare, the modern history of South and Southeast Asia has been a study in extremes. But as the turmoil of earlier decades fades across most of the region, many states have emerged as leaders in international commerce, technology, and finance. In an international age, they are capitalizing on the region's centuries-old tradition of bridging cultures and adapting new ideas. These qualities are seen clearly in the South and Southeast Asian art of the Modern period which blends the traditional with the new.

MODERN SOUTH ASIA

In the wake of World War II, the imperial powers of Europe began to shed their colonial domains. The attainment of self-rule had been five long decades in the making, when finally—chastened by the non-violent example of Mahatma Gandhi (1869–1948)—the British Empire relinquished its "Jewel in the Crown," which was

24-21 • Maqbool Fida Husain **VEDIC**
From the *Theorama* series, 1994. Limited
edition color print, 23½″ × 36″ (60 × 92 cm).

24-22 • PETRONAS TOWERS
Kuala Lumpur, Malaysia. 1998.

partitioned to form the modern nations of India, Pakistan, and (in 1972) Bangladesh. After independence in 1947, the exuberant young nations welcomed a modern, internationalist approach to art and architecture.

MAQBOOL FIDA HUSAIN One of India's most influential and prolific modern artists was M. F. Husain (1915–2011). Beginning his career in the 1940s, he embraced Modernism and used its techniques to express South Asian themes. He drew his subjects from diverse sources such as Hindu literature, historical events, and the natural world, as well as from the traditions of his Muslim upbringing. He was exceedingly productive and his range of subject matter at times drew controversy from religious groups who objected to his appropriation of religious imagery. These complaints led him reluctantly to spend the final years of his life in Qatar but he consistently returned to South Asian themes for his inspiration.

His simplified and schematic style can be seen in the *Theorama* series, which addresses nine of the world's major religions. Pictured here is **VEDIC** (FIG. 24–21), Hussain's tribute to Hinduism. Despite its abstraction, the figure of Krishna can be seen dancing on the serpent deity Kaliya, whose body merges with the story of the Churning of the Ocean of Milk (see FIG. 10–41). The event pivots on a triangular form with three faces reminiscent of the Shiva from Elephanta (see FIG. 10–22), and a goddess on elephant-back dispenses abundance in the form of coins or seeds falling from her outstretched hand. The composition is framed on the right by a seated ascetic whose head is a spoked wheel. This wheel may reference the spinning wheels whose use Gandhi advocated to break

dependence on British textiles, but it also reaches back further into the South Asian past and evokes the wheel of *dharma*.

MODERN SOUTHEAST ASIA

The transition from colonial control varied greatly across Southeast Asia, due largely to the range of colonial powers in the region and their varying attitudes toward relinquishing control. Some nations, like Thailand, managed to avoid imperial domination entirely, whereas others fought long wars to establish their independence. In some cases, the power vacuum was filled by local regimes that brought new hardship, like the horrors perpetrated by the Khmer Rouge in Cambodia. The region has gradually achieved stability and growing prosperity as exemplified by its internationally recognized artwork and contemporary architecture.

THE PETRONAS TOWERS, MALAYSIA Dominating the skyline of Kuala Lumpur, Malaysia, are the **PETRONAS TOWERS** (FIG. 24–22), which from 1998 to 2004 were the tallest structures in the world. These paired skyscrapers, linked by a sky bridge at the 41st and 42nd floors, are built primarily of reinforced concrete surrounded by a casing of steel and glass. They were designed collaboratively by Argentine architect César Pelli and Filipino-Malaysian engineer Deejay Cerico, who drew inspiration in their designs from traditional Malaysian Islamic forms. The towers stand 1,242 feet tall and took seven years to build. Today the buildings house many business offices, a shopping mall, and the Malaysian Philharmonic Orchestra, and are characteristic of the new growth and development across the region.

THINK ABOUT IT

24.1 Consider the paintings *Jahangir and Shah Abbas* (FIG. 24–8) and *Mother India* (FIG. 24–15). What are the political messages and at whom were they directed? Who would have seen these works?

24.2 Analyze the form of the Gateway of India (FIG. 24–14) in relation to the ancient Roman form of the triumphal arch—see, for example, the Arch of Titus (FIG. 6–36). Explain what aspects are European and which derive from South Asian architecture.

24.3 The Emerald Buddha and the Seated Buddha from the reign of Jayavarman VII are both closely associated with royal power. Explain how each image lends authority to the king; emphasize both similarities and differences between the two examples.

24.4 Consider the Qutb Minar (FIG. 24–5) and Fatehpur Sikri. Do these structures reveal differences in the way each kingdom viewed itself in relation to wider Indian culture? If so, explain how. Can similar differences be seen when comparing the Victoria Terminus and the Gateway of India? Explain.

CROSSCURRENTS

FIG. 24–1   FIG. 24–20

Consider some of the ways that Islamic art and culture impacted South and Southeast Asia. Explain how the Taj Mahal and the Kudus mosque minaret are similar. In what ways do they differ from one another? What historical and cultural influences help account for those differences?

✔—Study and review on myartslab.com

25-1 • Wang Hui **A THOUSAND PEAKS AND MYRIAD RAVINES**

Qing dynasty, 1693. Hanging scroll with ink on paper, 8′2½″ × 3′4½″ (2.54 × 1.03 m). National Palace Museum, Taibei, Taiwan, Republic of China.

Read the document related to *A Thousand Peaks and Myriad Ravines* on myartslab.com

Chinese and Korean Art after 1279

A THOUSAND PEAKS AND MYRIAD RAVINES (**FIG. 25-1**), painted by Wang Hui (1632–1717) in 1693, exemplifies the subjects of Chinese landscape painting: mountains, rivers, waterfalls, trees, rocks, temples, pavilions, houses, bridges, boats, wandering scholars, fishers—familiar motifs from a tradition now many centuries old. On it, the artist has written:

> Moss and weeds cover the rocks and mist hovers over the water.
> The sound of dripping water is heard in front of the temple gate.
> Through a thousand peaks and myriad ravines the spring flows,
> And brings the flying flowers into the sacred caves.
> In the fourth month of the year 1693, in an inn in the capital, I painted this based on a Tang-dynasty poem in the manner of [the painters] Dong [Yuan] and Ju[ran].
>
> (Translation by Chu-tsing Li)

The inscription refers to the artist's inspiration—for the subject, found in the lines of a Tang-dynasty poem, and for the style, found in the paintings of tenth-century painters Dong Yuan and Juran. Wang Hui's art embodies the ideals of the scholar in imperial China.

China's scholar class was unique, the product of an examination system designed to recruit the finest minds in the country for government service. Instituted during the Tang dynasty (618–907) and based on even earlier traditions, the civil service examinations were excruciatingly difficult, but for the tiny percentage who passed at the highest level, the rewards were great—prestige, position, power, and wealth. Steeped in philosophy, literature, and history, China's scholars—often called *wenren* (literati)—shared a common outlook. Following Confucianism, they became officials to fulfill their obligation to the world; pulled by Daoism, they retreated from society in order to come to terms with nature and the universe—to create a garden, to write poetry, to paint.

During the Song dynasty (960–1279) the examinations were expanded and regularized. More than half of all government positions came to be filled by scholars. In the subsequent Yuan and Ming periods, the tradition of **literati painting** (a style that reflected the taste of the educated class) further developed. When the Yuan period of foreign rule came to an end, the new Ming ruling house revived the court traditions of the Song. The Ming became the model for the rulers of Korea's Joseon dynasty, under whose patronage these styles achieved a distinctive and austere beauty.

In the Qing era, China was again ruled by an outside group, this time the Manchus. While maintaining their traditional connections to Tibet and inner Asia through their patronage of Tibetan Buddhism, the Manchu rulers also embraced Chinese ideals, especially those of the literati. Practicing painting and calligraphy, composing poetry in Chinese, and collecting esteemed Chinese works of art, these rulers amassed the great palace collections that can now be seen in Beijing and Taibei.

LEARN ABOUT IT

25.1 Explore the literati style and its relationship to the scholarly life in later Chinese and Korean art.

25.2 Understand the development and significance of the theme of landscape in Chinese and Korean painting.

25.3 Assess the influence of court life and patronage on art in China and Korea.

25.4 Analyze and learn to characterize the emergence of expression beyond representation as a valued aspect of art in China and Korea, from the thirteenth century to the present.

(((•—[Listen to the chapter audio on myartslab.com

THE MONGOL INVASIONS

At the beginning of the thirteenth century the Mongols, a nomadic people from the steppes north of China, began to amass an empire. Led first by Genghiz Khan (c. 1162–1227), then by his sons and grandsons, they swept westward into central Europe and overran Islamic lands from Central Asia through present-day Iraq. To the east, they quickly captured northern China, and in 1279, led by Kublai Khan, they conquered southern China as well. Grandson of the mighty Genghiz, Kublai proclaimed himself emperor of China and founded the Yuan dynasty (1279–1368).

The Mongol invasions were traumatic; their effect on China was long-lasting. During the Song dynasty, China had grown increasingly introspective. Rejecting foreign ideas and influences, intellectuals had focused on defining the qualities that constituted true "Chinese-ness." They drew a clear distinction between their own people, whom they characterized as gentle, erudite, and sophisticated, and the "barbarians" outside China's borders, whom they regarded as crude, wild, and uncivilized. Now, faced with the reality of foreign occupation, China's inward gaze intensified in spiritual resistance. For centuries to come, long after the Mongols had gone, leading scholars continued to seek intellectually more challenging, philosophically more profound, and artistically more subtle expressions of all that could be identified as authentically Chinese (see "Foundations of Chinese Culture," opposite).

YUAN DYNASTY

The Mongols established their capital in the northern city now known as Beijing (**MAP 25-1**). The cultural centers of China,

MAP 25-1 • CHINA AND KOREA

The map shows the borders of both contemporary China and Korea. The colored areas indicate the historical extent of the Qing-dynasty empire (1644–1911), including its tributary states.

Chinese culture is distinguished by its long and continuous development. Between 6000 and 2000 BCE a variety of Neolithic cultures flourished across China. Through long interaction these cultures became increasingly similar and they eventually gave rise to the three Bronze Age dynastic states with which Chinese history traditionally begins: the Xia, the Shang (c. 1700–1100 BCE), and the Zhou (1100–221 BCE).

The Shang developed traditions of casting ritual vessels in bronze, working jade in ceremonial shapes, and writing consistently in scripts that directly evolved into the modern Chinese written language. Society was stratified, and the ruling group maintained its authority in part by claiming power as intermediaries between the human and spirit worlds. Under the Zhou a feudal society developed, with nobles related to the king ruling over numerous small states.

During the latter part of the Zhou dynasty, states began to vie for supremacy through intrigue and increasingly ruthless warfare. The collapse of social order profoundly influenced China's first philosophers, who largely concerned themselves with the pragmatic question of how to bring about a stable society.

In 221 BCE, rulers of the state of Qin triumphed over the remaining states, unifying China as an empire for the first time. The Qin created the mechanisms of China's centralized bureaucracy, but their rule was harsh and the dynasty was quickly overthrown. During the ensuing Han dynasty (206 BCE–220 CE), China at last knew peace and prosperity. Confucianism was made the official state ideology, in the process assuming the form and force of a religion. Developed from the thought of Confucius (551–479 BCE), one of the many philosophers of the Zhou, Confucianism is an ethical system for the management of society based on establishing correct relationships among people. Providing a counterweight was Daoism, which also came into its own during the Han dynasty. Based on the thought of Laozi, a possibly legendary contemporary of Confucius, and the philosopher Zhuangzi (369–286 BCE), Daoism is a view of life that seeks to harmonize the individual with the Dao, or Way, the process of the universe. Confucianism and Daoism have remained central to Chinese thought—the one addressing the public realm of duty and conformity, the other the private world of individualism and creativity.

Following the collapse of the Han dynasty, China experienced a centuries-long period of disunity (220–589 CE). Invaders from the north and west established numerous kingdoms and dynasties, while a series of six precarious Chinese dynasties held sway in the south. Buddhism, which had begun to spread over trade routes from India during the Han era, now flourished. The period also witnessed the economic and cultural development of the south (previous dynasties had ruled from the north).

China was reunited under the Sui dynasty (581–618 CE), which quickly fell to the Tang (618–907), one of the most successful dynasties in Chinese history. Strong and confident, Tang China fascinated and, in turn, was fascinated by the cultures around it. Caravans streamed across central Asia to the capital, Chang'an, then the largest city in the world. Japan and Korea sent thousands of students to study Chinese culture, and Buddhism reached the height of its influence before a period of persecution signaled the start of its decline.

The mood of the Song dynasty (960–1279) was quite different. The martial vigor of the Tang gave way to a culture of increasing refinement and sophistication, and Tang openness to foreign influences was replaced by a conscious cultivation of China's own traditions. In art, landscape painting emerged as the most esteemed genre, capable of expressing both philosophical and personal concerns. With the fall of the north to invaders in 1126, the Song court set up a new capital in the south, which became the cultural and economic center of the country.

however, remained the great cities of the south, where the Song court had been located for the previous 150 years. Combined with the tensions of Yuan rule, this separation of China's political and cultural centers created a new dynamic in the arts.

Throughout most of Chinese history, the imperial court had set the tone for artistic taste: Artisans attached to the court produced architecture, paintings, gardens, and objects of jade, lacquer, ceramics, and silk especially for imperial use. Over the centuries, painters and calligraphers gradually moved higher up the social scale, for these "arts of the brush" were often practiced by scholars and even emperors, whose high status reflected positively on whatever interested them. With the establishment of an imperial painting academy during the Song dynasty, painters finally achieved a status equal to that of court officials. For the literati, painting came to be grouped with calligraphy and poetry as the trio of accomplishments suited to members of the cultural elite.

But while the literati elevated the status of painting by virtue of practicing it, they also began to develop their own ideas of what painting should be. Not needing to earn an income from their art, they cultivated an amateur ideal in which personal expression counted for more than professional skill. They created for themselves a status as artists totally separate from and superior to professional painters, whose art they felt was inherently compromised, since it was done to please others, and impure, since it was tainted by money.

The conditions of Yuan rule now encouraged a clear distinction between court taste, ministered to by professional artists and artisans, and literati taste. The Yuan dynasty continued to see patronage of the arts as an imperial responsibility, commissioning buildings, murals, gardens, paintings, and decorative arts. Western visitors, such as the Italian Marco Polo, were mightily impressed by the magnificence of the Yuan court (see "Marco Polo," page 796). But scholars, profoundly alienated from the new government, took little notice of these accomplishments. Nor did Yuan rulers have much use for scholars, especially those from the south. The civil service examinations were abolished, and the highest government positions were bestowed, instead, on Mongols and their foreign allies. Scholars now tended to turn inward, to search for solutions of their own, and to try to express themselves in personal and symbolic terms.

China under Kublai Khan was one of four Mongol khanates that together extended west into present-day Iraq and through Russia to the borders of Poland and Hungary. For roughly a century, travelers moved freely across this vast expanse, making the era one of unprecedented cross-cultural exchange. Diplomats, missionaries, merchants, and adventurers flocked to the Yuan court, and Chinese envoys were dispatched to the West. The most celebrated European traveler of the time was a Venetian named Marco Polo (c. 1254–1324), whose descriptions of his travels were for several centuries the only firsthand account of China available in Europe.

Marco Polo was still in his teens when he set out for China in 1271. He traveled with his uncle and father, both merchants, bearing letters for Kublai Khan from Pope Gregory X. After a four-year journey the Polos arrived at last in Beijing. Marco became a favorite of the emperor and spent the next 17 years in his service, during which time he traveled extensively throughout China. He eventually returned home in 1295.

Imprisoned later during a war between Venice and Genoa, rival Italian city-states, Marco Polo passed the time by dictating an account of his experiences to a fellow prisoner. The resulting book, *A Description of the World*, has fascinated generations of readers with its depiction of prosperous and sophisticated lands in the East. Translated into many European languages, it was an important influence in stimulating further exploration. When Columbus set sail across the Atlantic in 1492, one of the places he hoped to find was a country Marco Polo called Zipangu—Japan.

ZHAO MENGFU Zhao Mengfu (1254–1322) was a descendant of the imperial line of Song. Unlike many scholars of his time, he eventually chose to serve the Yuan government and was made a high official. A distinguished painter, calligrapher, and poet, Zhao was especially known for his carefully rendered paintings of horses. But he also cultivated another manner, most famous in his landmark painting **AUTUMN COLORS ON THE QIAO AND HUA MOUNTAINS** (**FIG. 25-2**).

Zhao painted this work for a friend whose ancestors came from Jinan, the present-day capital of Shandong Province, and the painting supposedly depicts the landscape there. Yet the mountains and trees are not painted in the accomplished naturalism of Zhao's own time but rather in the archaic yet elegant manner of the earlier Tang dynasty (618–907). The Tang had ruled during a great era in Chinese history, when the country was both militarily strong and culturally vibrant. Through his painting Zhao evoked a nostalgia not only for his friend's distant homeland but also for China's distant past.

This educated taste for the "spirit of antiquity" became an important aspect of literati painting in later periods. Also typical of literati taste are the unassuming brushwork, the subtle colors sparingly used (many literati paintings forgo color altogether), the use of landscape to convey personal meaning, and even the intended audience—a close friend. The literati did not paint for public display but for each other. They favored small formats such as handscrolls, **hanging scrolls**, or **album** leaves (book pages), which could easily be shown to friends or shared at small gatherings (see "Formats of Chinese Painting," page 799).

NI ZAN Of the considerable number of Yuan painters who took up Zhao's ideas, several became models for later generations. One was Ni Zan (1301–1374), whose most famous surviving painting is **THE RONGXI STUDIO** (**FIG. 25-3**). Done entirely in ink, the painting depicts the lake region in Ni's home district. Mountains, rocks, trees, and a pavilion are sketched with a minimum of detail using a dry brush technique—a technique in which the brush is not fully loaded with ink but rather is about to run out, so that white paper "breathes" through the ragged strokes. The result is a painting with a light touch and a sense of simplicity and purity. Literati styles were believed to reflect an individual painter's personality, and Ni's spare, dry style became associated with a noble spirit. Many later painters adopted it or paid homage to it.

25-2 • Zhao Mengfu AUTUMN COLORS ON THE QIAO AND HUA MOUNTAINS
Yuan dynasty, 1296. Handscroll with ink and color on paper, 11¼″ × 3⅜″ (28.6 × 9.3 cm). National Palace Museum, Taibei, Taiwan, Republic of China.

25-3 • Ni Zan THE RONGXI STUDIO
Yuan dynasty, 1372. Hanging scroll with ink on paper, height 29⅜"
(74.6 cm). National Palace Museum, Taibei, Taiwan, Republic of China.

The idea that a painting is not an attempt to capture the visual appearance of nature nor to satisfy others but is executed freely and carelessly for the artist's own amusement is at the heart of the literati aesthetic. Ni Zan once wrote this comment on a painting: "What I call painting does not exceed the joy of careless sketching with a brush. I do not seek formal likeness but do it simply for my own amusement. Recently I was rambling about and came to a town. The people asked for my pictures, but wanted them exactly according to their own desires and to represent a specific occasion. [When I could not satisfy them,] they went away insulting, scolding, and cursing in every possible way. What a shame! But how can one scold a eunuch for not growing a beard?" (translated in Bush and Shih, p. 266).

Ni Zan's eccentric behavior became legendary in the history of Chinese art. In his early years he was one of the richest men in the region, the owner of a large estate. His pride and his aloofness from daily affairs often got him into trouble with the authorities. His cleanliness was notorious. In addition to washing himself several times daily, he also ordered his servants to wash the trees in his garden and to clean the furniture after his guests had left. He was said to be so unworldly that late in life he gave away most of his possessions and lived as a hermit in a boat, wandering on rivers and lakes.

Whether these stories are true or not, they were important elements of Ni's legacy to later painters, for Ni's life as well as his art served as a model. Literati painting was associated with a viewpoint concerning what constituted an appropriate life. The ideal, as embodied by Ni Zan and others, was a brilliantly gifted scholar whose spirit was too refined for the dusty world of government service and who thus preferred to live as a recluse, or as one who had retired after having become frustrated by a brief stint as an official.

MING DYNASTY

The founder of the next dynasty, the Ming (1368–1644), came from a family of poor uneducated peasants. As he rose through the ranks in the army, he enlisted the help of scholars to gain power and solidify his following. Once he had driven the Mongols from Beijing and firmly established himself as emperor, however, he grew to distrust intellectuals. His rule was despotic, even ruthless. Throughout the nearly 300 years of Ming rule, most emperors shared his attitude, so although the civil service examinations were reinstated, scholars remained alienated from the government they were trained to serve.

COURT AND PROFESSIONAL PAINTING

The contrast between the luxurious world of the court and the austere ideals of the literati continued through the Ming dynasty.

A typical example of Ming court taste is **HUNDREDS OF BIRDS ADMIRING THE PEACOCKS**, a large painting on silk by Yin Hong, an artist active during the late fifteenth and early sixteenth centuries (**FIG. 25-4**). A pupil of well-known courtiers, Yin most probably served in the court at Beijing. This painting is an example of the birds-and-flowers genre, which had been popular with artists of the Song academy. Here the subject takes on symbolic meaning, with the homage of the birds to the peacocks representing the homage of court officials to the imperial state. Although the style is faithful to Song academic models, the large format and pervasive attention to detail are traits of the Ming.

A related, yet bolder and less constrained, landscape style was also popular during this period. It is sometimes called the Zhe style since its roots were in Hangzhou, Zhejiang Province, where the Southern Song court had been located. A representative example

25-4 • Yin Hong HUNDREDS OF BIRDS ADMIRING THE PEACOCKS
Ming dynasty, late 15th–early 16th century. Hanging scroll with ink and color on silk, 7′10½″ × 6′5″ (2.4 × 1.96 m). The Cleveland Museum of Art. Purchase from the J.H. Wade Fund (1974.31)

25-5 • Dai Jin RETURNING HOME LATE FROM A SPRING OUTING
Ming dynasty. Hanging scroll with ink on silk, 5′6″ × 2′8¾″ (1.68 × 0.83 m). National Palace Museum, Taibei, Taiwan, Republic of China.

is **RETURNING HOME LATE FROM A SPRING OUTING (FIG. 25-5)**, unsigned but attributed to Dai Jin (1388–1462). Zhe-style works such as this will become sources for Korean and Japanese artists such as An Gyeon (see FIG. 25-18) and Sesshu (see FIG. 26-3).

QIU YING A preeminent professional painter in the Ming period was Qiu Ying (1494–1552), who lived in Suzhou, a prosperous southern city. He inspired generations of imitators with

exceptional works, such as a long handscroll known as **SPRING DAWN IN THE HAN PALACE (FIG. 25-6)**. The painting is based on Tang-dynasty depictions of women in the court of the Han dynasty (206 BCE–220 CE). While in the service of a well-known collector, Qiu Ying had the opportunity to study many Tang paintings, whose artists usually concentrated on the figures, set on blank backgrounds. Qiu's graceful and elegant figures—although modeled after those in Tang works—are situated within a

25-6 • Qiu Ying SECTION OF SPRING DAWN IN THE HAN PALACE
Ming dynasty, 1500–1550. Handscroll with ink and color on silk, 1′ × 18′13⁄16″ (0.3 × 5.7 m). National Palace Museum, Taibei, Taiwan, Republic of China.

With the exception of large wall paintings that typically decorated palaces, temples, and tombs, most Chinese paintings were created from ink and water-based colors on silk or paper. Finished works were generally mounted as handscrolls, hanging scrolls, or leaves in an album.

An album comprises a set of paintings of identical size mounted in a book. (A single painting from an album is called an album leaf.) The paintings in an album are usually related in subject, such as various views of a famous site or a series of scenes glimpsed on one trip.

Album-sized paintings might also be mounted as a handscroll, a horizontal format generally about 12 inches high and anywhere from a few feet to dozens of feet long. More typically, however, a handscroll would be a single continuous painting. Handscrolls were not meant to be displayed all at once, the way they are commonly presented today in museums. Rather, they were unrolled only occasionally, to be savored in much the same spirit as we might view a favorite film. Placing the scroll on a flat surface such as a table, a viewer would unroll it a foot or two at a time, moving gradually through the entire scroll from right to left, lingering over favorite details. The scroll was then rolled up and returned to its box until the next viewing.

Like handscrolls, hanging scrolls were not displayed permanently but were taken out for a limited time: a day, a week, a season. Unlike a handscroll, however, the painting on a hanging scroll was viewed as

a whole—unrolled and hung on a wall, with the roller at the lower end acting as a weight to help the scroll hang flat. Although some hanging scrolls are quite large, they are still fundamentally intimate works, not intended for display in a public place.

Creating a scroll was a time-consuming and exacting process accomplished by a professional mounter. The painting was first backed with paper to strengthen it. Next, strips of paper-backed silk were pasted to the top, bottom, and sides, framing the painting on all four sides. Additional silk pieces were added to extend the scroll horizontally or vertically, depending on the format. The assembled scroll was then backed again with paper and fitted with a half-round dowel, or wooden rod, at the top of a hanging scroll or on the right end of a handscroll, with ribbons for hanging and tying, and with a wooden roller at the other end. Hanging scrolls were often fashioned from several patterns of silk, and a variety of piecing formats were developed and codified. On a handscroll, a painting was generally preceded by a panel giving the work's title and often followed by a long panel bearing colophons—inscriptions related to the work, such as poems in its praise or comments by its owners over the centuries. A scroll would be remounted periodically to better preserve it, and colophons and inscriptions would be preserved in each remounting. Seals added another layer of interest. A treasured scroll often bears not only the seal of its maker but also those of collectors and admirers through the centuries.

colophon panel

frontispiece

鵲華秋色

label

handscroll rolled for storage

handscroll

front

back

hanging scroll

carefully described setting of palace buildings. They engage in courtly pastimes, such as chess, music, calligraphy, and painting. With its antique subject matter, refined technique, brilliant color, and controlled composition, *Spring Dawn in the Han Palace* brought professional painting to another level (see a detail from this scroll in "A Closer Look," page 801).

DECORATIVE ARTS

Qiu Ying painted to satisfy his patrons in Suzhou. The cities of the south were becoming wealthy, and newly rich merchants collected paintings, antiques, and art objects. The court, too, was prosperous and lavishly funded the arts. In such a setting, the decorative arts thrived.

Marco Polo, it is said, was the one who named a new type of ceramic he found in China. Its translucent purity reminded him of the smooth whiteness of the cowry shell, *porcellana* in Italian. Porcelain is made from kaolin, an extremely refined white clay, and petuntse, a variety of the mineral feldspar. When properly combined and fired at a sufficiently high temperature (generally in the range of 1300° to 1400°C), the two materials fuse into a glasslike, translucent ceramic that is far stronger than it looks.

Porcelaneous stoneware, fired at lower temperatures, was known in China by the seventh century, but true porcelain was perfected during the Song dynasty. To create blue-and-white porcelain such as the flask in FIGURE 25–7, blue pigment was made from cobalt oxide, finely ground and mixed with water. The decoration was painted directly onto the unfired porcelain vessel, then a layer of clear glaze was applied over it. (In this technique, known as **underglaze** painting, the pattern is painted beneath the glaze.) After firing, the piece emerged from the kiln with a clear blue design set sharply against a snowy white background.

Entranced with the exquisite properties of porcelain, European potters tried for centuries to duplicate it. The technique was finally discovered in 1709 by Johann Friedrich Böttger in Dresden, Germany, who tried—but failed—to keep it a secret.

MING BLUE-AND-WHITE WARES Ming China became famous the world over for its exquisite ceramics, especially porcelain (see "The Secret of Porcelain," above). The imperial kilns in Jingdezhen, in Jiangxi Province, became the most renowned center for porcelain not only in China, but in all the world. Particularly noteworthy are the blue-and-white wares produced there during the ten-year reign of the ruler known as the Xuande Emperor (r. 1426–1435). The subtle shape, the refined yet vigorous decoration of dragons on the sea, and the flawless glazing of the **FLASK** in **FIGURE 25–7** are representative of the high achievement of Ming ceramic artists.

ARCHITECTURE AND CITY PLANNING

Centuries of warfare and destruction have left very few early Chinese architectural monuments intact. The most important remaining example of traditional architecture is **THE FORBIDDEN CITY**, the imperial palace compound in Beijing, whose principal buildings were constructed during the Ming dynasty (**FIG. 25–8**).

THE FORBIDDEN CITY The basic plan of Beijing was the work of the Mongols, who laid out their capital city according to traditional Chinese principles. City planning had begun early in China—in the seventh century, in the case of Chang'an (present-day Xi'an), the capital of the Sui and Tang emperors. The walled city of Chang'an was organized on a rectangular grid, with evenly spaced streets that ran north–south and east–west. At the northern end stood a walled imperial complex.

25-7 • FLASK

Ming dynasty, 1426–1435. Porcelain with decoration painted in underglaze cobalt blue. Collection of the Palace Museum, Beijing.

Dragons have featured prominently in Chinese folklore from earliest times—Neolithic examples have been found painted on pottery and carved in jade. In Bronze Age China, dragons came to be associated with powerful and sudden manifestations of nature, such as wind, thunder, and lightning. At the same time, dragons became associated with superior beings such as virtuous rulers and sages. With the emergence of China's first firmly established empire during the Han dynasty, the dragon was appropriated as an imperial symbol, and it remained so throughout Chinese history. Dragon sightings were duly recorded and considered auspicious. Yet even the Son of Heaven could not monopolize the dragon. During the Tang and Song dynasties the practice arose of painting pictures of dragons to pray for rain, and for Chan (Zen) Buddhists, the dragon was a symbol of sudden enlightenment.

A CLOSER LOOK | *Spring Dawn in the Han Palace*

by Qiu Ying. Ming dynasty, 1500–1550. Section of a handscroll with ink and color on silk.
1′ × 18′13⁄16″ (0.3 × 5.7 m). National Palace Museum, Taibei, Taiwan, Republic of China.

Two ladies unwrap a *qin*, the zither or lute that was the most respected of musical instruments.

A seated lady plays the *pipa*, an instrument introduced from Central Asia during the Tang dynasty.

Antique vessels of bronze, lacquer, and porcelain adorn the room and suggest the ladies' refined taste.

A tray landscape featuring an eroded rock provides a sculptural counterpart to landscape (mountain-and-water) painting and suggests a place where immortals might dwell.

Two ladies dance together letting their sleeves and sashes swirl.

View the Closer Look for *Spring Dawn in the Han Palace* on myartslab.com

Beijing, too, was developed as a walled, rectangular city with streets laid out in a grid. The palace enclosure occupied the center of the northern part of the city, which was reserved for the Mongols. Chinese lived in the southern third of the city. Later, Ming and Qing emperors preserved this division, with officials living in the northern or Inner City and commoners living in the southern or Outer City. The third Ming emperor, Yongle (ruled 1403–1424), rebuilt the Forbidden City as we see it today.

The approach was impressive. Visitors entered through the Meridian Gate, a monumental complex with perpendicular side wings (see FIG. 25–8). After passing through the Meridian Gate, visitors encountered a broad courtyard crossed by a bow-shaped waterway spanned by five arched marble bridges. At the opposite end of this courtyard is the Gate of Supreme Harmony, opening onto an even larger courtyard that houses three ceremonial halls raised on a broad platform. First is the Hall of Supreme Harmony, where, on the most important state occasions, the emperor sat on his throne, facing south. Beyond is the smaller Hall of Central Harmony, then the Hall of Protecting Harmony. Behind these vast ceremonial spaces, still on the central axis, is the inner court, again with a progression of three buildings, this time more intimate in scale. In its balance and symmetry the plan of the Forbidden City reflects ancient Chinese beliefs about the harmony of the universe, and it emphasizes the emperor's role as the Son of Heaven, whose duty was to maintain the cosmic order from his throne in the middle of the world.

25-8 • THE FORBIDDEN CITY
Now the Palace Museum, Beijing. Mostly Ming dynasty. View from the southwest.

 Explore the architectural panoramas of the Forbidden City on myartslab.com

THE LITERATI AESTHETIC

In the south, particularly in the district of Suzhou, literati paint-ing, associated with the educated men who served the court as government officials, remained the dominant artistic trend. One of the major literati painters from the Ming period is Shen Zhou (1427–1509), who had no desire to enter government service and spent most of his life in Suzhou. He studied the Yuan painters avidly and tried to recapture their spirit in such works as *Poet on a Mountaintop* (see "*Poet on a Mountaintop*," opposite). Although the style of the painting recalls the freedom and simplicity of Ni Zan (see FIG. 25-3), the motif of a poet surveying the landscape from a mountain plateau is Shen's creation.

LITERATI INFLUENCE ON FURNITURE, ARCHITEC-TURE, AND GARDEN DESIGN The taste of the literati also influenced the design of furniture, architecture, and especially gardens. Characteristic of Chinese furniture during the Ming period, the **ARMCHAIR** in **FIGURE 25-9** is constructed without the use of glue or nails. Instead, pieces fit together based on the

25-9 • ARMCHAIR
Ming dynasty, 16th–17th century. Huanghuali wood (hardwood), 39⅜″ × 27¼″ × 20″ (100 × 69.2 × 50.8 cm). Nelson-Atkins Museum of Art, Kansas City, Missouri. Purchase: William Rockhill Nelson Trust (46–78/1)

In earlier landscape paintings, human figures were typically shown dwarfed by the grandeur of nature. Travelers might be seen scuttling along a narrow path by a stream, while overhead towered mountains whose peaks conversed with the clouds and whose heights were inaccessible. In **FIGURE 25-10** the poet has climbed the mountain and dominates the landscape. Even the clouds are beneath him. Before his gaze, a poem hangs in the air, as though he were projecting his thoughts.

The poem, composed by Shen Zhou himself, and written in his distinctive hand, reads:

White clouds like a scarf enfold the mountain's
    waist;
Stone steps hang in space—a long, narrow
    path.
Alone, leaning on my cane, I gaze intently at
    the scene,
And feel like answering the murmuring brook
    with the music of my flute.

(Translation by Jonathan Chaves, *The Chinese Painter as Poet*, New York, 2000, p. 46.)

Shen Zhou composed the poem and wrote the inscription at the time he painted the album. The style of the calligraphy, like the style of the painting, is informal, relaxed, and straightforward—qualities that were believed to reflect the artist's character and personality.

The painting visualizes Ming philosophy, which held that the mind, not the physical world, was the basis for reality. With its tight synthesis of poetry, calligraphy, and painting, and with its harmony of mind and landscape, *Poet on a Mountaintop* represents the essence of Ming literati painting.

25-10 • Shen Zhou POET ON A MOUNTAINTOP
Leaf from an album of landscapes; painting mounted as part of a handscroll. Ming dynasty, c. 1500. Ink and color on paper, 15¼″ × 23¾″ (40 × 60.2 cm). The Nelson-Atkins Museum of Art, Kansas City, Missouri. Purchase: William Rockhill Nelson Trust (46-51/2)

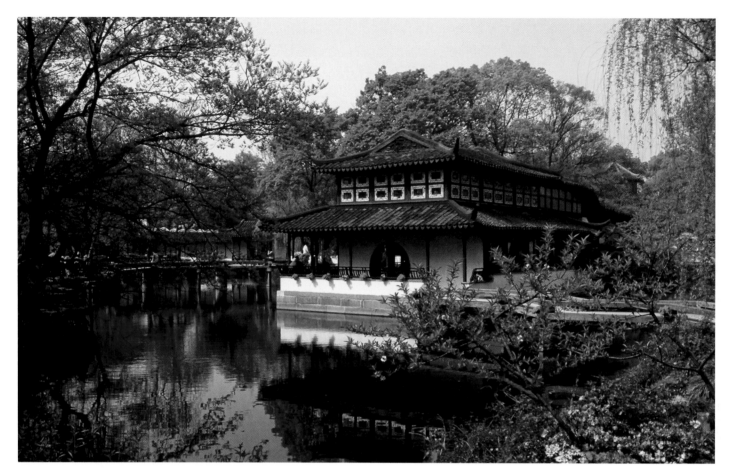

25-11 • GARDEN OF THE CESSATION OF OFFICIAL LIFE (ALSO KNOWN AS THE HUMBLE ADMINISTRATOR'S GARDEN)

Suzhou, Jiangsu. Ming dynasty, early 16th century.

Early in the sixteenth century, an official in Beijing, frustrated after serving in the capital for many years without promotion, returned home. Taking an ancient poem, "The Song of Leisurely Living," for his model, he began to build a garden. He called his retreat the Garden of the Cessation of Official Life to indicate that he had exchanged his career as a bureaucrat for a life of leisure. By leisure, he meant that he could now dedicate himself to calligraphy, poetry, and painting, the three arts dear to scholars in China.

---

principle of the mortise-and-tenon joint, in which a projecting element (tenon) on one piece fits snugly into a cavity (mortise) on another. Each piece of the chair is carved—not bent or twisted—and the joints are crafted with great precision. The patterns of the wood grain provide subtle interest, unconcealed by painting or other embellishment. The style, like that of Chinese architecture, is simple, clear, symmetrical, and balanced. The effect is formal and dignified but natural and simple—virtues central to the traditional Chinese view of proper human conduct as well.

The art of landscape gardening also flourished during the Ming dynasty, as many literati surrounded their homes with gardens. The most famous gardens were created in the southern cities of the Yangzi Delta, especially in Suzhou, including the largest surviving garden of the era—the **GARDEN OF THE CESSATION OF OFFICIAL LIFE** (FIG. 25-11). Although modified and reconstructed many times since the sixteenth century, it still reflects many of the basic ideas of the original Ming owner. About one third of the garden is devoted to water through artificially created

brooks and ponds. The landscape is dotted with pavilions, kiosks, libraries, studios, and corridors—many with poetic names, such as Rain Listening Pavilion and Bridge of the Small Flying Rainbow.

DONG QICHANG, LITERATI THEORIST The ideas underlying literati painting found their most influential expression in the writings of Dong Qichang (1555–1636). This high official in the late Ming period embodied the literati tradition as poet, calligrapher, and painter. He developed a view of Chinese art history that divided painters into two opposing schools, northern and southern. The categorization is unrelated to the actual geographic home of the painters—a painter from the south might well be classed as northern—but reflects parallels Dong perceived with the northern and southern schools of Chan (Zen) Buddhism in China. The southern school of Chan, founded by the eccentric monk Huineng (638–713), was unorthodox, radical, and innovative; the northern Chan school was traditional and conservative. Similarly, Dong's two schools of painters represented progressive and conservative traditions. In Dong's view, the conservative northern school was dominated by professional painters whose academic, often decorative, style emphasized technical skill. In contrast, the progressive southern school preferred ink to color and free brushwork to meticulous detail. Its painters aimed for poetry and personal expression. In promoting this theory, Dong privileged literati painting, which he positioned as the culmination of the southern school, and this viewpoint fundamentally influenced the way the Chinese viewed their own tradition.

Dong Qichang summarized his views on the proper training for literati painters in the famous statement "Read ten thousand books and walk ten thousand miles." By this he meant that one must first study the works of the great masters, then follow "heaven and earth," the world of nature. Such study would prepare the way for greater self-expression through brush and ink, the goal of literati painting. Dong's views rested on an awareness that a painting of scenery and the actual scenery are two very different things. The excellence of a painting does not lie in its degree of resemblance to the natural world—that gap can never be bridged—but in its expressive power. In this view, the expressive language of painting is inherently abstract, rooted in the construction of its brushstrokes. For example, in a painting of a rock, the rock itself is not expressive; rather, the brushstrokes that suggest the rock are expressive.

With such thinking Dong brought painting close to the realm of calligraphy, which had long been considered the highest form of artistic expression in China. More than a thousand years before Dong's time, a body of critical terms and theories had evolved to discuss calligraphy in relation to the formal and expressive properties of brushwork and composition. Dong incorporated some of these terms—categories such as opening and closing, rising and falling, and void and solid—into the criticism of painting.

Dong's theories take visual form in his painting of **THE QINGBIAN MOUNTAINS** (**FIG. 25-12**). As documented in his own inscription, he based this painting on a work by the tenth-century artist Dong Yuan. Dong Qichang's style, however, is quite different from the styles of the masters he admired. Although there is some indication of foreground, middle ground, and distant mountains, the space is ambiguous, as if all the elements were compressed to the surface of the picture. With this flattening of space, the trees, rocks, and mountains become more readily legible as semiabstract forms made of brushstrokes.

Six trees arranged diagonally at lower right define the extreme foreground and announce themes that the rest of the painting repeats, varies, and develops. The left-most of these foreground trees, with its outstretched branches and full foliage, is echoed first in the shape of another tree just across the river and again in a tree farther up and to the left. The tallest tree of the foreground grouping anticipates the high peak that towers in the distance almost directly above it, while the forms of the smaller foreground trees, especially the one with the darkest leaves, are repeated in numerous variations across the painting. At the same time, the simple and ordinary-looking boulder in the foreground is transformed in the

25-12 • Dong Qichang THE QINGBIAN MOUNTAINS
Ming dynasty, 1617. Hanging scroll with ink on paper, 21′8″ × 7′4⅜″ (6.72 × 2.25 m). Cleveland Museum of Art. Leonard C. Hanna, Jr., Fund

conglomeration of rocks, ridges, hills, and mountains above. This double reading—both abstract and representational, on the surface and into space—parallels the work's dual nature as a painting of a landscape and an interpretation of a traditional landscape painting.

The influence of Dong Qichang on the development of Chinese painting of later periods cannot be overstated. Indeed, nearly all Chinese painters since the early seventeenth century have engaged with his ideas in one way or another.

QING DYNASTY

In 1644, when the armies of the Manchu people to the northeast of China marched into Beijing, many Chinese reacted as though their civilization had come to an end. Yet, the Manchus had already adopted many Chinese customs and institutions before their conquest. After gaining control of all of China, a process that took decades, they showed great respect for Chinese tradition. All the major artistic trends of the late Ming dynasty eventually continued into the Manchu, or Qing, dynasty (1644–1911).

ORTHODOX PAINTING

Literati painting had been established as the dominant tradition; it now became orthodox. Scholars followed Dong Qichang's recommendation, basing their approach on the study of past masters—especially Song and Yuan artists—and imitating antique styles as a way of expressing their own learning, technique, and taste.

The Qing emperors of the late seventeenth and eighteenth centuries were painters themselves. They collected literati painting,

25-13 • Yun Shouping AMARANTH
Leaf from an album of flowers, bamboo, fruits, and vegetables. 1633–1690. Album of 10 leaves; ink and color on paper; each leaf 10″ × 13″ (25.3 × 33.5 cm). Collection of Phoenix Art Museum, Arizona. Gift of Marilyn and Roy Papp

The leaf is inscribed by the artist: "Autumn garden abounds in beauty, playfully painted by Ouxiangguan (Yun Shouping)." (Translation by Momoko Soma Welch)

25-14 • Shitao
LANDSCAPE
Leaf from *An Album of Landscapes*. Qing dynasty, c. 1700. Ink and color on paper, 9½″ × 11″ (24.1 × 28 cm). Collection C.C. Wang family.

and their taste was shaped mainly by artists such as Wang Hui (see FIG. 25-1). Thus literati painting, long associated with reclusive scholars, ultimately became an academic style practiced at court. Imbued with values associated with scholarship and virtue, these paintings constituted the highest art form of the Qing court. The emperors also valued a style of bird-and-flower painting developed by Yun Shouping (1633–1690) that, like the orthodox style of landscape painting, was embraced by literati painters, many of them court officials themselves. The style, most often seen in albums or fans, recalled aspects of Song- and Yuan-dynasty bird-and-flower painting, and artists cited their ancient models as a way to enrich both the meaning and the beauty of these small-format works. In a leaf from an album of flowers, bamboo, fruits and vegetables, which employs a variety of brush techniques (FIG. 25-13), Yun Shouping represents flowers of the autumn season.

INDIVIDUALIST PAINTING

The first few decades of Qing rule had been both traumatic and dangerous for those who were loyal—or worse, related—to the Ming. Some committed suicide, while others sought refuge in monasteries (e.g., Zhu Da, see Introduction, "A Closer Look," page xxxiv, FIG. B), or wandered the countryside. Among them were several painters who expressed their anger, defiance, frustration, and melancholy in their art. They took Dong Qichang's idea of painting as an expression of the artist's personal feelings very seriously and cultivated highly original styles. These painters have become known as the individualists.

SHITAO One of the individualists was Shitao (1642–1707), who was descended from the first Ming emperor and who took refuge in Buddhist temples when the dynasty fell. In his later life he brought his painting to the brink of abstraction in such works as **LANDSCAPE** (FIG. 25-14). A monk sits in a small hut, looking out onto mountains that seem to be in turmoil. Dots, used for centuries to indicate vegetation on rocks, here seem to have taken on a life of their own. The rocks also seem alive—as if about to swallow up the monk and his hut. Throughout his life Shitao continued to identify himself with the fallen Ming, and he felt that his secure world had turned to chaos with the Manchu conquest.

THE MODERN PERIOD

In the mid and late nineteenth century, China was shaken from centuries of complacency by a series of humiliating military defeats at the hands of Western powers and Japan. Only then did the government finally realize that these new rivals were not like the Mongols of the thirteenth century. China was no longer at the center of the world, a civilized country surrounded by "barbarians."

Spiritual resistance was no longer sufficient to solve the problems brought on by change. New ideas from Japan and the West began to filter in, and the demand arose for political and cultural reforms. In 1911, the Qing dynasty was overthrown, ending 2,000 years of imperial rule, and China was reconceived as a republic.

During the first decades of the twentieth century Chinese artists traveled to Japan and to Europe to study Western art. Returning to China, many sought to introduce the ideas and techniques they had learned, and they explored ways to synthesize the Chinese and the Western traditions. After the establishment of the present-day Communist government in 1949, individual artistic freedom was curtailed as the arts were pressed into the service of the state and its vision of a new social order. After 1979, however, cultural attitudes began to relax, and Chinese painters again pursued their own paths.

WU GUANZHONG One artist who emerged during the 1980s as a leader in Chinese painting was Wu Guanzhong (1919–2010). Combining his French artistic training with his Chinese background, Wu Guanzhong developed a semiabstract style to depict scenes from the Chinese landscape. He made preliminary sketches on site. Then, back in his studio, he developed these sketches into free interpretations based on his feeling and vision. An example of his work, **PINE SPIRIT**, depicts a scene in the Huang (Yellow) Mountains (**FIG. 25-15**). The technique, with its sweeping gestures of paint, is clearly linked to Abstract Expressionism, an influential Western movement of the post–World War II years (Chapter 33); yet the painting also claims a place in the long tradition of Chinese landscape as exemplified by such masters as Shitao.

Like all aspects of Chinese society, Chinese art has felt the strong impact of Western influence, and the question remains whether Chinese artists will absorb Western ideas without losing their traditional identity. Interestingly, landscape remains an important subject, as it has been for more than a thousand years, and calligraphy continues to play a vital role. Using the techniques and methods of the West, some of China's artists have joined an international avant-garde (see, for example, Wenda Gu in Chapter 33, FIG. 33-68), while other painters still seek communion with nature through their ink brushstrokes as a means to come to terms with human life and the world.

ARTS OF KOREA: THE JOSEON DYNASTY TO THE MODERN ERA

In 1392, General Yi Seonggye (1335–1408) overthrew the Goryeo dynasty (918–1392), establishing the Joseon dynasty (1392–1910), sometimes called the Yi dynasty. He first maintained his capital at Gaeseong, the old Goryeo capital, but moved it to Seoul in 1394, where it remained through the end of the dynasty. The Joseon regime rejected Buddhism, espousing Neo-Confucianism as the state philosophy. Taking Ming-dynasty China as its model, the new government patterned its bureaucracy on that of the Ming

25-15 • Wu Guanzhong PINE SPIRIT
1984. Ink and color on paper, 2′3⅝″ × 5′3½″ (0.70 × 1.61 m). Spencer Museum of Art, The University of Kansas, Lawrence.
Gift of the E. Rhodes and Leonard B. Carpenter Foundation (1991.0003)

emperors, even adopting as its own such outward symbols of Ming imperial authority as blue-and-white porcelain. The early Joseon era was a period of cultural refinement and scientific achievement, during which Koreans invented Han'geul (the Korean alphabet) and movable type, not to mention the rain gauge, astrolabe, celestial globe, sundial, and water clock.

JOSEON CERAMICS

Like their Silla and Goryeo forebears (see Chapter 11), Joseon potters excelled in the manufacture of ceramics, taking their cue from contemporaneous Chinese wares, but seldom copying them directly.

BUNCHEONG CERAMICS Descended from Goryeo celadons, Joseon-dynasty stonewares, known as *buncheong* wares, enjoyed widespread usage throughout the peninsula. Their decorative effect relies on the use of white slip that makes the humble stoneware resemble more expensive white porcelain. In fifteenth-century examples, the slip is often seen inlaid into repeating design elements stamped into the clay body.

Sixteenth-century *buncheong* wares are characteristically embellished with wonderfully fluid, calligraphic brushwork painted in iron-brown slip on a white slip ground. Most painted *buncheong* wares have stylized floral décor, but rare pieces, such as the charming **WINE BOTTLE** in **FIGURE 25–16**, feature pictorial decoration. In fresh, lively brushstrokes, a bird with outstretched wings grasps a fish that it has just caught in its talons; waves roll below, while two giant lotus blossoms frame the scene.

Japanese armies repeatedly invaded the Korean peninsula between 1592 and 1597, destroying many of the *buncheong* kilns, and essentially bringing ceramic production to a halt. Tradition holds that the Japanese took many *buncheong* potters home

with them to produce *buncheong*-style wares, which were greatly admired by connoisseurs of the tea ceremony. In fact, the spontaneity of Korean *buncheong* pottery has inspired Japanese ceramics to this day.

PAINTED PORCELAIN Korean potters produced porcelains with designs painted in underglaze cobalt blue as early as the fifteenth century, inspired by Chinese porcelains of the early Ming period (see **FIG. 25–7**). The Korean court dispatched artists from the royal painting academy to the porcelain kilns—located some 30 miles southeast of Seoul—to train porcelain painters. As a result, from the fifteenth century onward, the painting on the best Korean porcelains closely approximated that on paper and silk, unlike in China, where ceramic decoration followed a path of its own with little reference to painting traditions.

In another unique development, Korean porcelains from the sixteenth and seventeenth centuries often feature designs painted in underglaze iron-brown rather than the cobalt blue customary in Ming porcelain. Also uniquely Korean are porcelain jars with bulging shoulders, slender bases, and short, vertical necks, which appeared by the seventeenth century and came to be the most characteristic ceramic shapes in the later Joseon period. Painted in underglaze iron-brown, the seventeenth-century jar shown in **FIGURE 25–17** depicts a fruiting grape branch around its shoulder. In typical Korean fashion, the painting spreads over a surface unconstrained by borders, resulting in a balanced but asymmetrical design that incorporates the Korean taste for unornamented spaces.

JOSEON PAINTING

Korean secular painting came into its own during the Joseon dynasty. Continuing Goryeo traditions, early Joseon examples employ Chinese styles and formats, their range of subjects

25-16 • HORIZONTAL WINE BOTTLE WITH DECORATION OF A BIRD CARRYING A NEWLY CAUGHT FISH
Korea. Joseon dynasty, 16th century. Buncheong ware: light gray stoneware with decoration painted in iron-brown slip on a white slip ground, 6¹⁄₁₀″ × 9½″ (15.5 × 24.1 cm). Museum of Oriental Ceramics, Osaka, Japan. Gift of the Sumitomo Group (20773)

25-17 • BROAD-SHOULDERED JAR WITH DECORATION OF A FRUITING GRAPEVINE
Korea. Joseon dynasty, 17th century. Porcelain with decoration painted in underglaze iron-brown slip, height 22⅛″ (53.8 cm). Ewha Women's University Museum, Seoul, Republic of Korea.

Korean potters learned to make porcelain during the Goryeo dynasty, probably as early as the eleventh or twelfth century, though few Goryeo examples remain today. For many centuries, only the Chinese and Koreans were able to produce porcelains.

expanding from botanical motifs to include landscapes, figures, and a variety of animals.

Painted in 1447 by An Gyeon (b. 1418), **DREAM JOURNEY TO THE PEACH BLOSSOM LAND** (**FIG. 25-18**) is the earliest extant and dated Joseon secular painting. It illustrates a fanciful tale by China's revered nature poet Tao Qian (365–427), and recounts a dream about chancing upon a utopia secluded from the world for centuries while meandering among the peach blossoms of spring.

As with their Goryeo forebears, the monumental mountains and vast, panoramic vistas of such fifteenth-century Korean paintings echo Northern Song painting styles. Chinese paintings of the Southern Song (1127–1279) and Ming periods (1368–1644) also influenced Korean painting of the fifteenth, sixteenth, and seventeenth centuries, though these styles never completely supplanted the imprint of the Northern Song masters.

THE SILHAK MOVEMENT In the eighteenth century, a truly Korean style emerged, inspired by the *silhak* ("practical learning") movement, which emphasized the study of things Korean in addition to the Chinese classics. The impact of the movement is exemplified by the painter Jeong Seon (1676–1759), who chose well-known Korean vistas as the subjects of his paintings, rather than the Chinese themes favored by earlier artists. Among Jeong Seon's paintings are numerous representations of the Diamond Mountains (Geumgang-san), a celebrated range of craggy peaks along Korea's east coast. Painted in 1734, the scroll reproduced in **FIGURE 25-19** aptly captures the Diamond Mountains' needlelike peaks. The subject is Korean, and so is the energetic spirit and the intensely personal style, with its crystalline mountains, distant clouds of delicate ink wash, and individualistic brushwork.

Among figure painters, Sin Yunbok (b. 1758) is an important exemplar of the *silhak* attitude. Active in the late eighteenth and early nineteenth centuries, Sin typically depicted aristocratic

25-18 • An Gyeon DREAM JOURNEY TO THE PEACH BLOSSOM LAND
Korea. Joseon dynasty, 1447. Handscroll with ink and light colors on silk, 15¼″ × 41¾″ (38.7 × 106.1 cm). Central Library, Tenri University, Tenri (near Nara), Japan.

25-19 • Jeong Seon
PANORAMIC VIEW OF THE DIAMOND MOUNTAINS (GEUMGANG-SAN)
Korea. Joseon dynasty, 1734. Hanging scroll with ink and colors on paper, 40⅝″ × 37″ (130.1 × 94 cm). Lee'um, Samsung Museum, Seoul, Republic of Korea.

figures in native Korean garb. The album leaf entitled **PICNIC AT THE LOTUS POND** (**FIG. 25-20**) represents a group of Korean gentlemen enjoying themselves in the countryside on an autumn day in the company of several *gisaeng* (female entertainers). The figures are recognizably Korean—the women with their full coiffures, short jackets, and generous skirts, and the men with their beards, white robes, and wide-brimmed hats woven of horsehair and coated with black lacquer. The stringed instrument played by the gentleman seated at lower right is a *gayageum* (Korean zither), the most hallowed of all Korean musical instruments.

MODERN KOREA

Long known as "the Hermit Kingdom," the Joseon dynasty pursued a policy of isolationism, closing its borders to most of the world, except China, until 1876. Japan's annexation of Korea in 1910 brought the Joseon dynasty to a close, but effectively prolonged the country's seclusion from the outside world. The legacy of self-imposed isolation compounded by colonial occupation (1910–1945)—not to mention the harsh circumstances imposed by World War II (1939–1945), followed by the even worse conditions of the Korean War (1950–1953)—impeded Korea's

25-20 • Sin Yunbok PICNIC AT THE LOTUS POND
Leaf from an album of genre scenes. Korea. Joseon dynasty, late 18th century. Album of 30 leaves; ink and colors on paper, 11⅛″ × 13⅞″ (28.3 × 35.2 cm). Kansong Museum of Art, Seoul, Republic of Korea.

artistic and cultural development during the first half of the twentieth century.

A MODERNIST PAINTER FROM KOREA Despite these privations, some modern influences did reach Korea indirectly via China and Japan, and beginning in the 1920s and 1930s a few Korean artists experimented with contemporary Western styles, typically painting in the manner of Cézanne or Gauguin, but sometimes trying abstract, nonrepresentational styles. Among these, Gim Hwangi (1913–1974) was influenced by Constructivism and geometric abstraction and would become one of twentieth-century Korea's influential painters. Like many Korean artists after the Korean War, Gim wanted to examine Western modernism at its source. He visited Paris in 1956 and then, from 1964 to 1974, lived and worked in New York, where he produced his best-known works. His painting **5-IV-71** presents a large pair of circular radiating patterns composed of small dots and squares in tones of blue, black, and gray

(**FIG. 25-21**). While appearing wholly Western in style, medium, concept, and even in the adoption of the date of the work's creation as its title, *5-IV-71* also seems related to East Asia's venerable tradition of monochrome **ink painting**, while suggesting a transcendence that seems Daoist or Buddhist in feeling. Given that the artist was Korean, that he learned the Chinese classics in his youth, that he studied art in Paris, and that he then worked in New York, it is possible that his painting embodies all of the above. Gim's painting illustrates the dilemma faced by many modern artists seeking to find a distinctive, personal style: whether to paint in an updated version of a traditional style, in a wholly international style, in an international style with a distinctive local twist, or in an eclectic, hybrid style that incorporates both native and naturalized elements from diverse artistic traditions. By addressing these questions, Gim Hwangi blazed a trail for subsequent Korean-born artists, such as the renowned video artist Nam June Paik (1932–2006), whose work will be discussed in Chapter 33.

25-21 • Gim Hwangi 5-IV-71
Korea. 1971. Oil on canvas, 39½″ × 39½″ (100 × 100 cm). Whanki Museum, Seoul, Republic of Korea.

THINK ABOUT IT

25.1 Discuss the place of Dong Qichang's *The Qingbian Mountains* (FIG. 25–12) within the history of Chinese landscape painting, drawing specific comparisons with works that came before and after it.

25.2 Examine a work commissioned by the court at Beijing and distinguish which of its features are typical of court art.

25.3 Characterize the culture of the literati, including their values and their art patronage.

25.4 Theorize reasons for the emergence of individualist painting in China, using specific works to support your argument.

CROSSCURRENTS

FIG. 18–15

FIG. 25–10

Both of these expansive paintings use landscape, figures, and text, to create compositions that embody important ideas, values, and themes that are characteristic of two very different cultures. Discuss the meanings the artists embodied in these two works. How do they represent the aspirations of the artists who created them and the viewers who originally encountered them?

✓—[Study and review on myartslab.com

26–1 • Suzuki Harunobu THE FLOWERS OF BEAUTY IN THE FLOATING WORLD: MOTOURA AND YAEZAKURA OF THE MINAMI YAMASAKIYA

Edo period, 1769. Polychrome woodblock print on paper, 11⅜″ × 8½″ (28.9 × 21.8 cm). Chicago Art Institute. Clarence Buckingham Collection (1925.2116)

👁 **Watch** a video about *ukiyo-e* techniques on myartslab.com

Japanese Art after 1333

Perched on a window seat, a young woman pauses from smoking her pipe while the girl at her side peers intently through a telescope at boats in the bay below (**FIG. 26-1**). The scene takes place in the city of Edo (now Tokyo) in the 1760s, during an era of peace and prosperity that had started some 150 years earlier when the Tokugawa shoguns unified the nation. Edo was then the largest city in the world, with over 1 million inhabitants: samurai-bureaucrats and working-class townspeople. The commoners possessed a vibrant culture centered in urban entertainment districts, where geisha and courtesans, such as the lady and her young trainee portrayed in this woodblock print, worked.

In the 1630s, the Tokugawa shogunate banned Japanese citizens from traveling abroad and restricted foreign access to the country. Nagasaki became Japan's sole international port, which only Koreans, Chinese, and Dutch could enter—and they could not travel freely in the country once there. The government did this to deter Christian missionaries and to assert authority over foreign powers. Not until 1853, when Commodore Matthew Perry of the United States forced Japan to open additional ports, did these policies change. Even so, foreign influences and products could not be prevented, as the tobacco pipe and telescope in this print testify.

The Japanese had first encountered Westerners—Portuguese traders—in the mid sixteenth century. The Dutch reached Japan by 1600 and brought tobacco and, soon after that, the telescope and other exotic optical devices—including spectacles and microscopes—and curious objects, including books, many illustrated. The Japanese eagerly welcomed these foreign goods and imitated foreign customs, which conferred an air of sophistication on the user. Looking through telescopes like the one in this print was a popular amusement of courtesans and their customers. It conveyed the sort of sexual overtones—because of the telescope's phallic shape—that characterized the ribald humor then in vogue. Novel Western optical devices, all readily available by the mid eighteenth century, offered a new way of seeing that affected the appearance of Japanese pictorial art. As in the early history of Japanese art, however, Chinese influence remained strong and now spread throughout the population as never before, due to new efforts to educate the broader populace in Chinese studies. In varying degrees, the intermingling of diverse native and foreign artistic traditions continued to shape the arts of Japan.

LEARN ABOUT IT

26.1 Survey and evaluate the variety of styles and modes of Japanese art after 1333 that develop in relation to Zen Buddhism.

26.2 Explore the principal themes and subjects portrayed in secular art during the Edo period, especially the popularized imagery featured in *ukiyo-e*.

26.3 Compare art created in Kyoto with art made in Edo during the Edo period and evaluate the relationship of these works to the very different cultural and social climates of the two cities.

26.4 Understand and learn to characterize the way imported artistic traditions, from Europe as well as Asia, interacted with traditional Japanese practices to create new forms of art in the modern period.

((•—**Listen** to the chapter audio on myartslab.com

MUROMACHI PERIOD

By the year 1333, the history of Japanese art was already long and rich (see "Foundations of Japanese Culture," page 819). Very early, a particularly Japanese sensitivity to artistic production had emerged, including a love of natural materials, a fondness for representing elements of the natural world, and the cultivation of fine craft. Aesthetically, Japanese art manifested a taste for asymmetry, abstraction, boldness of expression, and humor—characteristics that will continue to distinguish Japanese art in its evolving history.

Late in the twelfth century, the authority of the emperor had been superseded by powerful and ambitious warriors (samurai) under the leadership of the shogun, the general-in-chief. But in 1333, Emperor Go-Daigo attempted to retake power. He failed and was forced into hiding in the mountains south of Kyoto where he set up a "southern court." Meanwhile, the shogunal family then in power, the Minamoto, was overthrown by warriors of the Ashikaga clan, who placed a rival to the upstart emperor on the throne in Kyoto, in a "northern court," and had him declare their clan head as shogun. They ruled the country from the Muromachi district in Kyoto, and finally vanquished the southern court emperors in 1392. The Muromachi period, also known as the Ashikaga era (1392–1573), formally began with this event.

The Muromachi period is marked by the ascendance of Zen Buddhism, introduced into Japan in the late twelfth century, whose austere ideals particularly appealed to the highly disciplined samurai. While Pure Land Buddhism, which had spread widely during the latter part of the Heian period (794–1185), remained popular, Zen (which means meditation) became the dominant cultural force in Japan among the ruling elite.

ZEN INK PAINTING

During the Muromachi period, the creation of brightly colored narrative handscrolls in traditional Japanese style continued, but monochrome painting in black ink and its diluted grays—which had just been introduced to Japan from the continent at the end of the Kamakura period (1185–1333)—reigned supreme. Muromachi ink painting was heavily influenced by the aesthetics of Zen, but unlike earlier Zen paintings that had concentrated on portrayals of important individuals associated with the Zen monastic tradition, many artists also began painting Chinese-style landscapes in ink. Traditionally, the monk-artist Shubun (active c. 1418–1463) is regarded as Japan's first great master of ink landscape painting. Unfortunately, no undisputed work of his survives. Two landscapes by Shubun's pupil Bunsei (active c. 1450–1460), however, do survive. The one reproduced in **FIGURE 26–2** is closely modeled on Korean ink landscape paintings that themselves copied Chinese models from the Ming period (such as **FIG. 25–5**). It contains a foreground consisting of a spit of rocky land with an overlapping series of motifs—a spiky pine tree, a craggy rock, a poet seated in a hermitage, and a brushwood fence surrounding a small garden of trees and bamboo. In the middle ground is open space—emptiness,

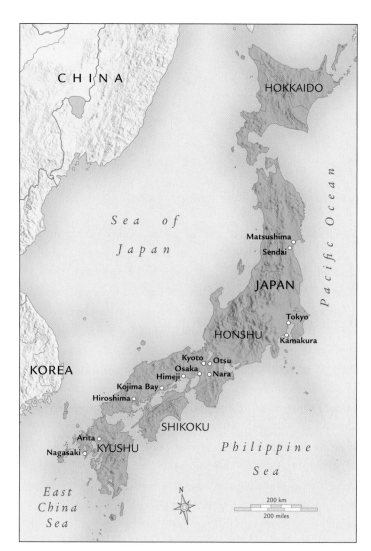

MAP 26–1 • JAPAN

Japan's wholehearted emulation of myriad aspects of Chinese culture began in the fifth century and was challenged by new influences from the West only in the mid nineteenth century after Western powers forced Japan to open its treaty ports to international trade.

the void. We are expected to "read" the unpainted expanse as water. Beyond the blank space, subtle tones of gray ink delineate a distant shore where fishing boats, a small hut, and two people stand. The two parts of the painting seem to echo each other across a deep expanse. The painting illustrates well the pure, lonely, and ultimately serene spirit of the poetic landscape tradition influenced by Zen.

SESSHU Another of Shubun's pupils, Sesshu (1420–1506), has come to be regarded as one of the greatest Japanese painters of all time. Although they completed training to become Zen monks, at the monastery, Shubun and his followers specialized in art rather than in religious ritual or teaching. This distinguished them from earlier Zen monk-painters for whom painting was but one facet of their lives. By Shubun's day, temples had formed their own professional painting ateliers in order to meet the large

Japan, where he could concentrate on painting unencumbered by monastic duties and entanglements with the political elite. His new temple was under the patronage of a wealthy warrior clan that engaged in trade with China. Funded by them, he had the opportunity to visit China in 1467 on a diplomatic mission. He traveled extensively there for three years, viewing the scenery, stopping at Chan (the Chinese word for Zen) monasteries, and studying Chinese paintings by professional artists rather than those by contemporary literati masters.

When Sesshu returned from China, he remained in the provinces to avoid the turmoil in Kyoto, at that time devastated by civil warfare that would last for the next hundred years. Only a few paintings created prior to his sojourn in China have recently come to light. They are in a style closer to Shubun, and Sesshu signed them with another name. In contrast, the paintings he produced after his return demonstrate a conscious break artistically with the refined landscape style of his teacher. These masterful later paintings exhibit a bold, new spirit, evident in his **WINTER LANDSCAPE** (FIG. 26–3). A cliff descending from the mist seems to cut

26–2 • Bunsei LANDSCAPE
Muromachi period, mid 15th century. Hanging scroll with ink and light colors on paper, 28¾″ × 13″ (73.2 × 33 cm). Museum of Fine Arts, Boston. Special Chinese and Japanese Fund (05.203)

26–3 • Sesshu WINTER LANDSCAPE
Muromachi period, c. 1470s. Hanging scroll with ink on paper, 18¼″ × 11½″ (46.3 × 29.3 cm). Collection of the Tokyo National Museum. National Treasure.

demand for paintings from warrior patrons. Sesshu trained as a Zen monk at Shokokuji, where Shubun had his studio. There, he worked in the painting atelier under Shubun for 20 years, before leaving Kyoto to head a small provincial Zen temple in western the composition in two parts. Sharp, jagged brushstrokes delineate a series of rocky hills, where a lone figure makes his way to a Zen monastery. Instead of a gradual recession into space, flat overlapping planes fracture the composition into crystalline facets. The white of the paper is left to indicate snow, while the sky is suggested by tones of gray. A few trees cling desperately to the rocky land. The harsh chill of winter is almost palpable.

THE ZEN DRY GARDEN

Zen monks led austere lives in their quest for the attainment of enlightenment. In addition to daily meditation, they engaged in manual labor to provide for themselves and maintain their temple properties. Many Zen temples constructed dry landscape courtyard gardens, not for strolling but for contemplative viewing. Cleaning and maintaining these gardens—pulling weeds, tweaking unruly shoots, and raking the gravel—was a kind of active meditation. It helped to keep their minds grounded.

The dry landscape gardens of Japan, *karesansui* ("dried-up mountains and water"), exist in perfect harmony with Zen Buddhism. The dry garden in front of the abbot's quarters in the Zen temple at Ryoanji is one of the most renowned Zen creations in Japan (**FIG. 26–4**). A flat rectangle of raked gravel, about 29 by 70 feet, surrounds 15 stones of different sizes in islands of moss.

The stones are set in asymmetrical groups of two, three, and five. Low, plaster-covered walls establish the garden's boundaries, but beyond the perimeter wall maple, pine, and cherry trees add color and texture to the scene. Called "borrowed scenery," these elements are a considered part of the design even though they grow outside the garden. This garden is celebrated for its severity and its emptiness.

Dry gardens began to be built in the fifteenth and sixteenth centuries in Japan. By the sixteenth century, Chinese landscape painting influenced the gardens' composition, and miniature clipped plants and beautiful stones were arranged to resemble famous paintings. Especially fine and unusual stones were coveted and even carried off as war booty, such was the cultural value of these seemingly mundane objects.

The Ryoanji garden's design, as we see it today, probably dates from the mid seventeenth century, at which point such stone and gravel gardens had become highly intellectualized, abstract reflections of nature. This garden has been interpreted as representing islands in the sea, or mountain peaks rising above the clouds, perhaps even a swimming tigress with her cubs, or constellations of stars and planets. All or none of these interpretations may be equally satisfying—or irrelevant—to a monk seeking clarity of mind through contemplation.

26-4 • ROCK GARDEN, RYOANJI, KYOTO
Muromachi period, c. 1480. Photographed spring 1993. UNESCO World Heritage Site, National Treasure.

The American composer John Cage once exclaimed that every stone at Ryoanji was in just the right place. He then said, "And every other place would also be just right." His remark is thoroughly Zen in spirit. There are many ways to experience Ryoanji. For example, we can imagine the rocks as having different visual "pulls" that relate them to one another. Yet there is also enough space between them to give each one a sense of self-sufficiency and permanence.

With the end of the last Ice Age roughly 15,000 years ago, rising sea levels submerged the lowlands connecting Japan to the Asian landmass, creating the chain of islands we know today as Japan (**MAP 26–1**). Not long afterward, early Paleolithic cultures gave way to a Neolithic culture known as Jomon (c. 11,000–400 BCE) after its characteristic cord-marked pottery. During the Jomon period, a sophisticated hunter-gatherer culture developed. Agriculture supplemented hunting and gathering by around 5000 BCE, and rice cultivation began some 4,000 years later.

A fully settled agricultural society emerged during the Yayoi period (c. 400 BCE–300 CE), accompanied by hierarchical social organization. As people learned to manufacture bronze and iron, use of those metals became widespread. Yayoi architecture, with its unpainted wood and thatched roofs, already showed the Japanese affinity for natural materials and clean lines, and the style of Yayoi granaries in particular persisted in the design of shrines in later centuries. The trend toward social organization continued during the Kofun period (c. 300–552 CE), an era characterized by the construction of large royal tombs, following the Korean practice. Veneration of leaders grew into the beginnings of the imperial system that has lasted to the present day.

The Asuka era (552–645 CE) began with a period of profound change as elements of Chinese civilization flooded into Japan, initially through the intermediary of Korea. The three most significant Chinese contributions to the developing Japanese culture were Buddhism (with its attendant art and architecture), a system of writing, and the structures of a centralized bureaucracy. The earliest extant Buddhist temple compound in Japan, Horyuji, which contains the oldest currently existing wooden buildings in the world, dates from this period.

The arrival of Buddhism also prompted some formalization of Shinto, the loose collection of indigenous Japanese beliefs and practices. Shinto is a religion that connects people to nature. Its rites are shamanistic and emphasize ceremonial purification. These include the invocation and appeasement of spirits, including those of the recently dead. Many Shinto deities are thought to inhabit various aspects of nature, such as particularly magnificent trees, rocks, and waterfalls, and living creatures such as deer. Shinto and Buddhism have in common an intense awareness of the transience of life, and as their goals are complementary—purification in the case of Shinto, enlightenment in the case of Buddhism—they have generally existed comfortably alongside each other to the present day.

The Nara period (645–794) takes its name from the location of Japan's first permanently established imperial capital. During this time the founding works of Japanese literature were compiled and Buddhism became the most important force in Japanese culture. Its influence at court grew so great that in 794 the emperor moved the capital from Nara to Heian-kyo (present-day Kyoto), far from powerful monasteries.

During the Heian period (794–1185) an extremely refined court culture thrived, embodied today in an exquisite legacy of poetry, calligraphy, and painting. An efficient method for writing the Japanese language was developed, and with it a woman at the court wrote Japan's most celebrated fictional story, which some describe as the world's first novel: *The Tale of Genji*. Esoteric Buddhism, as hierarchical and intricate as the aristocratic world of the court, became popular.

The end of the Heian period was marked by civil warfare as regional warrior (samurai) clans were drawn into the factional conflicts at court. Pure Land Buddhism, with its simple message of salvation, offered consolation to many in troubled times. In 1185, the Minamoto clan defeated their arch rivals, the Taira, and their leader, Minamoto Yoritomo, assumed the position of shogun (general-in-chief). While paying respect to the emperor, Minamoto Yoritomo took actual military and political power for himself, setting up his own capital in Kamakura. The Kamakura era (1185–1333) began a tradition of rule by shogun that lasted in various forms until 1868. It was also the time in which renewed contacts with China created the opportunity for Zen Buddhism, which was then flourishing in China (known there as Chan), to be introduced to Japan. By the end of the Kamakura period, numerous Zen monasteries had been founded in Kyoto and Kamakura, and Chinese and Japanese Chan/Zen monks were regularly visiting each other's countries.

MOMOYAMA PERIOD

The civil wars sweeping Japan laid bare the basic flaw in the Ashikaga system—samurai were primarily loyal to their own feudal lord (*daimyo*), rather than to the central government. Battles between feudal clans grew more frequent, and it became clear that only a warrior powerful and bold enough to unite the entire country could control Japan. As the Muromachi period drew to a close, three leaders emerged who would change the course of Japanese history.

The first of these leaders was Oda Nobunaga (1534–1582), who marched his army into Kyoto in 1568 and overthrew the reigning Ashikaga shogun in 1573, initiating a new age of Japanese politics. A ruthless warrior, Nobunaga went so far as to destroy a Buddhist monastery because the monks refused to join his forces. Yet he was also a patron of the most rarefied and refined arts. Having taken his own life to avoid succumbing to his enemies in the midst of a military campaign, Nobunaga was succeeded by one of his generals, Toyotomi Hideyoshi (1537–1598), who soon gained complete power in Japan. He, too, was a patron of the arts when not leading his army since he considered culture a vital adjunct to his rule. Hideyoshi, however, was overly ambitious. He believed he could conquer both Korea and China, and he wasted much of his resources on two ill-fated invasions. A stable and long-lasting military regime finally emerged soon after 1600 with the triumph of a third leader, Tokugawa Ieyasu (1543–1616), a former ally of Nobunaga who served as a senior retainer to Hideyoshi, and only asserted his power after Hideyoshi's death. But despite its turbulence, the era of Nobunaga and Hideyoshi, known as the Momoyama period (1573–1615), was one of the most creative eras in Japanese history.

Today the very word Momoyama conjures up images of bold warriors, luxurious palaces, screens shimmering with gold leaf, and, in contrast, rustic tea-ceremony ceramics. Europeans first made an impact in Japan at this time. After the arrival of a few wayward Portuguese explorers in 1543, traders and missionaries soon followed. It was only with the rise of Nobunaga, however, that Westerners were able to extend their activities beyond the ports of Kyushu, Japan's southernmost island. Nobunaga welcomed foreign traders, who brought him various products, the most influential of which were firearms.

ARCHITECTURE

European muskets and cannons quickly changed the nature of Japanese warfare and Japanese castle architecture. In the late sixteenth century, to protect castles from these new weapons, they became heavily fortified garrisons. Some were eventually lost to warfare or torn down by victorious enemies, and others have been extensively altered over the years. One of the most beautiful of the few that have survived intact is **HIMEJI**, not far from the city of Osaka (**FIG. 26-5**). Rising high on a hill above the plains, Himeji has been given the name White Heron. To reach the upper fortress, visitors must follow angular paths beneath steep walls, climbing from one area to the next past stone ramparts and through narrow fortified gates, all the while feeling as though lost in a maze, with no sense of direction or progress.

At the main building, a further climb up a series of narrow ladders leads to the uppermost chamber. There, the footsore visitor is rewarded with a stunning 360-degree view of the surrounding countryside.

DECORATIVE PAINTINGS FOR *SHOIN* ROOMS

Castles such as Himeji were sumptuously decorated, offering artists unprecedented opportunities to work on a grand scale. Interiors were divided into rooms by paper-covered sliding doors (**fusuma**), perfect canvases for large-scale murals. Free-standing folding screens (*byobu*) were also popular. Some had gold-leaf backgrounds, whose glistening surfaces not only reflected light back into the castle rooms but also displayed the wealth of the warrior leaders. Temples, too, commissioned large-scale paintings in these formats for grand reception rooms where the monks met with their wealthy warrior patrons (see "*Shoin* Design," opposite).

Daitokuji, a celebrated Zen monastery in Kyoto, has a number of subtemples for which Momoyama artists painted magnificent *fusuma*. The *fusuma* of one, the Jukoin, were painted by Kano Eitoku (1543–1590), one of the most brilliant painters from the hereditary lineage of professional artists known as the Kano school. Eitoku headed this school, which was founded by his grandfather. The Kano school painted for the highest-ranking warriors from

26-5 • HIMEJI CASTLE, HYOGO, NEAR OSAKA
Momoyama period, 1601–1609. UNESCO World Heritage Site, National Treasure.

The Japanese tea ceremony and *shoin*-style interior residential architecture are undoubtedly the most significant and most enduring expressions of Japanese taste to become established during the Momoyama period. **Shoin** combine a number of interior features in more-or-less standard ways, though no two rooms are ever the same. These features include wide verandas, walls divided by wooden posts, floors covered with woven straw *tatami* mats, recessed panels in ceilings, sometimes painted and sometimes covered with reed matting, several shallow alcoves for prescribed purposes, *fusuma* (paper-covered sliding doors), and **shoji** screens—wood frames covered with translucent rice paper. The *shoin* illustrated here was built in 1601 as a guest hall, called Kojoin, at the Buddhist temple of Onjoji near Kyoto.

The *shoin* is a formal room for receiving important upper-class guests. With some variations due to differences in status, these rooms were designed for buildings used by samurai, aristocrats, and even well-to-do commoners. They are found in various types of buildings: private residences; living quarters, guesthouses, and reception rooms at religious complexes (both Shinto shrines and Buddhist temples); and the finest houses of entertainment (such as seen in FIG. 26–1) where geisha and courtesans entertained important guests. The owner of the building or the most important guest would be seated in front of the main alcove (*tokonoma*), which would contain a hanging scroll, an arrangement of flowers, or a large painted screen. Alongside that alcove was another that featured staggered shelves, often for displaying precious objects. The veranda side of the room also contained a writing space fitted with a low writing desk.

The architectural harmony of a *shoin* is derived from standardization of its basic units, or modules. In Japanese carpentry, the common module of design and construction is the bay, reckoned as the distance from the center of one post to the center of another, which is governed in turn by the standard size of **tatami** floor mats. Although varying slightly from region to region, the size of a single *tatami* is about 3 by 6 feet. Room area in Japan is still expressed in terms of the number of *tatami* mats; for example, a room may be described as an eight-mat room.

shoji — veranda — writing alcove — *tokonoma* — *tatami* — staggered shelves — *fusuma*

26–6 • ARTIST'S RENDERING OF THE KOJOIN GUEST HOUSE AT ONJOJI
Otsu, Shiga prefecture. Momoyama period, 1601. National Treasure.

👁—**Watch** an architectural simulation about *shoin* design on myartslab.com

the sixteenth century through 1868. They perfected a new style that combined the Muromachi ink-painting tradition with the brightly colored and decorative *yamato-e* style, developed during the Heian period (see Chapter 12). **FIGURE 26–7** shows two of the three walls of Fusuma panels at Jukoin painted by Eitoku when he was in his mid twenties. To the left, the subject is the familiar Kano school theme of cranes and pines, both symbols of long life; to the right is a great gnarled plum tree, symbol of spring. The trees are so massive they seem to extend far beyond the panels. An island rounding both walls of the far corner provides a focus for the outreaching trees. Ingeniously, it belongs to both compositions at the same time, thus uniting them into an organic whole. Eitoku's vigorous use of brush and ink, his powerfully jagged outlines, and his dramatic compositions recall the style of Sesshu, but the bold new sense of scale in his works is a defining characteristic of the Momoyama period.

26-7 • Kano Eitoku FUSUMA
Depicting pine and cranes (left) and plum tree (right) from the central room of the Jukoin, Daitokuji, Kyoto. Momoyama period, c. 1563–1573. *Fusuma* (sliding door panels) with ink and gold on paper, height 5′9⅛″ (1.76 m). National Treasure.

THE TEA CEREMONY

Japanese art is never one-sided. Along with castles and their opulent interior decoration, there was an equal interest during the Momoyama period in the quiet, the restrained, and the natural. This was expressed primarily through the tea ceremony.

The term "tea ceremony," a phrase now in common use, does not convey the full meaning of *chanoyu*, the Japanese ritual drinking of tea. There is no counterpart in Western culture. Tea had been introduced to Japan in the ninth century, when it was molded into cakes and boiled. However, the advent of Zen brought to Japan a different way of preparing tea, with the leaves ground into powder and then whisked in bowls with hot water. Zen monks used such tea as a mild stimulant to aid meditation. Others found it had medicinal properties.

SEN NO RIKYU The most famous tea master in Japanese history was Sen no Rikyu (1522–1591). He conceived of the tea ceremony as an intimate gathering in which a few people, often drawn from a variety of backgrounds—warriors, courtiers, wealthy merchants—would enter a small rustic room, drink tea carefully prepared in front of them by their host, and quietly discuss the tea utensils or a Zen scroll hanging on the wall. He largely established the aesthetic of modesty, refinement, and rusticity that permitted the tearoom to serve as a respite from the busy and sometimes violent world outside. A traditional tearoom combines simple elegance and rusticity. It is made of natural materials such as bamboo and wood, with mud walls, paper windows, and a floor covered with *tatami*. One tearoom that preserves Rikyu's design is named **TAIAN** (**FIG. 26-8**). Built in 1582, it has a tiny door (guests must crawl to enter) and miniature *tokonoma* (alcove) for displaying a Zen scroll or a simple flower arrangement. At first glance, the room seems symmetrical. But a longer look reveals the disposition of the *tatami* does not match the spacing of the *tokonoma*, providing a subtle undercurrent of irregularity. The walls seem scratched

26-8 • Sen no Rikyu TAIAN TEAROOM
Myokian Temple, Kyoto. Momoyama period, 1582. National Treasure.

and worn with age, but the *tatami* are replaced frequently to keep them clean and fresh. The mood is quiet; the light is muted and diffused through three small paper windows. Above all, there is a sense of spatial clarity. Since nonessentials have been eliminated, there is nothing to distract from focused attention. This tearoom aesthetic became an important element in Japanese culture.

THE TEA BOWL Every utensil connected with tea, including the water jar, the kettle, the tea scoop, the whisk, the tea caddy, and, above all, the tea bowl, came to be appreciated for its aesthetic quality, and many works of art were created for use in *chanoyu*.

The age-old Japanese admiration for the natural and the asymmetrical found full expression in tea ceramics. Korean-style rice bowls made for peasants were suddenly considered the epitome of refined taste, and tea masters urged potters to mimic their imperfect shapes. But not every misshapen bowl would be admired. A rarified appreciation of beauty developed that took into consideration such factors as how well a tea bowl fitted into the hands, how subtly the shape and texture of the bowl appealed to the eye, and who had previously used and admired it. For this purpose, the inscribed storage box became almost as important as the ceramic that fitted within it, and if a bowl had been given a name by a leading tea master, it was especially treasured by later generations.

One of the finest surviving early **TEA BOWLS** (**FIG. 26-9**) is attributed to Chojiro (1516–1592), the founder of the Raku family of potters. Named *Yugure* ("Twilight") by tea master Sen no Sotan (1578–1658), a grandson of Rikyu, this bowl is an excellent example of red **raku** ware—a hand-built, low-fired ceramic of gritty red clay, developed especially for use in the tea ceremony. The effect created by the glaze-shaded red hue and lively surface texture evokes a gentle landscape, illuminated by the setting sun. With its small foot, straight sides, irregular shape, and crackled texture, this bowl exemplifies tea taste at the beginning of its development.

EDO PERIOD

When Tokugawa Ieyasu gained control of Japan, he forced the emperor to proclaim him shogun, a title neither Nobunaga nor Hideyoshi had held. His reign initiated the Edo period (1615–1868), named after the city that he founded (present-day Tokyo) as his capital. This period is alternatively known as the Tokugawa era. Under the rule of the Tokugawa family, peace and prosperity came at the price of a rigid and repressive bureaucracy. The problem of a potentially rebellious *daimyo* was solved by ordering all feudal lords to spend either half of each year, or every other year, in Edo, where their families were required to live. Zen Buddhism was supplanted as the prevailing intellectual force by a form of Neo-Confucianism, a philosophy formulated in Song-dynasty China that emphasized loyalty to the state, although the popularity of Buddhism among the commoner population surged at this time.

26-9 • Chojiro TEA BOWL, CALLED YUGURE ("TWILIGHT")
Momoyama period, late 16th century. Raku ware, height 3½″ (9 cm). The Gotoh Museum, Tokyo.

Connoisseurs developed a subtle vocabulary to discuss the aesthetics of tea. A favorite term was *sabi* ("loneliness"), which refers to the tranquility found when feeling alone. Other virtues were *wabi* ("poverty"), which suggests the artlessness of humble simplicity, and *shibui* ("bitter" or "astringent"), meaning elegant restraint. Tea bowls, such as this example, embody these aesthetics.

The shogunate officially divided Edo society into four classes. Samurai officials constituted the highest class, followed by farmers, artisans, and finally merchants. As time went on, however, merchants began to control the money supply, and in Japan's increasingly mercantile economy their accumulation of wealth soon exceeded that of the samurai, which helped, unofficially, to elevate their status. Reading and writing became widespread at all levels of society, and with literacy came intellectual curiosity and interest in the arts. All segments of the population—including samurai, merchants, townspeople, and rural peasants—were able to acquire art. A rich cultural atmosphere developed unlike anything Japan had experienced before, in which artists worked in a wide variety of styles that appealed to these different groups of consumers.

RINPA SCHOOL PAINTING

During the Edo period, Edo was the shogun's city while life in Kyoto took its cues from the resident emperor and his court. Kyoto was also home to wealthy merchants, artists, and craftsmakers who served the needs of the courtiers and shared their interest in refined pursuits, such as the tea ceremony, and also their appreciation of art styles that recalled those perfected by aristocratic artists in the Heian period. The most famous and original Kyoto painter who worked for this group of patrons was Tawaraya Sotatsu (active c. 1600–1640). Sotatsu is considered the first great painter of the Rinpa school, the modern name given to a group of artists whose art reinterpreted ancient courtly styles. These artists are grouped together because of their shared artistic interests;

This **LACQUER BOX** (**FIG. 26–10**) reflects collaborative artistic production and demonstrates the fluidity with which some Japanese artists were able to work in a variety of media. It was designed by the Rinpa-school painter Ogata Korin (1658–1716), who oversaw its execution, although he left the actual work to highly trained craftsmakers. He also frequently collaborated with his brother Kenzan, a celebrated potter. The upper tray housed writing implements, the larger bottom section stored paper (see "Inside a Writing Box," page 826). Korin's design sets a motif of irises and a plank bridge in a dramatic asymmetrical composition created from mother-of-pearl, silver, lead, and gold lacquer. The subject was one he frequently represented in painting because it was immensely popular with the educated Japanese of his day, who would have recognized the imagery as an allusion to a famous passage from the tenth-century Japanese literary classic *Tales of Ise*. A nobleman poet, having left his wife in the capital, pauses at a place called Eight Bridges, where a river branches into eight streams, each covered with a plank bridge. Irises are in full bloom, and his traveling companions urge the poet to write a *waka*—a five-line, 31-syllable

poem—beginning each line with a syllable from the word for "iris": *Kakitsubata* (*ka-ki-tsu-ba-ta*; *ba* is the voiced form of *ha*, which here begins the penultimate line). The poet responds:

> **Ka**ragoromo
> **ki**tsutsu narenishi
> **tsu**ma shi areba
> **ha**rubaru kinuru
> **ta**bi o shi zo omou.
> When I remember
> my wife, fond and familiar
> as my courtly robe,
> I feel how far and distant
> my travels have taken me.
>
> (Translated by Stephen Addiss)

The poem in association with the scene became so famous that any image of a group of irises, with or without a plank bridge, immediately called the episode to mind.

Lacquer is derived in Asia from the sap of the lacquer tree, *Rhus verniciflua*, indigenous to China but very early in history also grown commercially throughout East Asia. It is gathered by tapping into a tree and letting the sap flow into a container, and it can be colored with vegetable or mineral dyes. Applied in thin coats to a surface of wood or leather, lacquer

hardens into a glasslike protective coating that is waterproof, heat- and acid-resistant, and airtight. Its practical qualities made it ideal for storage containers, and vessels for food and drink. The creation of a piece of lacquer can take several years. First, the item is fashioned of wood and sanded smooth. Next, up to 30 layers of lacquer are thinly applied, each dried and polished before the next is brushed on.

Japanese craftsmakers exploited the decorative potential of lacquer to create expensive luxury items, such as this box, which was created when lacquer arts had been perfected. It features inlays of mother-of-pearl and precious metals in a style known as *makie* ("sprinkled design"), in which flaked or powdered gold or silver was embedded in a still-damp coat of lacquer.

26–10 • Ogata Korin EXTERIOR (A) AND VIEWS OF INTERIOR AND LID (B) OF A LACQUER BOX FOR WRITING IMPLEMENTS
Edo period, late 17th–early 18th century. Lacquer, lead, silver, and mother-of-pearl, 5⅝″ × 10¾″ × 7¾″ (14.2 × 27.4 × 19.7 cm). Tokyo National Museum, Tokyo. National Treasure.

26–11 • Tawaraya Sotatsu WAVES AT MATSUSHIMA
Edo period, 17th century. Pair of six-panel folding screens with ink, mineral colors, and gold leaf on paper; each screen 4′9⅞″ × 11′8½″ (1.52 × 3.56 m). Freer Gallery of Art, Smithsonian Institution, Washington, DC. Gift of Charles Lang Freer (F1906.231 & 232)

The six-panel screen format was a triumph of scale and practicality. Each panel consisted of a light wood frame surrounding a latticework interior covered with several layers of paper. Over this foundation was pasted a high-quality paper, silk, or gold-leaf ground, ready to be painted by the finest artists. Held together with ingenious paper hinges, a screen could be folded for storage or transportation, resulting in a mural-size painting light enough to be carried by a single person, ready to be displayed as needed.

they did not constitute a formal school, such as the Kano. Rinpa masters were not just painters, however: They sometimes collaborated with craftsmakers (see "Lacquer Box for Writing Implements," opposite).

One of Sotatsu's most famous pairs of screens probably depict the islands of Matsushima near the northern city of Sendai (**FIG.**

26–11). On the right screen (shown here on top), mountainous islands echo the swing and sweep of the waves, with stylized gold clouds reserved from the gold ground at upper left. On the left screen (here below) the gold clouds continue until they become a sand spit from which twisted pines grow. One branch to the left seems to stretch down toward a strange island in the lower

Writing boxes hold tools basic for both writing and painting: ink stick, ink stone, brushes, and paper—all beautiful objects in their own right.

Ink sticks are basically soot from burning wood or oil that is bound into a paste with resin and pressed into small stick-shaped or cake-shaped molds to harden.

Fresh ink is made for each writing or painting session by grinding the hard, dry ink stick in water against a fine-grained stone. A typical ink stone has a shallow well at one end sloping up to a grinding surface at the other. The artist fills the well with water from a waterpot. The ink stick, held vertically, is dipped into the well to pick up a small amount of water, then is rubbed in a circular motion firmly on the grinding surface. Grinding ink is viewed as a meditative task, time for collecting one's thoughts and concentrating on the painting or calligraphy ahead.

Brushes are made from animal hair set in simple bamboo or hollow-reed handles. Brushes taper to a fine point that responds sensitively to any shift in pressure. Although great painters and calligraphers do eventually develop their own styles of holding and using the brush, all begin by learning the basic position for writing. The brush is held vertically, grasped firmly between the thumb and first two fingers, with the fourth and fifth fingers often resting against the handle for more subtle control.

well

ink stone

ink stick

writing implements

brushes

left, composed of an organic, amoebalike form in gold surrounded by mottled ink. This mottled effect was a specialty of Rinpa school painters.

As one of the "three famous beautiful views of Japan," Matsushima was often depicted in art. Most painters showed from above the pine-covered islands that make the area famous. Sotatsu's genius was to portray them in an abbreviated manner and from a fresh vantage point, as though the viewer were passing the islands in a boat on the roiling waters. The artist's asymmetrical composition and his use of thick mineral colors in combination with soft, playful brushwork and sparkling gold leaf create the boldly decorative effect that is the hallmark of the Rinpa tradition.

NATURALISTIC PAINTING

NAGASAWA ROSETSU By the middle of the eighteenth century, the taste of wealthy Kyoto merchants had shifted, influencing the styles of artists who competed for their patronage. The public was enthralled with novel imagery captured in magnifying glasses, telescopes, and an optical device that enhanced the three-dimensional effects of Western-style perspective pictures. Schools of independent artists emerged in Kyoto to satisfy demands for naturalistic-style paintings that reflected this fascination. The most influential was founded by Maruyama Okyo, who had perfected methods to incorporate Western shading and perspective into a more native Japanese decorative style, creating a sense of volume new to East Asian painting, while still retaining a sense of familiarity.

Okyo's most famous pupil was Nagasawa Rosetsu (1754–1799), a painter of great natural talent who added his own boldness and humor to his master's tradition. Rosetsu delighted in surprising his viewers with odd juxtapositions and unusual compositions. One of his finest works is a pair of screens, the left one depicting a **BULL AND PUPPY** (FIG. 26–12). The bull is so immense that

26–12 • Nagasawa Rosetsu BULL AND PUPPY
Edo period, late 18th century. Left of a pair of six-panel screens with ink and gold wash on paper, 5'7¼" × 12'3" (1.70 × 3.75 m). Los Angeles County Museum of Art, California. Joe and Etsuko Price Collection (L.83.45.3a)

his mammoth body exceeds the borders of the screen, an effect undoubtedly influenced by new optical devices. The tiny puppy, white against the dark gray of the bull, helps to emphasize the bull's huge size through its contrasting smallness. The puppy's relaxed and informal pose, looking happily straight out at the viewer, gives this powerful painting a humorous touch that increases its charm. In the hands of a master such as Rosetsu, plebeian subject matter became simultaneously delightful and monumental.

LITERATI PAINTING

Because the city of Kyoto was far from the watchful eyes of the government in Edo, and the emperor resided there with his court, it enjoyed a degree of privilege and independence not found in any other Japanese city. These conditions allowed for the creation of art in the new Rinpa and naturalistic styles. They also encouraged the emergence of new schools of philosophy based on interpretations of Chinese Confucianism that disagreed with those taught at schools sponsored by Tokugawa shoguns. These new interpretations incorporated ideas from Chinese Daoism, which promoted cultivation of a person's uniqueness, thus encouraging artistic creativity. Kyoto's intellectuals, who admired Chinese culture, even created a new, more informal tea ceremony of their own, featuring steeped tea called *sencha* because it was the tea drunk by Ming-dynasty Chinese literati. They did this as political protest—by then *chanoyu* had become encumbered by rules and was closely associated with the repressive shogunate. Influenced by such new ideas, a Chinese manner of painting arose in the mid eighteenth century in emulation of literati painting. Artists who embraced this style—both professionals who painted for paying clients and amateurs who painted for their own enjoyment—quickly grew to number hundreds as its popularity spread throughout Japan along with increased interest in drinking *sencha*, as well as in other aspects of Chinese culture. These artists learned about Chinese literati painting not only from the paintings themselves, but also from woodblock-printed painting manuals imported from China, and also from Chinese emigrant monks and merchants who lived in Japan.

The best and most successful of these artists took Chinese literati painting models as starting points for their own original interpretations of literati themes. One of them was Ike Taiga (1723–1776), admired as much for his magnetic personality as for his art. He was born into a poor farming family near Kyoto and showed innate talent for painting at a young age. Moving to Kyoto in his teens, he became friends with Chinese scholars there, including those who promoted drinking *sencha*. Taiga became a leader in this group, attracting admirers who were enamored of both his quasi-amateurish painting style and his quest for spiritual self-cultivation. His character and personal style are seen in the scintillating, rhythmic layering of strokes used to define the mountains in his **VIEW OF KOJIMA BAY** (**FIG. 26–13**), which blends Chinese models, Japanese aesthetics, and personal brushwork. The gentle rounded forms of the mountains intentionally recall the

work of famous Chinese literati painters, and Taiga utilizes a stock landscape composition that separates foreground and background mountains with a watery expanse (compare FIG. 26–2). However, he did not paint an imaginary Chinese landscape but a personal vision of an actual Japanese place that he had visited—Kojima Bay—as a document accompanying the painting explains. Still, in deference to his admiration for Chinese literati, Taiga places two figures clad in Chinese robes on the right, midway up the mountain.

26-13 • Ike Taiga VIEW OF KOJIMA BAY
Edo period, third quarter of 18th century. Hanging scroll with ink and color on silk, 39¼″ × 14⅝″ (99.7 × 37.6 cm). Hosomi Museum, Kyoto.

The production of woodblock prints combined the expertise of three individual specialists: the artist, the carver, and the printer. Coordinating and funding this collaborative endeavor was a publisher, who commissioned the project and distributed the prints to stores or itinerant vendors, who would sell them.

The artist designed and supplied the master drawing for the print, executing its outlines with brush and ink on tissue paper. Colors might be indicated, but more often they were understood or determined later. The drawing was passed on to the carver, who pasted it face down on a

26-14 • Toshusai Sharaku **OTANI ONIJI IN THE ROLE OF YAKKO EDOBE**
Edo period, 1794. Polychrome woodblock print with ink, colors, and white mica on paper, 15″ × 9⅞″ (38.1 × 25.1 cm). Metropolitan Museum of Art, New York. Henry L. Phillips Collection, Bequest of Henry L. Phillips, 1939 (JP2822)

hardwood block—preferably cherrywood—so that the outlines were visible through the tissue paper in reverse. A light coating of oil might be brushed on to make the paper more transparent, allowing the drawing to stand out even more clearly. The carver then cut around the lines of the drawing with a sharp knife, always working in the same direction as the original brushstrokes. The rest of the block was then chiseled away, leaving only the outlines in relief. This block, which reproduced the master drawing, was called the **key block**. If the print was to be polychrome, involving multiple colors, prints made from the key block were in turn pasted face down on blocks that would be used as guides for the carver of the color blocks. Each color generally required a separate block, although both sides of a block might be used for economy.

Once the blocks were completed, the printer took over. Paper for printing was covered lightly with animal glue (gelatin), and before printing, the coated paper was lightly moistened so that it would take ink and color well. Water-based ink or color was brushed over the blocks, and the paper was placed on top and rubbed with a smooth, padded device called a *baren*, until the design was completely transferred. The key block was printed first, then the colors, one by one. Each block was carved with two small marks called **registration marks**, in exactly the same place in the margins, outside of the image area—an L in one corner, and a straight line in another. By aligning the paper with these marks before letting it fall over the block, the printer ensured that the colors would be placed correctly within the outlines. One of the most characteristic effects of later Japanese prints is a grading of color from dark to pale. This was achieved by wiping some of the color from the block before printing, or by moistening the block and then applying the color gradually with an unevenly loaded brush—a brush loaded on one side with full-strength color and on the other with diluted color.

👁—[**Watch** a video about the woodblock printmaking process on myartslab.com

UKIYO-E: PICTURES OF THE FLOATING WORLD

Edo served as the shogun's capital as well as the center of a flourishing popular culture associated with tradespeople. Deeply Buddhist, commoners were acutely aware of the transience of life, symbolized, for example, by the cherry tree which blossoms so briefly. Putting a positive spin on this harsh realization, they sought to live by the mantra: Let's enjoy it to the full as long as it lasts. This they did to excess in the restaurants, theaters, bathhouses, and brothels of the city's pleasure quarters, named after the Buddhist phrase *ukiyo* ("floating world"). Every major city in Japan

had these quarters, and most were licensed by the government. But those of Edo were the largest and most famous. The heroes of the floating world were not famous samurai or aristocratic poets. Instead, swashbuckling kabuki actors and beautiful courtesans were admired. These paragons of pleasure soon became immortalized in paintings and—because paintings were too expensive for common people—in woodblock prints known as **ukiyo-e** ("pictures of the floating world"; see "Japanese Woodblock Prints," above). Most prints were inexpensively produced by the hundreds and not considered serious fine art. Yet when first imported to Europe and America, they were immediately acclaimed and strongly influenced late nineteenth- and early twentieth-century Western art (see "Modern Artists and World Cultures: Japonisme," page 996).

HARUNOBU The first woodblock prints had no color, only black outlines. Soon artists were adding colors by hand, but to produce colored prints more rapidly they gradually devised a system to print colors using multiple blocks. The first artist to design prints that took advantage of this new technique, known as *nishiki-e* ("brocade pictures"), was Suzuki Harunobu (1724–1770), famous for his images of courtesans (see FIG. 26–1).

SHARAKU Toshusai Sharaku is one of the most mysterious, if today among the most admired, masters of *ukiyo-e*. He seems to have been active less than a year in 1794–1795, during which he produced 146 prints, of which all but ten are pictures of famous actors in a popular form of drama known as kabuki. He was renowned for half-length portraits that captured the dramatic intensity of noted performers outfitted in the costumes and makeup of the characters they played on stage. Much as people today buy posters of their favorite sports, music, or movie stars,

so, too, in the Edo period people clamored for images of their kabuki idols. The crossed eyes, craning neck, and stylized gestures of Sharaku's portrayal of actor **OTANI ONIJI** (FIG. 26-14) capture a frozen, tension-filled moment in an action-packed drama, precisely the sort of stylized intensity that was valued in kabuki performance.

HOKUSAI During the first half of the nineteenth century, pictures of famous sights of Japan grew immensely popular. The two most famous *ukiyo-e* printmakers, Utagawa Hiroshige (1797–1858; see "Modern Artists and World Cultures: Japonisme," page 996) and Katsushika Hokusai (1760–1849), specialized in this genre. Hiroshige's *Fifty-Three Stations of the Tokaido* and Hokusai's *Thirty-Six Views of Mount Fuji* became the most successful sets of graphic art the world has known. The woodblocks were printed, and printed again, until they wore out. They were then recarved, and still more copies were printed. This process continued for decades, and thousands of prints from the two series still survive.

    THE GREAT WAVE (FIG. 26-15) is the most famous of the scenes from *Thirty-Six Views of Mount Fuji*. The great wave rears up like a dragon with claws of foam, ready to crash down on the

26-15 • Katsushika Hokusai THE GREAT WAVE
From *Thirty-Six Views of Mount Fuji*. Edo period, c. 1831. Polychrome woodblock print on paper, 9⅞" × 14⅝" (25 × 37.1 cm). Honolulu Academy of Art. Gift of James A. Michener 1995 (HAA 13, 695)

Read the document related to Hokusai on myartslab.com

figures huddled in the boats below. Exactly at the point of imminent disaster, but far in the distance, rises Japan's most sacred peak, Mount Fuji, whose slopes, we suddenly realize, swing up like waves and whose snowy crown is like foam—comparisons the artist makes clear in the wave nearest us, caught just at the moment of greatest resemblance. In the late nineteenth century when Japonisme, or *japonism*, became the vogue in the West, Hokusai's art was greatly appreciated, even more so than it had been in Japan: The first book on the artist was published in France.

ZEN PAINTING: BUDDHIST ART FOR RURAL COMMONERS

Outside Japan's urban centers, art for commoners also flourished, much of it tied to their devotion to Buddhism. Deprived of the support of the samurai officials who now favored Confucianism, Buddhism nevertheless thrived during the Edo period through patronage from private individuals, many of them rural peasants. In the early eighteenth century, one of the great monks who preached in the countryside was the Zen master Hakuin Ekaku (1685–1769), born in a small village near Mount Fuji. After hearing a fire-and-brimstone sermon in his youth he resolved to become a monk and for years he traveled around Japan seeking out the strictest Zen teachers. He became the most important Zen master of the last 500 years, and composed many *koan* (questions posed to novices by Zen masters to guide their progression toward enlightenment during meditation), including the famous "What is the sound of one hand clapping?" He was also, in his later years, a self-taught painter and calligrapher, who freely gave away his scrolls to admirers—who included not only farmers but also artisans, merchants, and even samurai—as a way of spreading his religious message.

Hakuin's art differed from that of Muromachi period monk-painters like Bunsei and Sesshu (see FIGS. 26-2, 26-3). His work featured everyday Japanese subjects or Zen themes that conveyed his ideas in ways his humble followers could easily understand. He often painted Daruma (Bodhidharma in Sanskrit) (**FIG. 26-16**), the semilegendary Indian monk who founded Zen (see Chapter 12). Hundreds of Zen monks of the Edo period and later created simply brushed Zen ink paintings, largely within the standards that Hakuin had set.

CLOTH AND CERAMICS

The ingenuity and technical proficiency that contributed to the development of *ukiyo-e* came about because of Japan's long and distinguished history of what the Western tradition considers fine crafts production. Japanese artists had excelled in the design and production of textiles, ceramics, lacquer, woodwork, and metalwork for centuries, and in pre-modern Japan, unlike the West, no separate words distinguished fine arts (painting and sculpture) from "crafts." (The Japanese word for fine art and corresponding modern Japanese language words for various types of craft were not coined until 1872.) This was largely because professional Japanese artistic studios basically followed the same hereditary, hierarchical

structure, regardless of medium. A master artist directed all activity in a workshop of trainees, who gradually gained seniority through years of apprenticeship and innate talent. Sometimes, such as when a pupil was not chosen to succeed the master, he would leave to establish his own studio. Teamwork under masterful supervision was the approach to artistic production.

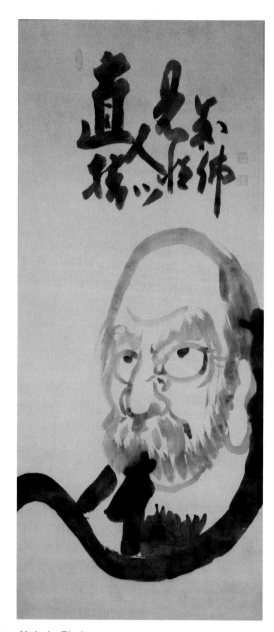

26-16 • Hakuin Ekaku GIANT DARUMA
Edo period, mid 18th century. Hanging scroll with ink on paper, 4'3½" × 1'9¾" (130.8 × 55.2 cm). Manyo'an Collection, New Orleans. (1973.2)

As a self-taught amateur painter, Hakuin's painting style is the very antithesis of that of consummate professionals, such as painters of the Kano or Rinpa schools. The appeal of his art lies in its artless charm, humor, and astonishing force. Here Hakuin has portrayed the wide-eyed Daruma during his nine years of meditation in front of a temple wall in China. Intensity, concentration, and spiritual depth are conveyed by a minimal number of broad, forceful brushstrokes. The inscription is the ultimate Zen message, attributed to Daruma himself: "Pointing directly to the human heart, see your own nature and become Buddha."

With design of bamboo fence and citrus tree (*tachibana*). Edo period, early 18th century.
White figured satin (*rinzu*), with embroidery (gold and silk thread) and stencil dyeing.
Length 62½" (158.8 cm).
Philadelphia Museum of Art. Gift of Mr. and Mrs. Rodolphe Meyer de Schauensee, 1951

Embroidery with vermilion threads gives a vibrant tonality to this citrus fruit and other motifs throughout the design.

The white silk damask fabric from which this robe is constructed is woven with a key-fret pattern, most visible with reflected light as the robe shifts with the movement of the wearer.

Some of the leaves and citrus fruits are embroidered with radiant gold threads. In a few instances, the gold threads have become loose, revealing the written inscriptions that informed the embroiderer which kind of thread to use.

The decoration flows up the back of the robe in the form of an inverted "C," leaving an area of unornamented silk at middle left. This design is characteristic of an early 18th-century taste for asymmetry.

There is extensive use of the *kata-kanoko* technique, in which stencils were used to create dotted patterns with the application of resist paste and dipping and/or painting with dye. This imitated the elaborate tie-dying that had been popular in earlier robes but was now too time-consuming to meet a growing demand for garments.

View the Closer Look for the woman's *kosode* on myartslab.com

KOSODE In the West, the robe most often known as a kimono has become as emblematic of Japanese culture as the "tea ceremony." These loose, unstructured garments, wrapping around the body and cinched with a sash, were the principal outer article of clothing for both men and women by the end of the fifteenth century. Robes with short sleeves were known as *kosode* ("small sleeves"). Because of the wear occasioned by their use, few *kosode* prior to the Edo period have survived, but the early examples that remain reveal the opulent tastes of affluent women at this time (see "A Closer Look," above). In this early eighteenth-century *kosode*, the curving branches of a citrus tree (the *tachibana*, native to Japan) emerge above a bamboo fence along the bottom of the robe to grow up its height and across its sleeves, creating an asymmetrical composition with an area of undecorated fabric concentrated at the center toward the left. The textile artists employed many techniques to create the rich interplay of textures and pictures on this gorgeous robe. The extensive use of stencil dyeing and embroidery associate this *kosode* with the tastes of wives of warriors during the early eighteenth century. The individual design elements and the principles of composition resemble those found in paintings and on ceramics during the Edo period, when the pattern books created for garment-makers disseminated motifs among artists working in a variety of media.

26-17 • PLATE WITH WISTERIA AND TRELLIS PATTERN
Edo period, 18th century. Nabeshima ware. Porcelain with underglaze blue decoration and overglaze enamels, diameter 12³⁄₁₆″ (31 cm). Kyushu National Museum, Japan. Important Cultural Property.

JAPANESE PORCELAIN While the history of ceramic production dates to the earliest days of Japanese civilization, production of glazed, high-fired stoneware ceramics proliferated in Japan only from the sixteenth century. The industry thrived in southern Japan, where, in the years following 1600, influxes of more highly skilled Korean potters helped native artisans learn new continental technologies that allowed them to manufacture porcelain for the first time. One town, Arita, became the center for the production of porcelain, created not only for domestic use but for export to the West. While tea ceremony aesthetics still favored rustic wares such as Chojiro's tea bowl (see FIG. 26-9), porcelain was more widely adopted for everyday use in response to a growing fashion for Chinese arts. Porcelains made in Arita are known by various names according to their dating and decorative schemes. The plate in **FIGURE 26-17** is an example of Nabeshima ware, produced in kilns that had been established in Arita by the Nabeshima samurai clan as early as 1628. Initially, ceramics from these kilns were reserved for family use or as gifts to the Tokugawa shogunate, but eventually Nabeshima ware was also acquired by other powerful noble families. The multicolor decorative motifs often juxtapose an organically irregular natural form (here a branch of flowering wisteria) and a more abstracted, stabilizing design drawn from the built environment (here a trellis on which the wisteria can grow). Contemporary textile designs—well known through the publication of pattern books that documented the latest fashion—frequently served as source material for the decoration of Nabeshima ware.

THE MODERN PERIOD

The tensions that resulted from Commodore Matthew Perry's forced opening of trade ports in Japan in 1853 precipitated the downfall of the Tokugawa shogunate. In 1868, the emperor was formally restored to power, an event known as the Meiji Restoration. The court soon moved from Kyoto to Edo, which was

26-18 • Yokoyama Taikan **FLOATING LIGHTS**
Meiji period, 1909. One of a pair of hanging scrolls with ink, colors, and gold on silk, 56½″ × 20½″ (143 × 52 cm).
Museum of Modern Art, Ibaraki.

renamed Tokyo ("Eastern Capital"). After a period of intense industrialization in the first two decades after the Meiji Restoration, influential private individuals and government officials, sometimes working cooperatively, created new arts institutions including juried exhibitions, artists' associations, arts universities, and cultural heritage laws. These rekindled appreciation for the art of the past, encouraged perpetuation of artistic techniques threatened by adoption of Western ways, and stimulated new artistic production. Many of these arts institutions still exist today.

MEIJI-PERIOD NATIONALIST PAINTING

The Meiji period (1868–1912) marked a major change for Japan. Japanese society adopted various aspects of Western education, governmental systems, clothing, medicine, industrialization, and technology in efforts to modernize the nation. Teachers of sculpture and oil painting came from Italy, while adventurous Japanese artists traveled to Europe and America to study.

A MEIJI PAINTER Ernest Fenollosa (1853–1908), an American who had recently graduated from Harvard, traveled to Japan in 1878 to teach philosophy and political economy at Tokyo University. Within a few years, he and a former student, Okakura Kakuzo (1862–1913), began urging artists to study traditional Japanese arts rather than focusing exclusively on Western art styles and media, but to infuse these traditional practices with a modern sensibility. Yokoyama Taikan (1868–1958) subsequently developed his personal style within the Nihonga (modern Japanese painting) genre promoted by Okakura. Encouraged by Okakura, who had gone there before him, Taikan visited India in 1903. He embraced Okakura's ideals of pan-Asian cultural nationalism, expressed in the first line of Okakura's book, *Ideals of the East* (1903), with the words "Asia is One." This outlook later contributed to fueling Japan's imperialist ambitions. Taikan's **FLOATING LIGHTS** (FIG. 26-18) was inspired by a visit to Calcutta (Kolkata), where he observed women engaged in divination on the banks of the Ganges. The naturalism of their semitransparent robes and the gently rippling water reveal his indebtedness to Western art. In contrast, the lightly applied colors and gracefully composed branches with delicate, mottled brushwork defining the leaves, recall techniques of Rinpa-school artists.

JAPAN AFTER WORLD WAR II

In the aftermath of World War II (1941–1945), Japan was a shambles, her great cities ruined. Nevertheless, under the U.S.-led Allied Occupation (1946–1952), the Japanese people immediately began rebuilding, unified by a sense of national purpose. Within ten years, Japan established nascent automobile, electronics, and consumer goods industries. Rail travel, begun in 1872, expanded and improved significantly after the war, and by the time of the Tokyo Olympics in 1964, the capital had an extensive commuter rail system. Japan became the world leader in city-to-city high-speed rail transit with its new Shinkansen (bullet train). As the rest of the world came to know Japan, foreign interest in its arts focused especially on the country's still thriving "crafts" traditions. Not only were these a source of national pride and identity, the skills and attitudes they fostered also served as the basis for Japan's national revival.

TANGE KENZO The **HIROSHIMA PEACE MEMORIAL MUSEUM** and Park (FIG. 25-19) was one of the first monuments constructed after World War II. A memorial to those who perished on August 6, 1945, and an expression of prayers for world peace, it attests the spirit of the Japanese people at this difficult juncture in history. Tange Kenzo (1913–2005), who would

26-19 • Tange Kenzo HIROSHIMA PEACE MEMORIAL MUSEUM
Showa period, 1955. Main building (center) repaired in Heisei period, 1991. East building (right), the former Peace Memorial Hall, which first opened in 1955, was rebuilt in June 1994 and attached to the main building. Designated UNESCO World Heritage site in 1996.

Throughout the history of Japanese art, there has been a salient sensitivity toward the surface quality of things, for polish, for line, for exquisite facture and stylish articulation. This is certainly the case with an exquisite wooden box (**FIG. 26-20**) created in 2006 by Eri Sayoko (1945–2007). In 2002, the government had designated her a Living National Treasure for her accomplishment in the art of cut-gold leaf (*kirikane*), traditionally used to decorate Buddhist sculpture and paintings (as in FIG. 12–17). The National Treasure designation originated in Japanese laws of 1897 that were intended to safeguard the nation's artistic heritage at a time when art was being bought by Western collectors but suffering neglect at home. In 1955, the government added provisions to honor living individuals who excel in traditional craft techniques with the title Living National Treasure. This historic preservation system is the most complex of its type in the world.

Eri was the third person awarded the title for cut-gold-leaf decoration and the first woman. In its encouragement of traditional arts, the Living National Treasure system has greatly assisted women in gaining much-deserved recognition. In pre-modern Japan (encompassing the prehistoric era up to the start of the Meiji period in 1868), women mostly operated in the private sphere of the home where they created crafts for their own enjoyment or for devotional purposes. By the eighteenth century, this situation had begun to change, so that women could be poets, calligraphers, and painters; the wives or daughters of famous male artists gained the most recognition. Among the most famous was Gyokuran, wife of the literati painter Ike Taiga (see FIG. 26–13). However, the conservative nature of traditional Japanese crafts workshops meant women could not hold leadership positions in them, and until the postwar period they were seldom recognized for their achievements. Eri Sayoko flourished in the new climate, as one of the first women to work in the medium of cut-gold, which she took up via an unorthodox route.

Eri specialized in Japanese painting in high school and in design-dyeing in junior college. After marriage to a traditional Buddhist sculptor she started producing Buddhist paintings and began an apprenticeship with a master *kirikane* craftsmaker. She was so talented that after only three years she was able to exhibit her work professionally. Her art is informed by her deep study of the history of the technique, and her special sensitivity for color betrays her training in dyeing. Eri's elegant, functional objects, typified by this box, are infused with modern sensibilities, proving that adherence to a traditional technique can still result in artistic originality.

26–20 • Eri Sayoko ORNAMENTAL BOX: DANCING IN THE COSMOS
Heisei period, 2006. Wood with polychrome and cut gold, height 33⅞″ (86 cm), width 6½″ (16.5 cm), depth 6½″ (16.5 cm). Collection of Eri Kokei.

eventually become one of the masters of Modernist architecture, designed the complex after winning an open competition as a young, up-and-coming architect.

The building's design befits the solemnity of its context. Concrete piers raise its compact concrete form 20 feet off the ground. The wood formwork of the concrete recalls the wooden forms of traditional Japanese architecture, but the use of concrete as a building material was inspired by Le Corbusier's 1920s Modernist villas (see Chapter 32). Evenly spaced vertical concrete fins lining the façade afford light shade. They suggest both the regular spacing of elements present in modular *shoin* architecture (see "Shoin Design," page 821) and the values of Modernist architects who demanded a strict correlation between structure and form. In this commission Tange infuses Modernist tendencies and materials with a Japanese sense of interval and refinement, characteristics still seen in the work of younger contemporary Japanese architects active today.

FUKAMI SUEHARU Perhaps because the arts of tea ceremony and flower arrangement both require ceramic vessels, the Japanese have long had a particular affection for pottery. While some ceramicists continue to create *raku* tea bowls and other

26–21 • Fukami Sueharu SKY II
Heisei period, c. 1990. Celadon-glazed porcelain with wood base, 3″ × 44⅛″ × 9½″ (7.7 × 112.1 × 24.2 cm).
Helen Foresman Spencer Museum of Art, University of Kansas, Lawrence, Kansas. Museum purchase: R. Charles and
Mary Margaret Clevenger Fund (1992.0072)

traditional wares, others experiment with new styles and innovative techniques.

Fukami Sueharu (b. 1947) is among the most innovative clay artists in Japan today. Yet his art has roots in the past—in his case, in Chinese porcelains with pale bluish-green glazes (*seihakuji*). Even so, his forms and fabrication methods, typified by his **SKY II**, are ultramodern (**FIG. 26–21**). He created the piece using a slip casting technique, in which he injected liquid clay into a mold using a high-pressure compressor. Although he sometimes makes functional pieces, mainly cylinders that could hold flower arrangements, *Sky II* shows his mastery of pure form. The title suggests sources of this abstract sculptural shape: a wing or a blade of an aircraft slicing through the sky. The pale sky-blue glaze only enhances this allusion. The fusion here of traditions, media, techniques, and forms looks back to a distinguished artistic heritage, but the suave mastery of abstraction and the subtle evocation of thematic meaning point forward to a global art world, where Japanese artists are clearly taking their place.

THINK ABOUT IT

26.1 Discuss how the Japanese tea ceremony works and observe the role that art plays within it. Explore the unique aesthetics of the tearoom and artistic practices associated with the ceremony, making reference to at least one work from this chapter.

26.2 Chose one woodblock print discussed in this chapter and explain how its subject matter represents the culture of the "floating world" in Edo.

26.3 Reflect on the differences between the styles practiced by artists from the cities of Kyoto and Edo. How do these distinctions relate to the variations in the social status and cultural and intellectual interests of the residents of these two cities? How would you fit the lacquer box by a Rinpa-school artist from Kyoto (FIG. 26–10) and the *kosode* robe made in Edo (see "A Closer Look," page 831) into your discussion?

26.4 Chose one of the three Japanese works in this chapter dating from the period after World War II and evaluate the ways in which it draws from both traditional Japanese and foreign artistic practices. Is there a larger debt to tradition or to innovation?

CROSSCURRENTS

FIG. 23–51

FIG. 26–4

Garden design weaves its way through the history of art during most times and places. These two distinguished examples were produced for two very different architectural complexes and to serve very different populations. Assess the way these two gardens were used and discuss how their form is related to their function. How are they representative of their cultural contexts?

✔—[**Study** and review on myartslab.com

27–1 • Julia Jumbo TWO GREY HILLS TAPESTRY WEAVING
Navajo, 2003. Handspun wool, 36″ × 24½″ (91.2 × 62.1 cm). Wheelwright Museum of the American Indian, Santa Fe, New Mexico.

Art of the Americas after 1300

According to Navajo mythology, the universe itself is a weaving, its fibers spun by Spider Woman out of sacred cosmic materials. Spider Woman taught the art of weaving to Changing Woman (a Mother Earth figure), and she in turn taught it to Navajo women, who continue to keep this art vital, seeing its continuation as a sacred responsibility. Early Navajo blankets were composed of simple horizontal stripes, but over time weavers have introduced more intricate patterns, and today Navajo rugs are woven in numerous distinctive styles.

The tapestry weaving in **FIGURE 27–1** is designed in the Two Grey Hills style that developed during the early twentieth century around a trading post of that name in northwest New Mexico. Weavers who work in this style use the natural colors of undyed sheep's wool (only the black wool is sometimes dyed) to create dazzling geometric patterns. Julia Jumbo (1928–2007), who learned to weave as a child, used her weavings to support her family. She raised her own sheep, and carded and spun her wool by hand before incorporating it into painstakingly made textiles. Jumbo is renowned for the clarity of her designs and the technical perfection of her fine weave.

When the first Europeans arrived, the Western Hemisphere was already inhabited from the Arctic Circle to Tierra del Fuego by peoples with long histories and rich cultural traditions (**MAP 27–1**). After 1492, when Christopher Columbus

and his companions first sailed to the New World, the arrival of Europeans completely altered the destiny of the Americas. In Mesoamerica and South America the break with the past was sudden and violent: two great empires—the Aztec in Mexico and the Inca in South America—that had risen to prominence in the fifteenth century were rapidly destroyed. In North America the change took place more gradually, but the outcome was much the same. In both North and South America, natives succumbed to European diseases to which they had no immunity, especially smallpox, leading to massive population loss and social disruption. Over the next 400 years, many Native Americans were displaced from their ancestral homelands, and many present-day Native American ethnic groupings were formed by combinations of various survivor groups.

Despite all the disruption, during the past century the indigenous arts of the Americas have undergone a re-evaluation that has renewed the conception of what constitutes "American art." Native artists like Julia Jumbo continue to revive and reimagine indigenous traditions, revisit traditional outlooks, and restate their ancient customs and ideas in new ways. After being pushed to the brink of extinction, Native American cultures are experiencing a revival in both North and South America, as Native Americans assert themselves politically and insist on the connections between their history and the land.

LEARN ABOUT IT

27.1 Explore the variety of styles, media, and techniques that characterize indigenous art and architecture across the Americas, both before and after contact with Europeans.

27.2 Recognize and understand the themes and symbols developed by Native American artists to express cultural, religious, and political ideas and values.

27.3 Explore how an understanding of the ritual and political use, as well as the practical function, of works are critical to interpreting their meaning in Native American arts.

27.4 Recognize and evaluate how indigenous arts have changed in the centuries since contact with Europeans.

((•—[Listen to the chapter audio on myartslab.com

THE AZTEC EMPIRE

In November 1519, the army of the Spanish soldier Hernán Cortés beheld for the first time the great Aztec capital of Tenochtitlan. The shimmering city, which seemed to be floating on the water, was built on an island in the middle of Lake Texcoco in the Valley of Mexico, and linked by broad causeways to the mainland. One of Cortés's companions later recalled the wonder the Spanish felt at that moment: "When we saw so many cities and villages built on the water and other great towns on dry land and that straight and level causeway going towards [Tenochtitlan], we were amazed … on account of the great towers and temples and buildings rising from the water, and all built of masonry. And some of our soldiers even asked whether the things that we saw were not a dream." (Bernal Díaz del Castillo, cited in Coe and Koontz 2005, p. 190.)

The Mexica people who lived in the remarkable city that Cortés found were then rulers of much of the land that later took their name, Mexico. Their rise to power had been recent and swift. Only 400 years earlier, according to their own legends, they had been a nomadic people living far north of the Valley of Mexico in a distant place called Aztlan. The term Aztec derives from the word Aztlan, and refers to all those living in Central Mexico who came from this mythical homeland, not just to the Mexica of Tenochtitlan.

The Mexica arrived in the Valley of Mexico in the thirteenth century. They eventually settled on an island in Lake Texcoco where they had seen an eagle perching on a prickly pear cactus (*nochtli*) growing out of a stone (*tetl*), a sign that their god Huitzilopochtli told them would mark the end of their wandering. They called the place Tenochtitlan. The city on the island was gradually expanded by reclaiming land from the lake, and serviced by a grid of artificial canals. In the fifteenth century, the Mexica—joined by allies in a triple alliance—began an aggressive campaign of

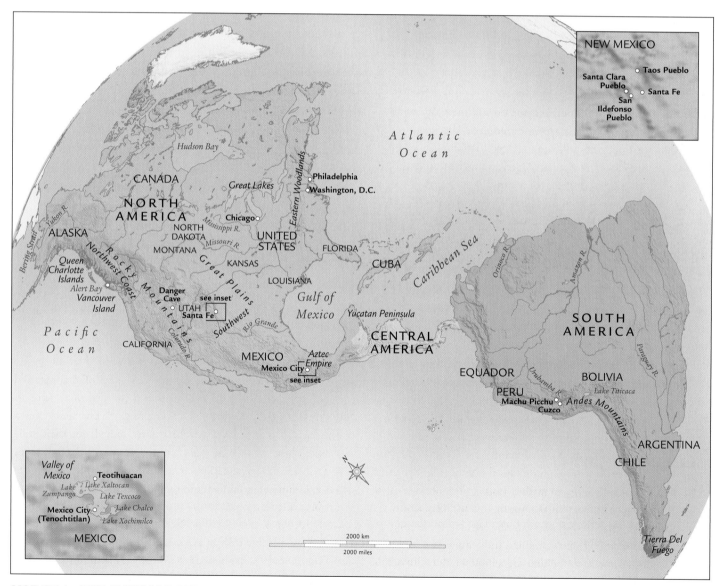

MAP 27–1 • THE AMERICAS AFTER 1300

Diverse cultures inhabited the Americas, each shaping a distinct artistic tradition.

expansion. The tribute they exacted from all over Mexico transformed Tenochtitlan into a glittering capital.

Aztec religion was based on a complex pantheon that combined Aztec deities with more ancient ones that had long been worshiped in Central Mexico. According to Aztec belief, the gods had created the current era, or sun, at the ancient city of Teotihuacan in the Valley of Mexico (see Chapter 13). The continued existence of the world depended on human actions, including rituals of bloodletting and human sacrifice. Many Mesoamerican peoples believed that the world had been created multiple times before the present era. But while most Mesoamericans believed that they were living in the fourth era, or sun, the Mexica asserted that they lived in the fifth sun, a new era that coincided with the Aztec Empire. The Calendar Stone (see "A Closer Look," page 841) boldly makes this claim, using the dates of the destructions of the four previous eras to form the glyph that names the fifth sun, 4 Motion. The end of each period of 52 years in the Mesoamerican calendar was a particularly dangerous time that required a special fire-lighting ritual.

TENOCHTITLAN

An Aztec scribe drew an idealized representation of the city of Tenochtitlan and its sacred ceremonial precinct (**FIG. 27-2**) for the Spanish viceroy in 1545. It forms the first page of the Codex Mendoza. An eagle perched on a prickly pear cactus growing out of a stone—the symbol of the city—fills the center of the page. Waterways divide the city into four quarters, and indicate the lake surrounding the city. Early leaders of Tenochtitlan are shown sitting in the four quadrants. The victorious warriors at the bottom of the page represent Aztec conquests, and a count of years surrounds the entire scene. This image combines historical narration with idealized cartography, showing the city in the middle of the lake at the moment of its founding.

At the center of Tenochtitlan was the sacred precinct, a walled enclosure that contained dozens of temples and other buildings. This area has been the site of intensive archaeological excavations in Mexico City since 1978, work that has greatly increased our understanding of this aspect of the Aztec city. The focal point of the sacred precinct was the Great Pyramid (or Templo Mayor), with paired temples on top: The one on the north was dedicated to Tlaloc, an ancient rain god with a history extending back to Teotihuacan, and the one on the south to Huitzilopochtli, the solar god of the newly arrived Mexica tribe (**FIG. 27-3**). During the winter rainy season the sun rose behind the temple of Tlaloc, and during the dry season it rose behind the temple of Huitzilopochtli. The double temple thus united two natural forces, sun and rain, or fire and water. During the spring and autumn equinoxes, the sun rose between the two temples.

27-2 • THE FOUNDING OF TENOCHTITLAN
Page from Codex Mendoza. Mexico. Aztec, 1545. Ink and color on paper, 12⅜″ × 8⁷⁄₁₆″ (31.5 × 21.5 cm). Bodleian Library, University of Oxford, England. MS. Arch Selden. A.1, fol. 2r

Two steep staircases led up the west face of the pyramid from the plaza in front. Sacrificial victims climbed these stairs to the temple of Huitzilopochtli, where priests threw them over a stone, quickly cut open their chests, and pulled out their still-throbbing hearts, a sacrifice that ensured the survival of the sun, the gods, and the Aztecs. The bodies were then rolled down the stairs and dismembered. Thousands of severed heads were said to have been kept on a skull rack in the plaza, represented in FIGURE 27-2 by the rack with a single skull to the right of the eagle. In addition to major works of Aztec sculpture, current excavations have uncovered a series of deep shafts containing multiple levels of offerings—precious objects as well as animals—and some believe that eventually human burials will be discovered, perhaps those of Aztec kings.

27-3 • RECONSTRUCTION OF THE GREAT PYRAMID (TEMPLO MAYOR) OF TENOCHTITLAN, c. 1500

SCULPTURE

Aztec sculpture was monumental, powerful, and often unsettling. A particularly striking example is an imposing statue of **COATLICUE**, mother of the Mexica god Huitzilopochtli (**FIG. 27-4**). Coatlicue means "she of the serpent skirt," and this broad-shouldered figure with clawed feet has a skirt of twisted snakes. The sculpture may allude to the moment of Huitzilopochtli's birth: When Coatlicue conceived Huitzilopochtli from a ball of down, her other children—the stars and the moon—jealously conspired to kill her. As they attacked, Huitzilopochtli emerged from his mother's body fully grown and armed, drove off his half-brothers, and destroyed his half-sister, the moon goddess Coyolxauhqui. Coatlicue, however, did not survive the encounter. In this sculpture, she has been decapitated and a pair of serpents, symbols of gushing blood, rise from her neck to form her head. Their eyes are her eyes; their fangs, her tusks. Around her stump of a neck hangs a necklace of human hands, hearts, and a dangling skull. Despite the surface intricacy, the statue's massive form creates an impression of

27-4 • THE GODDESS COATLICUE
Mexico. Aztec, c. 1500. Basalt, height 8′6″ (2.65 m). Museo Nacional de Antropología, Mexico City.

 View the Closer Look for *The Goddess Coatlicue* on myartslab.com

A CLOSER LOOK | Calendar Stone

Mexico. Aztec, c. 1500. Diameter 11'6¾" (3.6 m).
Museo Nacional de Antropología, Mexico City.

According to Mexica belief, the gods created the world four times before the present era. These cartouches name the days on which the four previous suns were destroyed: 4 Jaguar, 4 Wind, 4 Rain, and 4 Water.

Together, these four calendrical glyphs and the face and claws of the central god combine to form the glyph for 4 Motion, the day on which the fifth sun will be destroyed by a giant earthquake.

This central face combines elements of the sun god as the night sun in the underworld with the clawed hands and flint tongue of earth gods, symbolizing the night sun and the hungry earth.

This band forms the Aztec symbol for the sun, a round disk with triangular projections denoting the sun's rays.

This band contains the 20 day signs of the 260-day ritual calendar.

Two fire serpents encircle the outer part of the disk. Stylized flames rise off their backs. Their heads meet at the bottom, and human faces emerge from the mouths of the serpents.

View the Closer Look for the calendar stone on myartslab.com

solidity, and the entire sculpture leans forward, looming over the viewer. The colors with which it was originally painted would have heightened its dramatic impact.

FEATHERWORK

Indeed Aztec art was colorful. An idea of its iridescent splendor is captured in the **FEATHER HEADDRESS** (**FIG. 27–5**) said to have been given by the Aztec emperor Moctezuma to

27–5 • FEATHER HEADDRESS OF MOCTEZUMA
Mexico. Aztec, before 1519. Quetzal, blue cotinga, and other feathers and gold on a fiber frame, 45⅝" × 68⅞" (116 × 175 cm). Museo Nacional de Antropología, Mexico City, Mexico.

Cortés, and thought to be the one listed in the inventory of treasures Cortés shipped to Charles V, the Habsburg emperor in Spain, in 1519. Featherwork was one of the glories of Mesoamerican art, but very few of these extremely fragile artworks survive. The tropical feathers in this headdress exemplify the exotic tribute paid to the Aztecs; the long iridescent green feathers that make up most of the headdress are the exceedingly rare tail feathers of the quetzal bird—each male quetzal has only two such plumes. The feathers were gathered in small bunches, their quills reinforced with reed tubes, and then sewn to the frame in overlapping layers, the joins concealed by small gold plaques. Featherworkers were esteemed artists. After the Spanish invasion, they turned their exacting skills to "feather paintings" of Christian subjects.

MANUSCRIPTS

Aztec scribes also created brilliantly colored books: histories, maps, and divinatory almanacs. Instead of being bound on one side like European books, Mesoamerican books took the form of a screen-fold, accordion-pleated so that each page was connected only to the two adjacent pages. This format allowed great flexibility: a book could be opened to show two pages, or unfolded to show six or eight pages simultaneously; different sections of the book could also be juxtaposed. A rare manuscript that survived the Spanish conquest provides a concise summary of Mesoamerican cosmology (**FIG. 27–6**). Mesoamerican peoples recognized five key directions: north, south, east, west, and center. At the center of the image is Xiuhtecuhtli, god of fire, time, and the calendar. Radiating from him are the four cardinal directions—each associated with a specific color, a deity, and a tree with a bird in its branches. The 260 dots that trace the eight-lobed path around the central figure refer to the 260-day Mesoamerican divinatory calendar; the 20 day signs of this calendar are also distributed throughout the image. By linking the 260-day calendar to the four directions, this image speaks eloquently of the unity of space and time in the Mesoamerican worldview.

The Aztec Empire was short-lived. Within two years of their arrival in Mexico, the Spanish conquistadors and their indigenous allies overran Tenochtitlan. They built their own capital, Mexico City, over its ruins and established their own cathedral on the site of Tenochtitlan's sacred precinct.

27-6 • A VIEW OF THE WORLD
Page from Codex Fejervary-Mayer. Mexico. Aztec or Mixtec, c. 1400–1519. Paint on animal hide, each page 6⅞″ × 6⅞″ (17.5 × 17.5 cm), total length 13′3″ (4.04 m). National Museums, Liverpool.

THE INCA EMPIRE

At the beginning of the sixteenth century the Inca Empire was one of the largest states in the world. It extended more than 2,600 miles along western South America, encompassing most of modern Peru, Ecuador, Bolivia, and northern Chile and reaching into present-day Argentina. Like the Aztec Empire, its rise was rapid and its destruction sudden.

The Incas called their empire the "Land of the Four Quarters." At its center was their capital, Cuzco, "the navel of the world," located high in the Andes Mountains. The Inca state began as one of many small competing kingdoms that emerged in the highlands. In the fifteenth century the Incas began to expand, suddenly and rapidly, and had subdued most of their vast domain—through conquest, alliance, and intimidation—by 1500.

To hold this linguistically and ethnically diverse empire together, the Inca ("Inca" refers to both the ruler and the people) relied on religion, an efficient bureaucracy, and various forms of labor taxation, in which the payment was a set amount of time spent performing tasks for the state. In return the state provided gifts through local leaders and sponsored lavish ritual entertainments. Men might cultivate state lands, serve in the army, or work periodically on public works projects—building roads and terracing hillsides, for example—while women wove cloth as tribute. No Andean civilization ever developed writing, but the Inca kept detailed accounts and historical records on knotted and colored cords (*quipu*).

To move their armies and speed transport and communication within the empire, the Incas built more than 23,000 miles of roads. These varied from 50-foot-wide thoroughfares to 3-foot-wide paths. Two main north–south roads, one along the coast and the other through the highlands, were linked by east–west roads. Travelers journeyed on foot, using llamas as pack animals. Stairways helped them negotiate steep mountain slopes, and rope suspension bridges allowed river gorge crossings. All along the roads, storehouses and lodgings—more than a thousand have been found—were spaced a day's journey apart. A relay system of runners could carry messages between Cuzco and the farthest reaches of the empire in about a week.

CUZCO

Cuzco, a capital of great splendor, was home to the Inca, ruler of the empire. Its urban plan was said to have been designed by the

---

ELEMENTS OF ARCHITECTURE | Inca Masonry

Working with the simplest of tools—mainly heavy stone hammers—and using no mortar, Inca builders created stonework of great refinement and durability: roads and bridges that linked the entire empire, terraces for growing crops, and structures both simple and elaborate. The effort expended on stone construction by the Inca was prodigious. Fine Inca masonry consisted of either rectangular blocks or irregular polygonal blocks (see FIG. 27-7). In both types, adjoining blocks were painstakingly shaped to fit tightly together without mortar. Their stone faces might be slightly beveled along their edges so that each block presented a "pillowed" shape expressing its identity, or walls might be smoothed into a continuous flowing surface in which the individual blocks form a seamless whole. At a few Inca sites, the stones used in construction were boulder-size: up to 27 feet tall. In Cuzco, and elsewhere in the Inca Empire, Inca masonry has survived earthquakes that have destroyed later structures.

At Machu Picchu (see FIGS. 27-7, 27-8), all buildings and terraces within its 3-square-mile extent were made of granite, the hard stone occurring at the site. Commoners' houses and some walls were constructed of irregular stones that were carefully fitted together, while fine polygonal or smoothed masonry distinguished palaces and temples.

polygonal-stone wall

smooth-surfaced wall

👁️ **Watch** an architectural simulation about Inca masonry on myartslab.com

27-7 • INCA MASONRY, DETAIL OF A WALL AT MACHU PICCHU
Peru. Inca, 1450–1530.

27-8 • MACHU PICCHU
Peru. Inca, 1450–1530.

👁 **Watch** a video about Machu Picchu on myartslab.com

Inca Pachacuti (r. 1438–1471) in the shape of a puma, its head the fortress of Sacsahuaman, and its belly the giant plaza at the center of town. The city was divided into upper and lower parts, reflecting the dual organization of Inca society. Cuzco was the symbolic as well as the political center of the Inca Empire: everyone had to carry a burden when entering the city, and gold, silver, or textiles brought into the city could not afterward be removed from it.

Cuzco was a showcase of the finest Inca masonry, some of which can still be seen in the present-day city (see "Inca Masonry," page 843). Architecture was a major expressive form for the Inca, the very shape of individually worked stones conveying a powerful aesthetic impact (**FIG. 27-7**). In contrast to the massive walls, Inca buildings had gabled, thatched roofs. Doors, windows, and niches were trapezoids, narrower at the top than the bottom.

MACHU PICCHU

MACHU PICCHU, one of the most spectacular archaeological sites in the world, provides an excellent example of Inca architectural planning (**FIG. 27-8**). At 9,000 feet above sea level, it straddles a ridge between two high peaks in the eastern slopes of the Andes and looks down on the Urubamba River. Stone buildings, today lacking only their thatched roofs, occupy terraces around central

27-9 • TUNIC
Peru. Inca, c. 1500. Camelid fiber and cotton, 35⅞″ × 30″ (91 × 76.5 cm). Dumbarton Oaks Research Library and Collections, Pre-Columbian Collection, Washington, DC.

plazas, and narrow agricultural terraces descend into the valley. The site, near the eastern limits of the empire, was the royal estate of the Inca ruler Pachacuti. The court might retire to this warmer, lower-altitude palace when the Cuzco winter became too harsh to enjoy. Important diplomatic negotiations and ceremonial feasts may also have taken place at this country retreat. The entire complex is designed with great sensitivity to its surroundings, with walls and plazas framing stupendous vistas of the surrounding landscape, and carefully selected stones echoing the shapes of the mountains beyond.

TEXTILES

The production of fine textiles was already an important art in the Andes by the third millennium BCE (see "Andean Textiles," page 397). Among the Incas, textiles of cotton and camelid fibers (from llama, vicuña, and alpaca) were an indication of wealth. One form of labor taxation required the manufacture of fibers and cloth, and textiles as well as agricultural products filled Inca storehouses. Cloth was deemed a fitting gift for the gods, so fine garments were draped around statues, and even burned as sacrificial offerings.

The patterns and designs on garments were not simply decorative; they carried symbolic messages, including indications of a person's ethnic identity and social rank. In the elaborate **TUNIC** in **FIGURE 27-9**, each square represents a miniature tunic with a different pattern and meaning. For example, tunics with checkerboard patterns were worn by military officers and royal escorts; the four-part motifs may refer to the empire as the

Land of the Four Quarters. While we may not be sure what was meant in every case, patterns and colors appear to have been standardized like uniforms in order to convey information at a glance. Perhaps an exquisite tunic such as this, containing patterns associated with multiple ranks and statuses, was woven as a royal garment.

METALWORK

When they arrived in Peru in 1532, the Spanish were far less interested in Inca cloth than in their vast quantities of gold and silver. The Inca valued objects made of gold and silver not for their precious metal, but because they saw in them symbols of the sun and the moon. They are said to have called gold the "sweat of the sun" and silver the "tears of the moon." On the other hand, the Spanish exploration of the New World was propelled by feverish tales of native treasure. Whatever gold and silver objects the Spanish could obtain were melted down to enrich their royal coffers. Only a few small figures buried as offerings, like the little **LLAMA** shown in **FIGURE 27-10**, escaped destruction. The llama was thought to have a special connection with the sun, with rain, and with fertility, and a llama was sacrificed to the sun every morning in Cuzco. In this small silver figurine, the essential character of a llama is rendered with a few well-chosen details, but in keeping with the value that Andeans placed on textiles the blanket on its back is carefully described.

THE AFTERMATH OF THE SPANISH CONQUEST

Native American populations in Mexico and Peru declined sharply after the conquest because of the exploitative policies of the conquerors and the ravages of smallpox and other European diseases against which the indigenous people had no immunity. This demographic collapse meant that the population of the Americas declined by as much as 90 percent in the century after contact with Europe. European missionaries suppressed local beliefs and practices and worked to spread Christianity throughout the Americas. Although increasing numbers of Europeans began to settle and dominate the land, the production of art did not end with the Spanish conquest. Traditional media, including fine weaving, continue to flourish to this day, transforming and remaining vital as indigenous peoples adjust to a changing world.

NORTH AMERICA

In America north of Mexico, from the upper reaches of Canada and Alaska to the southern tip of Florida, many different peoples with widely varying cultures coexisted. Here, the Europeans came less as military men seeking riches to plunder than as families seeking land to farm. Unlike the Spaniards, they found no large cities with urban populations to resist them. However, although they imagined that the lands they settled were an untended wilderness, in fact nearly all of North America was populated and possessed by indigenous peoples. Over the next 400 years, by means of violence, bribery, and treaties, the English colonies and, in turn, the United States displaced nearly all Native Americans from their ancestral homelands. For example, beginning in the 1830s and continuing through the nineteenth century, thousands of Native Americans (46,000 by 1938) were relocated from their ancestral homelands to newly assigned territory in present-day Oklahoma, a forced migration that became known as the Trail of Tears.

The indigenous art Euro-Americans encountered they viewed as a curiosity, not art. Native American works were small, portable, fragile, and impermanent—appreciated not for their aesthetic qualities, but collected as anthropological artifacts, curiosities, or souvenirs, often under coercive conditions. Today, Native peoples have begun to reclaim sacred objects and human remains that were forcibly taken from them, and museums are beginning to work with Native communities to present their art in respectful and culturally sensitive ways. Here, we will be able to look at art from only four North American cultural areas: the Eastern Woodlands, the Great Plains, the Northwest Coast, and the Southwest (**MAP 27-2**).

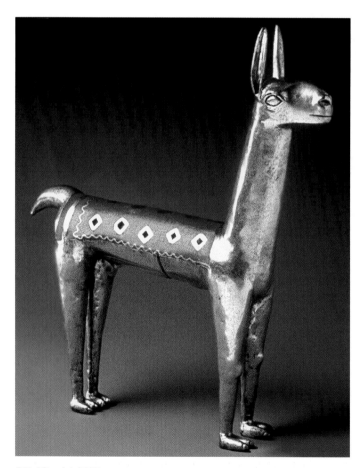

27-10 • LLAMA
From Bolivia or Peru, found near Lake Titicaca, Bolivia. Inca, 15th century. Cast silver with gold and cinnabar, 9″ × 8½″ × 1¾″ (22.9 × 21.6 × 4.4 cm). American Museum of Natural History, New York.

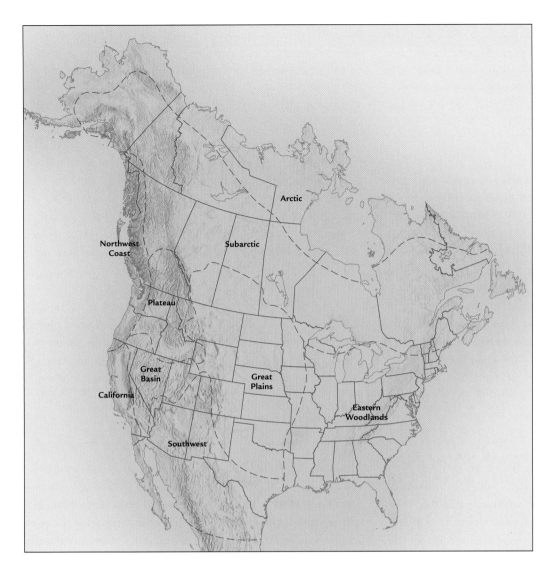

MAP 27-2 • NORTH AMERICAN CULTURAL AREAS

The varied geographic regions of North America supported diverse cultures adapted to their distinct environments.

THE EASTERN WOODLANDS

In the Eastern Woodlands, after the decline of the great Mississippian centers (see Chapter 13), most tribes lived in stable villages, and they combined hunting, gathering, and agriculture for their livelihood. In the sixteenth century, the Iroquois formed a powerful confederation of five northeastern Native American nations, which played a prominent military and political role until after the American Revolution. The Huron and Illinois also formed sizable confederacies.

In the seventeenth century, the arrival on the Atlantic coast of a few boatloads of Europeans seeking religious freedom, farmland, and a new life for themselves brought major changes. Trade with these settlers gave the Woodlands peoples access to things they valued, while on their part the colonists learned Native forms of agriculture, hunting, and fishing—skills they needed in order to survive. In turn, Native Americans traded furs for such useful items as metal tools, cookware, needles, and cloth, and they especially prized European glass beads and silver. These trade items largely replaced older materials, such as crystal, copper, and shell.

WAMPUM Woodlands peoples made belts and strings of cylindrical purple and white shell beads called wampum. The Iroquois and Delaware peoples used wampum to keep records (the purple and white patterns served as memory devices) and exchanged belts of wampum to conclude treaties (**FIG. 27-12**). Few actual wampum treaty belts have survived, so this one, said to commemorate an unwritten treaty when the land now comprising the state of Pennsylvania was ceded by the Delawares in 1682, is especially prized. The belt, with two figures of equal size holding hands, suggests the mutual respect enjoyed by the Delaware and Penn's Society of Friends (Quakers), a respect that later collapsed into land fraud and violence. In general, wampum strings and belts had the authority of legal agreement and also symbolized a moral and political order.

QUILLWORK Woodlands art focused on personal adornment—tattoos, body paint, elaborate dress—and fragile arts such as **quillwork**. Quillwork involved dyeing porcupine and bird quills with a variety of natural dyes, soaking the quills to soften them, and then working them into rectilinear, ornamental surface patterns

Basketry is the weaving of reeds, grasses, and other plant materials to form containers. In North America the earliest evidence of basketwork, found in Danger Cave, Utah, dates to as early as 8400 BCE. Over the subsequent centuries, Native American women, notably in California and the American Southwest, developed basketry into an art form that combined utility with great beauty.

There are three principal basket-making techniques: coiling, twining, and plaiting. **Coiling** involves sewing together a spiraling foundation of rods with some other material. **Twining** twists multiple elements around a vertical warp of rods. Plaiting weaves strips over and under each other.

The coiled basket shown here was made by a Pomo woman in California (**FIG. 27–11**). According to Pomo legend, the Earth was dark until their ancestral hero stole the sun and brought it to Earth in a basket. He hung the basket first just over the horizon, but, dissatisfied with the light it gave, he kept suspending it in different places across the dome of the sky. He repeats this process every day, which is why the sun moves across the sky from east to west. In the Pomo basket, the structure of coiled willow and bracken fern root produces a spiral surface into which the artist worked sparkling pieces of clam shell, trade beads, and soft tufts of woodpecker and quail feathers. The underlying basket, the glittering shells, and the soft, moving feathers make this an exquisite container. Such baskets were treasured possessions, cremated with their owners at death.

27-11 • FEATHERED BASKET
California. Pomo culture, c. 1877. Willow, bulrush, fern, feather, shells, glass beads. Height 5½″ (14 cm), diameter 12″ (36.5 cm). The Philbrook Museum of Art, Inc., Tulsa, Oklahoma. Gift of Clark Field (1948.39.37)

on deerskin clothing and on birch-bark items like baskets and boxes. A Sioux legend recounts how a mythical ancestor, Doublewoman ("double" because she was both beautiful and ugly, benign and dangerous), appeared to a woman in a dream and taught her the art of quillwork. As the legend suggests, quillwork was a woman's art form, as was basketry (see "Basketry," above). The Sioux **BABY CARRIER** in **FIGURE 27-13** is richly decorated with symbols of protection and well-being, including bands of antelopes in profile and thunderbirds flying with their heads turned and tails outspread. The thunderbird was an especially

27-12 • WAMPUM BELT, TRADITIONALLY CALLED WILLIAM PENN'S TREATY WITH THE DELAWARE
1680s. Shell beads, 17⅜″ × 6⅛″ (44 × 15.5 cm). Royal Ontario Museum, Canada.

27-13 • BABY CARRIER
Upper Missouri River area. Eastern Sioux, 19th century.
Wooden board, buckskin, porcupine quill, length 31″
(78.8 cm). Department of Anthropology, Smithsonian
Institution Libraries, Washington, DC. Catalogue No. 7311

beneficent symbol, thought to be capable of protecting against both human and supernatural adversaries.

BEADWORK In spite of the use of shell beads in wampum, decorative beadwork did not become commonplace until after European contact. In the late eighteenth century, Native American artists began to acquire European colored-glass beads, and in the nineteenth century they favored the tiny seed beads from Venice and Bohemia. Early beadwork mimicked the patterns and colors of quillwork. In the nineteenth century it largely replaced quillwork and incorporated European designs. Among other sources of inspiration, Canadian nuns introduced the young women in their schools to embroidered European floral motifs, and Native embroiderers began to adapt these designs, as well as European needlework techniques and patterns from European garments, into their own work. Functional aspects of garments might be transformed into purely decorative motifs; for example, a pocket would be replaced by an area of beadwork shaped like a pocket. A **BANDOLIER BAG** from Kansas, made by a Delaware woman (**FIG. 27-14**), is covered with curvilinear plant motifs in contrast to the rectilinear patterns of traditional quillwork. White lines outline brilliant pink and blue leaf-shaped forms on both bag and shoulder straps, heightening the intensity of the colors, which alternate within repeated patterns, exemplifying the evolution of beadwork design and its adaptation to a changing world.

27-14 • BANDOLIER BAG
Kansas. Delaware people, c. 1860. Wool fabric, cotton fabric and thread, silk ribbon, and glass beads, 22″ × 17″ (56 × 43 cm); bag without strap, 8⅝″ × 7¾″ (22 × 19.7 cm). The Detroit Institute of Arts. Founders Society Purchase (81.216)

The very shape of this bandolier bag is adapted from European military uniforms.

THE GREAT PLAINS

Between the Eastern Woodlands region and the Rocky Mountains to the west lay an area of prairie grasslands called the Great Plains. On the Great Plains, two differing ways of life developed, one a relatively recent and short-lived (1700–1870) nomadic lifestyle—dependent on the region's great migrating herds of buffalo for food, clothing, and shelter—and the other, a much older sedentary and agricultural lifestyle. Horses, from wild herds descended from feral horses brought to America by Spanish explorers in the sixteenth and seventeenth centuries, made travel, and thus a nomadic way of life, easier for the dispossessed eastern groups that moved to the plains.

European settlers on the eastern seaboard put increasing pressure on the Eastern Woodlands peoples, seizing their farmlands and forcing them westward. Both Native Americans and backcountry settlers were living in loosely village-based, farming societies and thus were competing for the same resources. The resulting interaction of Eastern Woodlands artists with one another and with Plains artists led in some cases to the emergence of a new hybrid style, while other artists consciously fought to maintain their own traditional cultures.

PORTABLE ARCHITECTURE The nomadic Plains peoples hunted buffalo for food and hides from which they created clothing and a light, portable dwelling known as a tipi (formerly spelled teepee) (**FIG. 27-15**). The tipi was well adapted to withstand the strong and constant wind, the dust, and the violent storms of the prairies. The framework of a tipi consisted of a stable pyramidal frame of three or four long poles, filled out with about 20 additional poles, in a roughly oval plan. The framework was covered with hides specially prepared to make them flexible and waterproof—or, later, with canvas—to form a conical structure. Between 20 and 40 hides were used to make a tipi, depending on its size. An opening at the top served as the smoke hole for a central hearth. The tipi leaned slightly into the prevailing west wind while the flap-covered door and smoke hole faced east, away from the wind. An inner lining covered the lower part of the walls and the perimeter of the floor to protect the occupants from drafts.

Tipis were the property and responsibility of women, who set them up at new encampments and lowered them when the group moved on. Blackfoot women could set up their huge tipis in less than an hour. Women quilled, beaded, and embroidered tipi linings, as well as backrests, clothing, and equipment. The patterns with which tipis were decorated, like their proportions and colors, varied from nation to nation, family to family, and individual to individual. In general, the bottom was covered with traditional motifs and the center section held personal images. When disassembled and packed to be dragged by a horse to another location, the tipi served as a platform for transporting other possessions. The Sioux arranged their tipis in two half-circles—one for the sky people and one for the earth people—divided along an east–west axis. When the Blackfoot people gathered in the summer for their ceremonial Sun Dance, their encampment contained hundreds of tipis in a circle a mile in circumference.

PLAINS INDIAN PAINTING Plains men recorded their exploits in paintings on tipis and on buffalo-hide robes. The earliest documented painted buffalo-hide robe, presented to Lewis and Clark during their transcontinental expedition, illustrates a battle fought in 1797 by the Mandan (of what is now North Dakota) and their allies against the Sioux (**FIG. 27-16**). The painter, trying to capture the full extent of a conflict in which five nations took part, shows a party of warriors in 22 separate episodes. The party is led by a man with a pipe and an elaborate eagle-feather headdress, and the warriors are armed with bows and arrows, lances, clubs, and flintlock rifles. Details of equipment and emblems of rank—headdresses, sashes, shields, feathered lances, powder horns for the rifles—are depicted carefully. Horses are shown in profile with stick legs, C-shaped hooves, and either clipped or flowing manes.

The figures stand out clearly against the light-colored background of the buffalo hide. The painter pressed lines into the hide, then filled in the forms with black, red, green, yellow, and brown pigments. A strip of colored porcupine quills runs down the spine of the buffalo hide. The robe would have been worn draped over the shoulders of the powerful warrior whose deeds it commemorates. As the wearer moved, the painted horses and warriors would seem to come alive, transforming him into a living representation of his exploits.

Life on the Great Plains changed abruptly in 1869, when the transcontinental railway linking the east and west coasts of

27-15 • BLACKFOOT WOMEN RAISING A TIPI
Photographed c. 1900. Montana Historical Society Research Center.

27-16 • BATTLE SCENE, HIDE PAINTING

North Dakota. Mandan, 1797–1800. Tanned buffalo hide, dyed porcupine quills, and black, red, green, yellow, and brown pigment, 7'10" × 8'6" (2.44 × 2.65 m). Courtesy of the Peabody Museum of Archaeology and Ethnology, Harvard University. Peabody 99-12-10/53121

This robe, "collected" in 1804 by Meriwether Lewis and William Clark on their expedition into western lands acquired by the United States in the Louisiana Purchase, is the earliest documented example of Plains painting. It was one of a number of Native American artworks that Lewis and Clark sent to President Thomas Jefferson, who displayed the robe in the entrance hall of his home at Monticello, Virginia.

the United States was completed, providing easy access to Native American lands. Between 1871 and 1890, Euro-American hunters killed off most of the buffalo, and soon ranchers and then farmers moved into the Great Plains. The U.S. government forcibly moved the outnumbered and outgunned Native Americans to reservations, land considered worthless until the later discovery of oil and, in the case of the Black Hills, gold.

THE NORTHWEST COAST

From southern Alaska to northern California, the Pacific coast of North America is a region of unusually abundant resources. Its many rivers fill each year with salmon returning to spawn. Harvested and dried, the fish could sustain large populations throughout the year. The peoples of the Northwest Coast—among them the Tlingit, the Haida, and the Kwakwaka'wakw (formerly spelled

Kwakiutl)—exploited this abundance to develop a complex and distinctive way of life in which the arts played a central role.

ANIMAL IMAGERY Animals feature prominently in Northwest Coast art because each extended family group (clan) claimed descent from a mythic animal or animal-human ancestor, from whom the family derived its name and the right to use certain animals and spirits as totemic emblems, or crests. These emblems appear frequently in Northwest Coast art, notably in carved cedar house poles and the tall, free-standing mortuary poles erected to memorialize dead chiefs. Chiefs, who were males in the most direct line of descent from the mythic ancestor, validated their status and garnered prestige for themselves and their families by holding ritual feasts known as potlatches, during which they gave valuable gifts to the invited guests. Shamans, who were sometimes also chiefs, mediated between the human and spirit worlds. Some shamans were female, giving them unique access to certain aspects of the spiritual world.

Northwest Coast peoples lived in large, elaborately decorated communal houses made of massive timbers and thick planks. Carved and painted partition screens separated the chief's quarters from the rest of the house. The Tlingit screen illustrated in **FIGURE 27-17** came from the house of Chief Shakes of Wrangell (d. 1916), whose family crest was the grizzly bear. The image of a rearing grizzly painted on the screen is itself made up of smaller bears and bear heads that appear in its ears, eyes, nostrils, joints, paws, and body. The oval door opening is a symbolic vagina; passing through it re-enacts the birth of the family from its ancestral spirit.

TEXTILES Blankets and other textiles produced collaboratively by the men and women of the Chilkat Tlingit had great prestige among Northwest Coast peoples (**FIG. 27-18**). Men drew the patterns on boards, and women wove them into the blankets, using shredded cedar bark and mountain-goat wool. The weavers did not use looms; instead, they hung cedar warp threads from a rod and twined colored goat wool back and forth through them to make the pattern, which in this technique can be defined by curving lines. The ends of the warp form the fringe at the bottom of the blanket.

The popular design used here is known as the diving whale—the central panel shows the downward-facing whale(s), while the panels to the sides have been interpreted as this animal's body or seated ravens seen in profile. Characteristic of Northwest painting and weaving, the images are composed of two basic elements: the ovoid (a slightly bent rectangle with rounded corners) and the formline (a continuous, shape-defining line). Here, subtly swelling black formlines define gently curving ovoids and C shapes. When the blanket was worn, its two-dimensional shapes would have become three-dimensional, with the dramatic central figure curving over the wearer's back and the intricate side panels crossing over his shoulders and chest.

MASKS To call upon guardian spirits, many Native American cultures staged ritual dance ceremonies in which dancers wore complex costumes and striking carved and painted wooden masks. Among the most elaborate masks were those used by the Kwakwaka'wakw in the Winter Ceremony that initiated members into the shamanistic Hamatsa society (see "Hamatsa Masks," page 854). The dance re-enacted the taming of Hamatsa, a cannibal spirit, and his three attendant bird spirits. Magnificent carved and painted masks transformed the dancers into Hamatsa and the bird attendants, who searched for victims to eat. Strings allowed the dancers to manipulate the masks so that the beaks opened and snapped shut with spectacular effect. Isolated in museums as "art," the masks doubtless lose some of the shocking vivacity they have in performance; nevertheless their bold forms and color

27-17 • GRIZZLY BEAR HOUSE-PARTITION SCREEN
From the house of Chief Shakes of Wrangell, Canada. Tlingit people, c. 1840. Cedar, paint, and human hair, 15′ × 8′ (4.57 × 2.74 m). Denver Art Museum Collection. Native Arts acquisition funds (1951.315)

27-18 • CHILKAT BLANKET
Southeast Alaska. Tlingit people,
c. 1850. Mountain-goat wool,
yellow cedar bark, linen thread,
approx. 55″ × 72″ (130 × 183 cm).
Thaw Collection, Fenimore Art
Museum, Cooperstown, New York.

schemes retain power and meaning that can be activated by the viewer's imagination.

THE SOUTHWEST

The Native American peoples of the southwestern United States include, among others, the Puebloans (sedentary village-dwelling groups) and the Navajo. The modern Puebloans are heirs of the Ancestral Puebloans (Anasazi) and Hohokam cultures (see Chapter 13). The Ancestral Puebloans built apartmentlike villages and cliff dwellings whose ruins are found throughout the Four Corners region of New Mexico, Colorado, Arizona, and Utah. The Navajo, who arrived in the region sometime between 1100 and 1500 CE, developed a semisedentary way of life based on agriculture and (after the introduction of sheep by the Spaniards) shepherding. Being among the very few Native American tribal groups whose reservations are located on their actual ancestral homelands, both groups have succeeded in maintaining the continuity of their traditions despite Euro-American pressure. Today, their arts reflect the adaptation of traditional forms to new technologies, new media, and the influences of the dominant American culture that surrounds them.

THE PUEBLOS Some Pueblo villages, like those of their ancient ancestors, consist of multi-storied dwellings made of adobe. One of these, **TAOS PUEBLO**, shown in **FIGURE 27–19** in a photograph taken in 1947 by the American photographer of the Southwest, Laura Gilpin (1891–1979), is located in north-central New

Mexico. Continually occupied and modified for over 500 years, the up to five-story house blocks of Taos Pueblo provide flexible, communal dwellings. Ladders provide access to the upper stories and to insulated inner rooms, entered through holes in the ceiling. Two large house blocks are arrayed around a central plaza that opens toward the neighboring mountains, rising in a stepped

27–19 • Laura Gilpin TAOS PUEBLO
Taos, New Mexico. Photographed 1947. © 1979 Amon Carter Museum of American Art, Fort Worth, Texas. Bequest of the artist (P1979.208.698)

Laura Gilpin, photographer of the landscape, architecture, and people of the American Southwest, began her series on the Pueblos and Navajos in the 1930s. She published her work in four volumes of photographs between 1941 and 1968.

During the harsh winter season, when spirits are thought to be most powerful, many Northwest Coast peoples seek spiritual renewal through their ancient rituals—including the potlatch, or ceremonial gift giving, and the initiation of new members into the prestigious Hamatsa society. With snapping beaks and cries of "Hap! Hap! Hap!" ("Eat! Eat! Eat!"), Hamatsa, the people-eating spirit of the north, and his three assistants—horrible masked monster birds—begin their wild ritual dance. The dancing birds threaten and even attack the Kwakwaka'wakw people who gather for the Winter Ceremony.

In the Winter Ceremony, youths are captured, taught the Hamatsa lore and rituals, and then in a spectacular theater-dance performance are "tamed" and brought back into civilized life. All the members of the community, including singers, gather in the main room of the great house, which is divided by a painted screen (see FIG. 27–17). The audience members fully participate in the performance; in early times, they brought containers of blood so that when the bird-dancers attacked them, they could appear to bleed and have flesh torn away.

Whistles from behind the screen announce the arrival of the Hamatsa (danced by an initiate), who enters through the central hole in the screen in a flesh-craving frenzy. Wearing hemlock, a symbol of the spirit world, he crouches and dances wildly with outstretched arms as attendants try to control him. He disappears but returns again, now wearing red cedar and dancing upright. Finally tamed, a full member of society, he even dances with the women.

Then the masked bird-dancers appear—first Raven-of-the-North-End-of-the-World, then Crooked-Beak-of-the-End-of-the-World, and finally the untranslatable Huxshukw, who cracks open skulls with his beak and eats the brains of his victims. Snapping their beaks, these masters of illusion enter the room backward, their masks pointed up as though the birds are looking skyward. They move slowly counterclockwise around the floor. At each change in the music they crouch, snap their beaks, and let out their wild cries of "Hap! Hap! Hap!" Essential to the ritual dances are the huge carved and painted wooden masks, articulated and operated by strings worked by the dancers. Among the finest masks are those by Willie Seaweed (1873–1967), a Kwakwaka'wakw chief, whose brilliant colors and exuberantly decorative carving style determined the direction of twentieth-century Kwakwaka'wakw sculpture (FIG. 27–20).

The Canadian government, abetted by missionaries, outlawed the Winter Ceremony and potlatches in 1885, claiming the event was injurious to health, encouraged prostitution, endangered children's education, damaged the economy, and was cannibalistic. But the Kwakwaka'wakw refused to give up their "oldest and best" festival—one that spoke powerfully to them in many ways, establishing social rank and playing an important role in arranging marriages. By 1936, the government and the missionaries, who called the Kwakwaka'wakw "incorrigible," gave up. But not until 1951 could the Kwakwaka'wakw people gather openly for winter ceremonies, including the initiation rites of the Hamatsa society.

27–20 • Attributed to Willie Seaweed KWAKWAKA'WAKW BIRD MASK
Alert Bay, Vancouver Island, Canada. Prior to 1951. Cedar wood, cedar bark, feathers, and fiber, 10″ × 72″ × 15″ (25.4 × 183 × 38.1 cm). Collection of the Museum of Anthropology, Vancouver, Canada. (A6120)

The name "Seaweed" is an anglicization of the Kwakwaka'wakw name *Siwid*, meaning "Paddling Canoe," "Recipient of Paddling," or "Paddled To"—referring to a great chief to whose potlatches guests paddled from afar. Willie Seaweed was not only the chief of his clan, but a great orator, singer, and tribal historian who kept the tradition of the potlatch alive during years of government repression.

27-21 • Maria Montoya Martinez and Julian Martinez BLACKWARE STORAGE JAR
New Mexico. c. 1942. Ceramic, height 18¾″ (47.6 cm), diameter 22½″ (57.1 cm). Museum of Indian Arts and Culture/Laboratory of Anthropology, Museum of New Mexico, Santa Fe.

fashion to provide a series of roof terraces that can serve as viewing platforms. The plaza and roof terraces are centers of communal life and ceremony, as can be seen in Pablita Velarde's painting of the winter solstice celebrations (see FIG. 27-22).

CERAMICS Traditionally, pottery was women's art among Pueblo peoples. Wares were made by coiling and other hand-building techniques, and then fired at low temperature in wood fires. The best-known twentieth-century Pueblo potter was Maria Montoya Martinez (1887–1980) of San Ildefonso Pueblo in New Mexico. Inspired by prehistoric pottery that was unearthed at nearby archaeological excavations and by the then-fashionable Art Deco style, she and her husband, Julian Martinez (1885–1943), developed a distinctive **blackware** ceramic style notable for its elegant forms and subtle textures (**FIG. 27-21**). Maria Martinez made pots covered with a slip that was then burnished. Using additional slip, Julian Martinez painted the pots with designs that interpreted traditional Pueblo and Ancestral Puebloan imagery. After firing, the burnished ground became a lustrous black and the slip painting retained a matte surface. By the 1930s, production of blackware in San Ildefonso had become a communal enterprise. Family members and friends all worked making pots, and Maria Martinez signed all the pieces so that, in typical Pueblo communal solidarity, everyone profited from her fame within the art market.

THE SANTA FE INDIAN SCHOOL In the 1930s, Anglo-American art teachers and dealers worked with Native Americans of the Southwest to create a distinctive, stereotypical "Indian" style in several media—including jewelry, pottery, weaving, and painting—to appeal to tourists and collectors. A leader in this effort was Dorothy Dunn (1903–1991), who taught painting in the Santa Fe

Indian School, an off-reservation government boarding school in New Mexico, from 1932 to 1937. Dunn inspired her students to create a painting style that combined the outline drawing and flat colors of folk art, the decorative qualities of Art Deco, and exotic "Indian" subject matter. She and her students formed the Studio School. Restrictive as the school was, Dunn's success made painting a viable occupation for young Native American artists.

Pablita Velarde (1918–2006), from Santa Clara Pueblo in New Mexico and a 1936 graduate of Dorothy Dunn's school, was only a teenager when one of her paintings was selected for exhibition at the Chicago World's Fair in 1933. Thereafter, Velarde documented Pueblo ways of life in a large series of murals for Bandelier National Monument, launching a long and successful career. In smaller works on paper, such as the one illustrated here, she continued this focus on Pueblo life. **KOSHARES OF TAOS** (**FIG. 27-22**) illustrates a moment during a ceremony celebrating the winter solstice when *koshares*, or clowns, take over the plaza from the Katsinas. Katsinas—the supernatural counterparts of animals, natural phenomena like clouds, and geological features like mountains—are central to traditional Pueblo religion. They manifest themselves in the human dancers who impersonate them during ceremonies throughout the year, as well as in the small figures known as Katsina dolls that are given to children as educational aids in learning to identify the masks. Velarde's painting combines bold, flat colors and a simplified decorative line with European perspective. Her paintings, with their Art Deco abstraction, helped establish the popular idea of the "Indian" style in art.

THE NAVAJOS While some Navajo arts, like sand painting, have deep traditional roots, others have developed over the centuries of European contact. Navajo weaving (see FIG. 27-1) depends on the

27-22 • Pablita Velarde KOSHARES OF TAOS
New Mexico. 1940s. Watercolor on paper, 13⁷⁄₈″ × 22³⁄₈″ (35.3 × 56.9 cm). Philbrook Museum of Art, Tulsa, Oklahoma.
Museum Purchase (1947.37)

wool of sheep introduced by the Spaniards, and the designs and colors of Navajo blankets continue to evolve today in response to tourism and changing aesthetics. Similarly, jewelry made of turquoise and silver did not become an important Navajo art form until the mid nineteenth century. Traditionally, Navajo arts had strict gender divisions: women wove cloth, and men worked metal.

Sand painting, a traditional Navajo art, is the exclusive province of men. Sand paintings are made to the accompaniment of chants by shaman-singers in the course of healing and blessing ceremonies, and they have great sacred significance. The Night Chant, sung toward the end of the ceremony, signals the restoration of inner harmony and balance:

> In beauty (happily) I walk.
> With beauty before me I walk.
> With beauty behind me I walk.
> With beauty below me I walk.
> With beauty all around me I walk.
> It is finished (again) in beauty.
> It is finished in beauty.

Navajo sand paintings depict mythic heroes and events; and as ritual art, they follow prescribed rules and patterns that ensure their power. To make them, the singer dribbles pulverized colored stones, pollen, flowers, and other natural colors over a hide or sand ground. The rituals are intended to cure by restoring harmony to the world. The paintings are not meant to be seen by the public and certainly not to be displayed in museums. They are meant to be destroyed by nightfall of the day on which they are made.

In 1919, a respected shaman-singer named Hosteen Klah (1867–1937) began to incorporate sand-painting images into weaving, breaking with the traditional prohibitions. Many Navajos took offense at Klah both for recording the sacred images and for doing so in what was traditionally a woman's art form. Klah had learned to weave from his mother and sister. The Navajo traditionally recognize at least three genders; Hosteen Klah was a *nadle*, or Navajo third-gender. Hence, he could learn both female and male arts; that is, he was trained both to weave and to heal. Hosteen Klah was not breaking artistic barriers in a conventional sense, but rather exemplifying the complexities of the traditional Navajo gender system. Klah's work was ultimately accepted because of his great skill and prestige.

The **WHIRLING LOG CEREMONY** sand painting, woven into tapestry (**FIG. 27-23**), depicts part of the Navajo creation myth. The Holy People create the earth's surface and divide it into four parts. They create humans, and bring forth corn, beans, squash, and tobacco—the four sacred plants. A male–female pair

In many cultures, the distinction between "fine art" and "craft" does not exist. The traditional Western academic hierarchy of materials—in which marble, bronze, oil, and fresco are valued more than ceramic, glass, and watercolor—and the equally artificial hierarchy of subjects—in which history painting, including religious history, stands supreme—are irrelevant to non-Western art, and to much art produced in the West before the modern era.

The indigenous peoples of the Americas did not produce objects as works of art to be displayed in museums. In their eyes all pieces were utilitarian objects, adorned in ways necessary for their intended purposes. A work was valued for its effectiveness and for the role it played in society. Some, like a Sioux baby carrier (see FIG. 27-13), enrich mundane life with their aesthetic qualities. Others, such as Pomo baskets (see "Basketry," page 848), commemorate important events. The function of an Inca tunic may have been to identify or confer status on its owner or user through its material value or symbolic associations. And as with art in all cultures, many pieces had great spiritual or magical power. Such works of art cannot be fully comprehended or appreciated when they are seen only on pedestals or encased in glass boxes in museums or galleries. They must be imagined, or better yet seen, as acting in their societies. How powerfully might our minds and emotions be engaged if we saw Kwakwaka'wakw masks (see FIG. 27-20) functioning in religious drama, changing not only the outward appearance, but also the very essence of the individual.

At the beginning of the twentieth century, European and American artists broke away from the academic bias that extolled the Classical heritage of Greece and Rome. They found new inspiration in the art—or craft, if you will—of many different non-European cultures. Artists explored a new freedom to use absolutely any material or technique that effectively challenged outmoded assumptions and opened the way for a free and unfettered delight in, and an interest in understanding, Native American art as well as the art of other non-Western cultures. The more recent twentieth- and twenty-first-century conception of art as a multimedia adventure has helped validate works of art once seen only in ethnographic collections. Today, objects once called "primitive" are recognized as great works of art and acknowledged to be an essential dimension of a twenty-first-century worldview. The line between "art" and "craft" seems more artificial and less relevant than ever before.

---

of humans and one of the sacred plants stand in each of the four quarters, defined by the central cross. The four Holy People (the elongated figures) surround the image, and the guardian figure of Rainbow Maiden frames the scene on three sides. Like all Navajo artists, Hosteen Klah hoped that the excellence of the work would make it pleasing to the spirits. Recently, shaman-singers have made permanent sand paintings on boards for sale, but they usually introduce slight errors in them to render the paintings ceremonially harmless.

A NEW BEGINNING

While Native American art has long been displayed in anthropology and natural history museums, today the art of indigenous peoples is finally achieving full recognition by the art establishment (see "Craft or Art?" above). The Institute of American Indian Arts (IAIA), founded in 1962 in Santa Fe and attended by Native American students from all over North America, supports Native American aspirations in the arts today just as Dorothy Dunn's Studio School did in the 1930s. Staffed by Native American artists, the school encourages the incorporation of indigenous ideals in the arts without creating an official "style." As alumni achieved distinction and the IAIA museum in Santa Fe established a reputation for excellence, the institute has led Native American art into the mainstream of contemporary art (see Chapter 33).

To cite just one example, contemporary Native American artist Jaune Quick-to-See Smith (b. 1940) borrowed a well-known image by Leonardo da Vinci for **THE RED MEAN** (FIG. 27-24). She describes the work as a self-portrait, and indeed the center of the work has a bumper sticker that reads "Made in the U.S.A." above an identification number. The central figure quotes Leonardo's *Vitruvian Man* (see "The Vitruvian Man," page 639), but the message here is autobiographical. Leonardo inscribed the human form within perfect geometric shapes to emphasize the perfection

27-23 • Hosteen Klah WHIRLING LOG CEREMONY
Sand painting; tapestry by Mrs. Sam Manuelito. Navajo, c. 1925. Wool, 5′5″ × 5′10″ (1.69 × 1.82 m). Heard Museum, Phoenix, Arizona.

27-24 • Jaune Quick-to-See Smith **THE RED MEAN: SELF-PORTRAIT**

1992. Acrylic, newspaper collage, and mixed media on canvas, 90″ × 60″ (228.6 × 154.4 cm). Smith College Museum of Art, Northampton, Massachusetts. © Jaune Quick-to-See Smith. Part gift from Janet Wright Ketcham, class of 1953, and part purchase from the Janet Wright Ketcham, class of 1953, Acquisition Fund. (SC 1993:10a.b.)

of the human body, while Smith put her silhouette inside the red X that signifies nuclear radiation. This image alludes both to the uranium mines found on some Indian reservations and to the fact that many have become temporary repositories for nuclear waste. The image's background is a collage of Native American tribal newspapers. Her self-portrait thus includes her ethnic identity and life on the reservation as well as allusions to the history of Western art.

Other artists, such as Canadian Haida artist Bill Reid (1920–1998), have sought to sustain and revitalize traditional art in their work. Trained as a woodcarver, painter, and jeweler, Reid revived the art of carving totem poles and dugout canoes in the Haida homeland of Haida Gwaii—"Islands of the People"—known on maps today as the Queen Charlotte Islands. Late in life he began to create large-scale sculptures in bronze. With their black patina, these works recall traditional Haida carvings in shiny black argillite.

Reid's imposing **THE SPIRIT OF HAIDA GWAII** now stands outside the Canadian Embassy in Washington, DC (**FIG. 27-25**). This sculpture, which Reid viewed as a metaphor for modern Canada's multicultural society, depicts a boatload of figures from the natural and mythic worlds struggling to paddle forward. The dominant figure is a shaman in a spruce-root basket hat and Chilkat blanket holding a speaker's pole. On the prow, the place reserved for the chief in a war canoe, sits the Bear. He faces backward rather than forward, and is bitten by an Eagle, with formline-patterned wings. The Eagle, in turn, is bitten by the Seawolf. The Eagle and the Seawolf, together with the man behind them, nevertheless continue paddling. At the stern, steering the canoe, is the Raven, the trickster in Haida mythology. The Raven is assisted by Mousewoman, the traditional guide and escort of humans in the spirit realms. According to Reid, the work represents a "mythological and environmental lifeboat," where "the entire family of living things ... whatever their differences, ... are paddling together in one boat, headed in one direction" (Bringhurst, 1991).

THE NATIONAL MUSEUM OF THE AMERICAN INDIAN In September 2004, the National Museum of the American Indian finally opened on the Mall in Washington, DC, directly below Capitol Hill and across from the National Gallery of Art. Inspired by the colors, textures, and forms of the American Southwest, the museum building establishes a new presence for Native Americans on the Mall (**FIG. 27-26**). Symbolizing the

27-25 • Bill Reid THE SPIRIT OF HAIDA GWAII
Haida, 1991. Bronze, approx. 13′ × 20′ (4 × 6 m). Canadian Embassy, Washington, DC.

27-26 • NATIONAL MUSEUM OF THE AMERICAN INDIAN
The Smithsonian Institution, Washington, DC. Opened September, 2004. Architectural design: GBQC in association with Douglas Cardinal (Blackfoot). Architectural consultants: Johnpaul Jones (Cherokee-Choctaw) and Ramona Sakiestewa (Hopi). Landscape consultant: Donna House (Navajo-Oneida), ethno-botanist.

Native relationship to the environment, the museum is surrounded by boulders ("Grandfather Rocks"), water, and plantings that recall the varied landscapes of North America, including wetlands, meadows, forest, and traditional cropland with corn, squash, and tomatoes. The entrance to the museum on the east side faces the morning sun and recalls the orientation of prairie tipis. Inside the building a Sun Marker of stained glass in the south wall throws its dagger of light across the vast atrium as the day progresses. Once again the great spirits of earth and sky take form in a creation of the art of the Americas.

THINK ABOUT IT

27.1 Distinguish characteristic styles and techniques developed by two Native American cultures—one in the north, and one in the south—and discuss their realization in one specific work from each culture.

27.2 Explain how symbols and themes are used in FIGURE 27-6 to articulate the Aztec worldview.

27.3 Choose a work of art in this chapter that is best understood in connection with its use in religious or political ritual. Discuss its meaning in relation to its ceremonial context. How can such works be displayed in museums in such a way that viewers will be able to understand this critical aspect of their meaning?

27.4 Evaluate the ways in which two Native North American works from this chapter exhibit influence from European culture.

CROSSCURRENTS

FIG. 21–6

FIG. 27–24

As is frequently the case in the history of art, artist Jaune Quick-to-See Smith has drawn, in *The Red Mean: Self-Portrait*, on a famous work of art from the past—in this case Leonardo da Vinci's *Vitruvian Man*. Discuss how grasping the meaning of Smith's work depends on the viewer's understanding of Leonardo's drawing. Does thinking about the comparison change the way you understand the earlier work?

 Study and review on myartslab.com

28-1 • THE BARUNGA STATEMENT

Various artists from Arnhem Land and central Australia. 1988. Ochers on composition board with collage of printed text on paper, 48″ × 47¼″ (122 × 120 cm). Reproduced with permission of the Northern and Central Land Councils.

Art of Pacific Cultures

In 1788, when Captain James Cook arrived in Australia, it was home to at least 300,000 Indigenous Australians, whose ancestors had arrived 50,000 years earlier, and who spoke over 250 languages. For 40,000 years the Indigenous Australians had been creating rock art and were the oldest continuous culture in the world. Nevertheless, Cook claimed Australia for Britain as a *terra nullius*, a land that belonged to no one. Within a few decades, European diseases had killed 50 percent of Indigenous Australians. Colonization and the arrival of missionaries would change their lives forever.

Two hundred years later, Indigenous Australians presented what is now known as **THE BARUNGA STATEMENT** (**FIG. 28–1**) to the then prime minister Bob Hawke. It was inspired by the Yirrkala Bark Petitions, which 25 years earlier had gained national attention when indigenous land rights claims were presented to the government on traditional bark paintings from Arnhem Land in the Northern Territory. The Barunga Statement placed its call for broader Aboriginal rights in text on paper collaged onto composition board decorated with two different styles of indigenous painting: one from Arnhem Land (on the left; see also **FIG. 28–3**) and the other from Australia's Central Desert area (on the right; see also "A Closer Look," page 878). Painted in natural ochers,

the cross hatching (*rarrk*) and zigzag patterns from the north contrast with the more fluid curved lines and dots that fill the central desert painting. In both, the artists used a dazzling array of symbols to retell stories about the adventures of ancestral beings.

In 1992, the Australian High Court rejected Cook's *terra nullius* argument and granted land rights to Indigenous Australians. When no treaty between the national government and Indigenous Australians followed, Galarrwuy Yunupingu, an indigenous leader, asked for the Barunga Statement back so that he could bury it. Today, however, it still hangs in Parliament and the struggle for full rights for Indigenous Australians continues.

Throughout the Pacific, contact with the West has had a significant impact on indigenous cultures, though to different degrees. In New Zealand, for example, the Treaty of Waitangi (1840) recognized Maori ownership of land and gave Maori the rights of British subjects, establishing early on a different political dynamic. Nonetheless, although numerous issues remain there, as well as in other parts of the region, Pacific islanders continue to use the arts to express and preserve their own rich and distinctive cultural identities.

LEARN ABOUT IT

28.1 Recognize how the availability of raw materials affects artistic choices and styles throughout the Pacific.

28.2 Examine the role the human body plays as a subject and medium in Pacific art.

28.3 Investigate ways that ancestor rituals influence the art in different Pacific cultures.

28.4 Assess the impact of Western contact on art in the Pacific.

(((•─[Listen to the chapter audio on myartslab.com

THE PEOPLING OF THE PACIFIC

On a map with the Pacific Ocean as its center, only the peripheries of the great landmasses of Asia and the Americas appear. Nearly one-third of the earth's surface is taken up by this vast watery expanse. Europeans arriving in Oceania in the late eighteenth and early nineteenth centuries noted four distinct but connected cultural-geographic areas: Australia, Melanesia, Micronesia, and Polynesia (**MAP 28–1**). Australia includes the continent, as well as the island of Tasmania to the southeast. Melanesia ("black islands," a reference to the dark skin color of its inhabitants) includes New Guinea and the string of islands that extends eastward from it as far as Fiji and New Caledonia. Micronesia ("small islands"), to the north of Melanesia, is a region of small islands and coral atolls. Polynesia ("many islands") is scattered over a huge, triangular region defined by New Zealand in the south, Rapa Nui (Easter Island) in the east, and the Hawaiian islands to the north. The last region on earth to be inhabited by humans, Polynesia covers some 7.7 million square miles, of which fewer than 130,000 square miles are dry land—and most of that is New Zealand. With the exception of temperate New Zealand, with its marked seasons and snowcapped mountains, Oceania is in the tropics, that is, between the tropic of Cancer in the north and the tropic of Capricorn to the south.

Australia, Tasmania, and New Guinea formed a single continent during the last Ice Age, which began some 2.5 million years ago. About 50,000 years ago, when the sea level was about 330 feet lower than it is today, people moved to this continent from Southeast Asia, making at least part of the journey over open water. Around 27,000 years ago, humans were settled on the large islands north and east of New Guinea as far south as San Cristobal, but they ventured no farther for another 25,000 years. By about 4000 BCE—possibly as early as 7000 BCE—the people of Melanesia were raising pigs and cultivating taro, a plant with edible rootstocks. As the glaciers melted, the sea level rose, flooding low-lying coastal land. By around 4000 BCE a 70-mile-wide waterway, now called the Torres Strait, separated New Guinea from Australia, whose indigenous people continued their hunting and gathering way of life into the twentieth century.

The settling of the rest of the islands of Melanesia and the westernmost islands of Polynesia—Samoa and Tonga—coincided with the spread of the Lapita culture, named for a site in New Caledonia. The Lapita people were Austronesian speakers who probably migrated from Taiwan to Melanesia about 6,000 years ago. They spread throughout the islands of Melanesia, beginning around 1500 BCE. They were farmers and fisherfolk who cultivated taro and yams, and brought with them dogs, pigs, and chickens, animals that these colonizers needed for food. They also carried with them the distinctive ceramics whose remnants today enable us to trace the extent of their travels. Lapita potters produced dishes, platters, bowls, and jars. Sometimes they covered their wares with a red slip, and they often decorated them with bands of incised and stamped patterns—dots, lines, and hatching—that may also have been used on bark cloth and in tattoos. Most of the decoration was geometric, but some was figurative. The human face that appears in the example in **FIGURE 28–2** is among the earliest representations of a human being, one of the most important subjects in Oceanic art. The Lapita people were skilled shipbuilders and navigators and engaged in inter-island trade. Over time the Lapita culture lost its widespread cohesion and evolved into various local forms. Its end is generally dated to the early centuries of the Common Era.

Polynesian culture emerged in the eastern Lapita region on the islands forming Tonga and Samoa. Just prior to the beginning of the first millennium CE, daring Polynesian seafarers, probably in double-hulled sailing canoes, began settling the scattered islands of Far Oceania and eastern Micronesia. Voyaging over open water, sometimes for thousands of miles, they reached Hawaii and Rapa Nui after about 500 CE and settled New Zealand around 800/900–1200 CE.

While this history of migrations across Melanesia to Polynesia and Micronesia allowed for cross-cultural borrowings, there are distinctions between these areas and within the regions as well. The islands that make up Micronesia, Melanesia, and Polynesia include both low-lying coral atolls and the tall tops of volcanic mountains that rise from the ocean floor. Raw materials available to residents of these islands vary greatly, and islander art and architecture utilize these materials in different ways. The soil of volcanic islands can be very rich, supporting densely populated settlements with a local diversity of plants and animals. On the other hand, the poorer soil of coral atolls cannot support large populations. In a like manner, whereas volcanic islands provide good stone for tools and building (as at Nan Madol, see FIG. 28–10), coral is sharp but not particularly

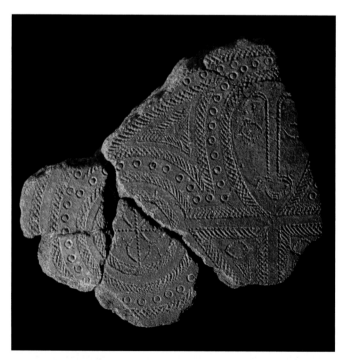

28–2 • FRAGMENTS OF A LARGE LAPITA JAR
From Venumbo Reef, Santa Cruz Island, Solomon Islands. c. 1200–1100 BCE. Clay, height of human face motif approx. 1½″ (4 cm).

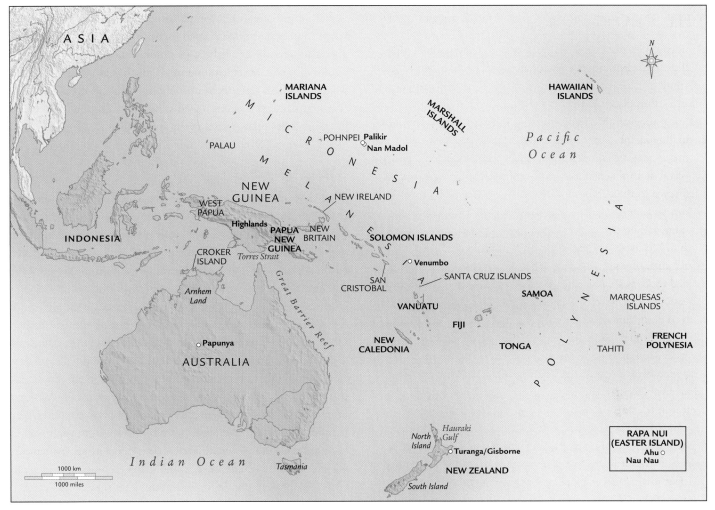

MAP 28-1 • PACIFIC CULTURAL-GEOGRAPHIC REGIONS

The Pacific cultures are spread over four vast areas: Australia, Melanesia, Micronesia, and Polynesia.

hard, and the strongest tools on a coral atoll are often those made from giant clam shells. Generally, the diversity of both plants and animals decreases from west to east among the Pacific islands.

The arts of this vast and diverse region display an enormous variety that is closely linked to each community's ritual and religious life. In this context, the visual arts were often just one strand in a rich weave that also included music, dance, and oral literature.

AUSTRALIA

Until European settlers disrupted their way of life, the hunter-gatherers of Australia were closely attuned to the environments in which they lived. Their only modification of the landscape was regular controlled burning of the underbrush, which encouraged new plant life and attracted animals. Their intimate knowledge of plants, animals, and water sources enabled them to survive and thrive in a wide range of challenging environments.

Indigenous Australian life is intimately connected with the concept of the Dreamtime, or the Dreaming. Not to be confused

with our notions of sleep and dreams, the Dreaming refers to the period before humans existed. (The term, a translation from Arrente, one of the more than 250 languages spoken in Australia when Europeans arrived, was first used in the late nineteenth century in an attempt to understand the indigenous worldview.) According to this complex belief system, the world began as a flat, featureless place. Ancestral Spirit Beings emerged from the earth or arrived from the sea, taking many different forms. The Spirit Beings had numerous adventures, and in crossing the continent, they created all of its physical features: mountains, sand hills, creeks, and water holes. They also brought about the existence of animals, plants, and humans and created the ceremonies and sacred objects needed to ensure that they themselves were remembered, a system sometimes referred to as Aboriginal Laws. The Spirit Beings eventually returned to the earth or became literally one of its features. Thus, they are identified with specific places, which are honored as sacred sites. Indigenous Australians who practice this traditional religion believe that they are descended from the Spirit Beings and associate themselves with particular places related to the ancestors' stories and transformations.

Knowledge of the Dreaming stories, and of the objects related to them, is sacred and secret. Multiple levels of meaning are learned over a lifetime and restricted to those properly trained and initiated to know each level. As a result, an outsider's understanding of the stories and related art (objects and motifs) is strictly limited to what is allowed to be public. Some stories are shared by many tribes across great distances, while others are specific to one area. Men and women have their own stories, women's often associated with food and food gathering.

Since the Dreaming has never ceased, the power of the ancestral Spirit Beings still exists. Indigenous Australians have developed a rich artistic life to relive the stories of the ancestors and transmit knowledge about them to subsequent generations. Ceremonial art forms include paintings on rock and bark, sand drawings, and ground sculptures. Sacred objects, songs, and dances are used to renew the supernatural powers of the ancestors in ceremonial meetings, called corroborees. In **FIGURE 28-3**, Western Arnhem Land artist Jimmy Midjaw Midjaw depicts such a meeting held by a group of Mimi, spirits who live in the narrow spaces between rocks by day and come out at night. Specific to this area, they taught humans how to hunt and cook animals, as well as to dance, sing, and play instruments in ceremonies. Tall, thin, humanlike figures, often in motion, they were painted in ancient rock shelters, and since at least the late nineteenth century, on eucalyptus bark.

Bark paintings are found throughout northern Australia, where numerous regional styles exist. In Western Arnhem Land, the background is usually a monochromatic red ocher wash, with figures in white, black, and red pigments. In the 1950s and 1960s, Midjaw Midjaw was part of a prolific group of artists on Minjilang (Croker Island) that became well known through the anthropologists and collectors working in the area.

MELANESIA

Since they usually rely at least partially on agriculture for survival, the inhabitants of Melanesia live in permanent settlements, many of which feature spaces set aside for ritual use. Social position and status are not inherited or determined by birth, but are achieved by the accumulation of wealth (often in the form of pigs), by the demonstration of leadership, and, often, by participation in men's societies. Much ceremony is related to rituals associated with these societies, including initiation into different levels or grades. Other important rituals facilitate relationships with the deceased and with supernatural forces. Melanesian art is often bold and dazzling. Masking and body decoration, often as part of ceremonial performances, are important, though often ephemeral. Men are prominent in the sculptural and masking traditions; women play significant roles as audience and are also known for their skill in making bark cloth, woven baskets, pottery, and other aesthetically pleasing objects.

28-3 • Jimmy Midjaw Midjaw **THREE DANCERS AND TWO MUSICIANS: CORROBOREE OF MIMI, SPIRITS OF THE ROCKS**
Minjilang (Croker Island), West Arnhem Land, Australia. Mid 20th century. Natural pigments on eucalyptus bark, 23″ × 35″ (59 × 89 cm). Musée du Quai Branly, Paris, France. (MNAO 64.9.103)

NEW GUINEA

New Guinea, the largest island in the Pacific (and, at 1,500 miles long and 1,000 miles wide, the second-largest island in the world), is today divided between two countries. Its eastern half is part of the modern nation of Papua New Guinea; the western half is West Papua, a province of present-day Indonesia. Located near the equator and with mountains that rise to 16,000 feet, the island affords its inhabitants a variety of environments, from coastal mangrove marshes to grasslands, from dense rainforests to swampy river valleys. The population is equally diverse, with coastal fishermen, riverine hunters, slash-and-burn agriculturalists, and more stable farmers in the highlands. Between New Guinea itself and the smaller neighboring islands, more than 700 languages have been identified.

THE *KORAMBO* OR CEREMONIAL HOUSE OF THE ABELAM OF PAPUA NEW GUINEA The Abelam, who live in the foothills of the mountains on the north side of the Sepik River in Papua New Guinea, raise pigs and cultivate yams, taro, bananas, and sago palms. In traditional Abelam society, people live in extended families or clans in hamlets. Wealth among the Abelam is measured in pigs, but men gain status from participation in a yam cult that has a central place in Abelam society. The yams that are the focus of this cult—some of which reach an extraordinary 12 feet in length—are associated with clan ancestors and the potency of their growers. Village leaders renew their relationship with the forces of nature as represented by yams during the Long Yam Festival, which is held at harvest time and involves processions, masked figures, singing, and the ritual exchange of the finest yams.

An Abelam hamlet includes sleeping houses, cooking houses, storehouses for yams, a central space for rituals, and a ceremonial or spirit house, the **korambo** (*haus tambaran* in Pidgin). In this ceremonial structure reserved for the men of the village, the objects associated with the yam cult and with clan identity are kept hidden from women and uninitiated boys. Men of the clan gather in the *korambo* to organize rituals, especially initiation rites, and to conduct community business. The prestige of a hamlet is linked to the quality of its *korambo* and the size of its yams. Constructed on a frame of poles and rafters and roofed with split cane and thatch, *korambo* are built with a triangular floor plan, the side walls meeting at the back of the building. The elaborately decorated façade consists of three parts, beginning at the bottom: a woven mat, a painted and carved wooden lintel, and painted sago bark panels (**FIG. 28-4**). In this example, built about 1961, red, white, and black faces of spirits (*nggwal*) appear on the façade's bark panels, and the figure at the top is said to represent a female flying witch. This last figure is associated with the feminine power of the house itself. The projecting pole at the top of the *korambo* is the only male element of the architecture, and is said to be the penis of the house. The small door at the lower right is a female element, a womb; entering and exiting the house is the symbolic equivalent to death and rebirth. The Abelam believe the paint itself has magical qualities. Regular, ritual repainting revitalizes the images and ensures their continued potency.

Every stage in the construction of a *korambo* is accompanied by ceremonies, which are held in the early morning while women and boys are still asleep. The completion of the façade of a house is celebrated with a ceremony called *mindja*, which includes all-night dancing, and which may continue for six months, until the roof is completely thatched. Women participate in these inaugural ceremonies and are allowed to enter the new house, which afterward is ritually cleansed and closed to them.

28-4 • EXTERIOR OF KORAMBO (HAUS TAMBARAN)
Kinbangwa village, Sepik River, Papua New Guinea. Abelam, 20th century.

***BILUM*—CONTEMPORARY NET BAGS OF HIGHLAND NEW GUINEA** Women's arts in Papua New Guinea tend to be less spectacular and more subtle than men's, but nonetheless significant. Both functionally and symbolically, they contribute to a balance between male and female roles in society. **Bilum**, for example, are netted bags made mainly by women throughout the central highlands of New Guinea (**FIG. 28-5**). Looped from a single long thread spun on the thigh, *bilum* are very strong and, as

28-5 • WOMEN WEARING NET BAGS (BILUM)
Wahgi Valley, Western Highlands Province, Papua New Guinea. 1990.

loosely woven work bags, are used to carry items from vegetables to beer. The bones of a deceased man may be stored in a special *bilum* in a village's men's house (which is similar in function to the Abelam *korambo* in FIGURE 28-4), while his widow wears his personal bag as a sign of mourning. Women wear decorative *bilum*, into which marsupial fur is often incorporated, as adornment, exchange them as gifts, and use them to carry babies.

Bilum are rich metaphorical symbols. Among the women of the Wahgi tribe, who live in the Wahgi Valley of the central highlands, seen in FIGURE 28-5, the term *bilum* may be used as a synonym for womb and bride, and they are also associated with ideas of female attractiveness; depending on how they are worn, they can indicate whether a girl is eligible for marriage.

In the past, *bilum* were made from natural fibers, most commonly the inner bark of a ficus plant. Today, while the technique for making them remains unchanged, a wide array of colorful contemporary fibers, including nylon and acrylic yarn, are used, and new designs incorporating complicated patterns and words are constantly appearing. *Bilum* are now made by women throughout Papua New Guinea, not just in the highlands. They are sold commercially in markets and towns, and have become one of the country's national symbols.

SPIRIT POLES OF THE ASMAT OF WEST PAPUA The Asmat, who live along rivers in the coastal swamp forests of the southwest coast, were known in the past as warriors and headhunters. In Asmat culture, trees are identified with human beings, their fruit with human heads. Fruit-eating birds were thus the equivalent of headhunters, and were often represented in war and mortuary arts, along with the praying mantis, whose female bites off the head of the male during mating. In the past, the Asmat believed that death was always caused by an enemy, either by direct killing or through magic, and that it required revenge, usually in the form of taking an enemy's head, to appease the spirit of the person who had died and thus maintain balance between hostile groups.

Believing that the spirit of the dead person remained in the village, the Asmat erected elaborately sculpted memorial poles (FIG. 28-6), known as *bisj* (pronounced bish), which embodied the spirits of the ancestors and paid tribute to them. Placed in front of special houses belonging to the village's men's society, *bisj* poles are generally carved from mangrove trees, although some in a museum in Leiden recently have been identified as wild nutmeg wood. The felling of a tree is a ritual act in which a group of men attack the tree as if it were an enemy. The figures on the poles represent the dead individuals who are to be avenged; small figures represent dead children. The bent pose of the figures associates them with the praying mantis. The large, lacy phalluses emerging from the figures at the top of the poles are carved from the projecting roots of the tree and symbolize male fertility, while the surface decoration suggests body ornamentation. The poles faced the river to ensure that the spirits of the dead would travel to the realm of the ancestors (*safan*), which lay beyond the sea. The *bisj* pole also served symbolically as the dugout canoe that would take the spirit of the deceased down the river to *safan*.

By carving *bisj* poles (usually for several deceased at the same time) and organizing a *bisj* feast, relatives publicly indicated their responsibility to avenge their dead in a headhunting raid. As part of the ceremonies, mock battles were held, the men boasting of their bravery, the women cheering them on. After the ceremonies, the poles were left in the swamp to deteriorate and transfer their supernatural power back to nature. Today, Asmat continue to carve *bisj* poles and use them in funerary ceremonies, although they stopped headhunting in the 1970s. Poles are also made to sell to outsiders.

NEW IRELAND

MALAGAN DISPLAY OF NEW IRELAND New Ireland is one of the large eastern islands of the nation of Papua New Guinea. The northern people on the island still practice a complex set of death and commemorative rites known as *malagan* (pronounced malang-gan), which can take place as much as two years after a person's death. In the past, clan leaders rose to prominence primarily through *malagan* ceremonies that honored their wives' recently deceased family members. The greater the *malagan* ceremony, the greater prominence the clan leader had achieved.

Malagan also include rites to initiate young men and women into adulthood. After several months' training in seclusion in a ritual enclosure, they are presented to the public and given carved and

28-6 • ASMAT ANCESTRAL SPIRIT POLES (BISJ)
Buepis village, Fajit River, West Papua Province, Indonesia. c. 1960. Wood, paint, palm leaves, and fiber, height approx. 18′ (5.48 m).

28-7 • MALAGAN DISPLAY
Medina village, New Ireland, Papua New Guinea. c. 1930. Height 6′10⅝″ (2.1 m), width 11′5¾″ (3.5 m).
Museum für Völkerkunde, Basel, Switzerland.

painted figures. The combined funerary and initiation ceremonies include feasts, masked dances, and the creation of a special house to display elaborately carved and painted sculptures (**FIG. 28-7**) that honor the dead. The display house illustrated, which dates to the early 1930s, is more than 14 feet wide and honors 12 deceased individuals. The carvings are large (the first on the left is nearly 6 feet in height) and take the form of horizontal friezes, standing figures, and poles containing several figures. They are visually complex, with tensions created between solids and voids, and between the two-dimensional painted patterns on three-dimensional sculptural forms. Such displays are kept secret until their unveiling at the climax of festivities. After the ceremonies they are no longer considered ritually "active" and are destroyed or, since the late nineteenth century, sold to outsiders. *Malagan* figures are still being carved in association with continuing ceremonies.

NEW BRITAIN

TUBUAN MASK OF NEW BRITAIN In the Papua New Guinea province of New Britain—including the Duke of York Islands—Tubuan masks represent the Tolai male secret society, which has different levels or grades of increasing knowledge and power, and wields both spiritual and social control, especially during the three months of ceremonies known as the "Time of the Tubuan." Though initiation to the society is the main purpose of the ceremonies, the men of the village, who have achieved power through the accumulation of wealth, and in the past through bravery in war, use this period to call up the spirits represented by the

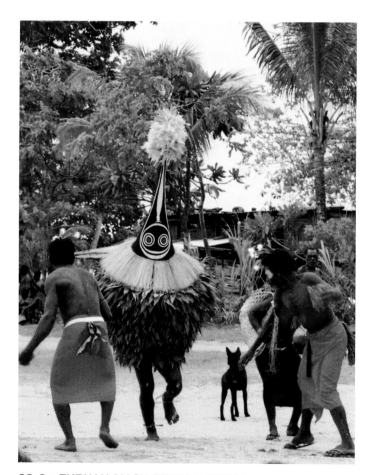

28-8 • TUBUAN MASK BEING DANCED
Tolai people, Duke of York Islands, New Britain, Papua New Guinea.
c. 1990. Cloth, paint, fiber, and feathers.

masks, who have the authority to settle disputes, stop fights, punish lawbreakers, and force the payment of debts. Political power and authority are underscored and enhanced by their appearance. In the past they had the power of life and death.

The masks represent both female and male spirits, though all the masks are danced by men. Local stories say women originally owned the masks and that men stole them. The **TUBUAN MASK** (**FIG. 28-8**) represents the Mother, who gives birth to her children, the Duk Duk masks, representing the new initiates into the society. With the appearance, first of the Mother masks, then of the Duk Duk masks, the initiates return to the village from the bush, where they have undergone intensive preparation to enter the society. The Tubuan mask has a distinctive, tall conical shape and prominent eyes formed by concentric white circles. The green leaf skirt is a very sacred part of the mask, which is itself made from painted bark cloth, various fibers, and feathers. Black feathers on top indicate a more powerful spirit than white feathers.

MICRONESIA

The majority of Micronesia's islands are small, low-lying coral atolls, but in the western region several are volcanic in origin. The eastern islands are more closely related culturally to Polynesia, while those in the west show connections to Melanesia, especially in the men's houses found on Palau and Yap. The atolls—circular coral reefs surrounding lagoons where islands once stood—have a limited range of materials for creating objects of any kind. Micronesians are known especially for their navigational skills and their fine canoes. They also create textiles from banana and coconut fibers, bowls from turtle shells, and abstract human figures from wood, which is scarce. As in other parts of the Pacific, tattooing and performative arts remain central to life.

WAPEPE **NAVIGATION CHART** Sailors from the Marshall Islands relied on celestial navigation—using the sun and moon and stars—as well as a detailed understanding of the ocean currents and trade winds to travel from one island to another. To teach navigation to younger generations, elders traditionally used stick charts (*wapepe* or *mattang*)—maps that showed land, but also the path from one island to the next, the water sailors would cross during their voyage.

In common use until the 1950s, stick charts (**FIG. 28-9**) were schematic diagrams of the prevailing ocean currents and the characteristic wave patterns encountered between islands. Currents are represented by sticks held together by coconut fibers; attached shells mark islands along the route. The arrangement of sticks around a shell indicates a zone of distinctive waves shaped by the effect of an island deflecting the prevailing wind. Such refracted waves enable a navigator to sense the proximity of land without being able to see it, and to discern the least difficult course for making landfall. Although *wapepe* are primarily functional, their combination of clarity, simplicity, and abstraction has an aesthetic impact.

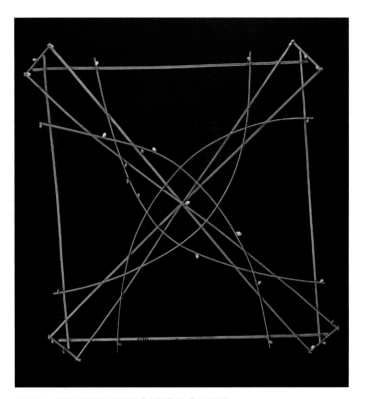

28-9 • WAPEPE NAVIGATION CHART
Marshall Islands. 19th century. Sticks, coconut fiber, and shells, 29½″ × 29½″ (75 × 75 cm). Peabody Essex Museum, Salem.

NAN MADOL The basalt cliffs of the island of Pohnpei provided the building material for one of the largest and most remarkable stone architectural complexes in Oceania. Nan Madol, on its southeast coast, consists of 92 artificial islands set within a network of canals covering about 170 acres (**MAP 28-2**). Seawalls and breakwaters 15 feet high and 35 feet thick protect the area from the ocean. When it was populated, openings in the breakwaters gave canoes access to the ocean and allowed seawater to flow in and out with the tides, flushing clean the canals. While other similar complexes have been identified in Micronesia, Nan Madol is the largest and most impressive, reflecting the importance of the kings who ruled from the site. The artificial islands and the buildings atop them were constructed between the early thirteenth century and the dynasty's political decline in the seventeenth. The site had already been abandoned by the time Europeans discovered it in the nineteenth century.

Nan Madol was an administrative and ceremonial center for powerful kings, who commanded a local labor force to construct this monumental city of as many as 1,000 people. Both the buildings and the underlying islands are built of massive masonry set in alternating layers of log-shaped stones and boulders of prismatic basalt. The largest of the artificial islets is more than 100 yards long, and one basalt cornerstone alone is estimated to weigh about 50 tons. The stone logs were split from the cliffs by alternately heating the stone and dousing it with water. Most of the islands are oriented northeast–southwest, receiving the benefit of the cooling prevailing winds.

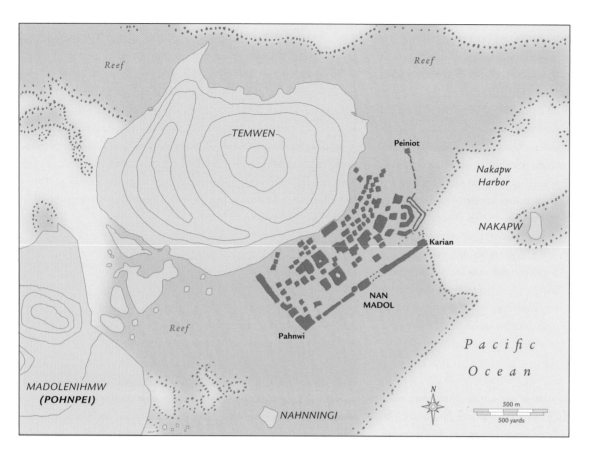

MAP 28-2 • THE COMPLEX OF NAN MADOL

Pohnpei, Federated States of Micronesia. c. 1200/1300– c. 1500/1600.

The walls of the **ROYAL MORTUARY COMPOUND**, which once dominated the northeast side of Nan Madol (**FIG. 28-10**), rise in subtle upward and outward curves to a height of 25 feet. To achieve the sweeping, rising lines, the builders increased the number of stones in the header courses (those with the ends of the stones laid facing out along the wall) relative to the stretcher courses (those with the lengths of the stones laid parallel to the wall) as they came to the corners and entryways. The plan of the structure consists of progressively higher rectangles within rectangles—the outer walls leading by steps up to interior walls that lead up to a central courtyard with a small, cubical tomb.

POLYNESIA

The settlers of the far-flung islands of Polynesia developed distinctive cultural traditions but also retained linguistic and cultural affinities that reflect their common origin. Traditional Polynesian society was generally far more stratified than Melanesian society: A person's genealogy, tracing his or her descent from an ancestral god, determined his or her place in society. First-born children of the hereditary elite were considered the most sacred because they inherited more spiritual power (*mana*) at their birth. *Mana* could

28-10 • ROYAL MORTUARY COMPOUND, NAN MADOL
Pohnpei, Federated States of Micronesia. Basalt blocks, wall height up to 25′ (7.62 m).

be gained through leadership, courage, or skill, but it could be lost because of failure in warfare. It was protected by strict laws of conduct called *tapu*, a word that came into the English language as "taboo."

All of the arts in Polynesia were sacred, and their creation was a sacred act. Master artists were also ritual specialists. Objects were crafted from a variety of materials, some of which, like jadeite in New Zealand, were considered spiritually powerful. Some objects were practical, such as canoes, fishhooks, and weapons; others indicated the status and rank of the society's elite. Objects had their own *mana,* which could increase or decrease depending on how successful they were in performing their functions. Quality and beauty were important. Objects were made to endure, and many were handed down as heirlooms from generation to generation. In addition, the human body itself was the canvas for the art of tattoo (*tatau* in several Polynesian languages).

Polynesian religions included many levels of gods, from creator gods and semidivine hero-gods (such as Maui, who appears in the stories of many of the Polynesian cultures) to natural forces, but the most important were ancestors, who became gods at their death. Since they remained influential in daily life, they had to be honored and placated, and their help was sought for important projects and in times of trouble. Throughout much of Polynesia, figures in human form—often generically called *tiki*—were carved in stone, wood, and in some places, including the Marquesas Islands, human bone. These statues represented the ancestors and were often placed on sacred ritual sites attended by ritual specialists (see FIG. 28–13) or, as in New Zealand, incorporated into meeting houses (see "Te-Hau-ki-Turanga," page 872).

MARQUESAS ISLANDS

TATTOO IN THE MARQUESAS ISLANDS The art of tattoo was widespread and ancient in Oceania. Tattoo chisels made of bone have been found in Lapita sites. They are quite similar to the tools used to decorate Lapita pottery, suggesting some symbolic connection between the marking of both pottery and human skin. The Polynesians, descendants of the Lapita people, brought tattooing with them as they migrated throughout the Pacific, and as they became isolated from each other over time, distinctive styles evolved. Spirals became a hallmark of the Maori facial tattoo (*moko*), and rows of triangles became prominent in Hawaiian designs.

The people of the Marquesas Islands—an archipelago about 900 miles northeast of Tahiti—were the most extensively tattooed of all Polynesians. The process of tattooing involves shedding blood, the most *tapu* (sacred) substance in Polynesia. In the Marquesas, the process for a young man of high social rank began around age 18; by age 30 he would be fully tattooed. Because of the sacredness and prestige of the process, some men continued to be tattooed until their skin was completely covered and the designs disappeared. Marquesan women were also tattooed, usually on the hands, ankles, lips, and behind the ears.

Tattooing was painful and expensive. Though women could be tattooed with little ceremony in their own homes, in the case of both men and women of high rank, special houses were built for the occasion. The master tattooer and his assistants had to be fed and paid, and at the end of the session a special feast was held to display the new tattoos. Each design had a name and a meaning. Tattooing marked passages in people's lives and their social positions; it commemorated special events or accomplishments. Some tattoos denoted particular men's societies or eating groups. Especially for men, tattoos demonstrated courage and were essential to their sexual attractiveness to women.

Tattooing was forbidden in the nineteenth century by French colonial administrators and Catholic missionaries, and it died out in the Marquesas. Beginning in the 1970s, however, there was a resurgence of the art throughout the Pacific, and in 1980 **TEVE TUPUHIA** became the first Marquesan in modern times to be fully tattooed (**FIG. 28–11**). He went to Samoa—the only place in Polynesia where the traditional art form continued—to be tattooed by master Samoan artist Lese I'io. The process took six weeks and cost $35,000. Teve based his tattoo designs on drawings made by George Langsdorff, a German naturalist who visited

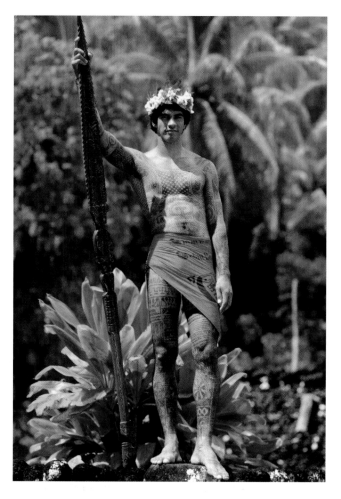

28-11 • TEVE TUPUHIA
Marquesan man tattooed in 1980 by Samoan Lese I'io.

New Zealand was settled sometime after 800 CE by intrepid seafaring Polynesians now known as the Maori. As part of the process of adapting their Polynesian culture to the temperate New Zealand environment, they began to build wooden-frame homes, the largest of which, the chief's house, evolved after Western contact into the meeting house (*whare nui*). The meeting house stands on an open plaza (*marae*), a sacred place where a Maori tribe (*iwi*) or subtribe (*hapu*) still today greets visitors, discusses important issues, and mourns the dead. In it, tribal history and genealogy are recorded and preserved. Created by the master carver Raharuhi Rukupo and his 18 named assistants in the early 1840s, **TE-HAU-KI-TURANGA** is the oldest existing,

fully decorated meeting house in New Zealand (**FIG. 28–12**). Built by Rukupo as a memorial to his elder brother, its name refers to the region of New Zealand where it was made—Turanga, today Gisborne and its region, on the northeast coast of North Island—and has been translated as "The Breezes of Turanga" or "The Spirit of Turanga."

In this area of New Zealand, the meeting house symbolizes the tribe's founding ancestor, for whom it is often named. The ridgepole is the backbone, the rafters are the ribs, and the slanting bargeboards—the boards attached to the projecting end of the gable—are the outstretched enfolding arms. The face appears in the gable mask. Relief figures of ancestors cover the support poles,

wall planks, and the lower ends of the rafters. The ancestors, in effect, support the house. They were thought to take an active interest in community affairs and to participate in the discussions held in the meeting house. Rukupo, an important political and religious leader as well as a master carver, included an unusual naturalistic portrait of himself among them.

Painted curvilinear patterns (**kowhaiwhai**) decorate the rafters in white on a red and black background. The **koru** pattern, a curling stalk with a bulb at the end that resembles the young tree fern, dominates the design system. Lattice panels (**tukutuku**) made by women fill the spaces between the wall planks. Because ritual prohibitions, or taboos, prevented

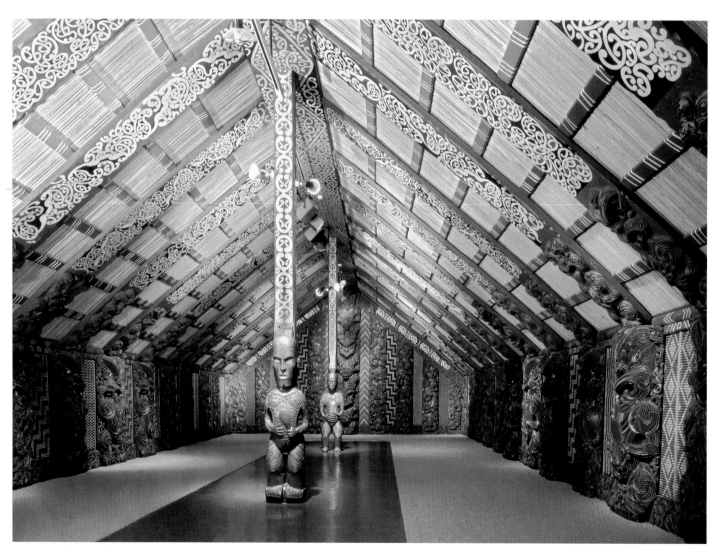

28–12 • Raharuhi Rukupo, master carver TE-HAU-KI-TURANGA (MAORI MEETING HOUSE)
Gisborne/Turanga, New Zealand; built and owned by the Rongowhakaata people of Turanga. 1842–1843, restored in 1935. Wood, shell, grass, flax, and pigments. Museum of New Zealand/Te Papa Tongarewa, Wellington. (Neg. B18358)

women from entering the meeting house, they worked from the outside and wove the panels from the back. They created the black, white, and orange patterns from grass, flax, and flat slats. Each pattern has a symbolic meaning: chevrons representing the teeth of the sea monster Taniwha, steps the stairs of heaven climbed by the hero-god Tawhaki, and diamonds the flounder.

When Captain Cook arrived in New Zealand in the second half of the eighteenth century, each tribe and geographical region had its own style. A storehouse doorway from the Ngäti Päoa tribe (FIG. 28–13), who lived in the Hauraki Gulf area to the west of Turanga, dates to this period of time (or earlier) and shows the soft, shallow surface carving resulting from the use of stone tools. In comparison, a

house panel (**poupou**) from Te-Hau-ki-Turanga (FIG. 28–14), carved with steel tools, shows the deeply cut, very precisely detailed surface carving characteristic of that time.

As is typical throughout Polynesia (see FIG. 28–16), the figures face frontally and have large heads with open eyes. The Hauraki Gulf figure has both hands placed on its stomach and represents a male ancestor, while the Te-Hau-ki-Turanga figure is a female ancestor nursing a child. In both, a small figure, representing their descendants, stands between their legs.

Considered a national treasure by the Maori, this meeting house was restored in 1935 by Maori artists who knew the old, traditional methods; it is now preserved at the Museum of New Zealand/Te Papa Tongarewa in Wellington and considered *taonga* (cultural treasure).

28–13 • CARVED FIGURE FROM STOREHOUSE DOORWAY
Ngäti Päoa, Hauraki Gulf, New Zealand. 1500–1800. Wood, height 33⅞″ (86 cm). Museum of New Zealand/Te Papa Tongarewa, Wellington.

28–14 • POUPOU (PANEL)
From Te-Hau-ki-Turanga. Wood and red pigment, height 4′7″ (140 cm). Museum of New Zealand/Te Papa Tongarewa, Wellington.

front

interior side wall

Parts of the meeting house

interior rear wall

the Marquesas in 1804 as part of a Russian scientific expedition. Today, Marquesan-style tattoo designs are seen throughout French Polynesia.

HAWAII

FEATHER CLOAK FROM HAWAII The Hawaiian islanders had one of the most highly stratified of all Polynesian societies, with valleys and whole islands ruled by high chiefs. Soon after contact with the West, the entire archipelago was unified for the first time under the rule of Kamehameha I (r. 1810–1819), who assumed the title of king in the European manner.

Among the members of the Hawaiian elite, feathered capes and cloaks were emblems of high social status. A full-length cloak made with thousands of red and yellow feathers (**FIG. 28-15**), was reserved for the highest ranks of the elite men and called an *'ahu 'ula* ("red cloak")—the color red is associated with high status and rank throughout Polynesia. Often given as gifts to important visitors to Hawaii, this particular cloak was presented in 1843 to Commodore Lawrence Kearny, commander of the USS *Constellation*, by King Kamehameha III (r. 1825–1854).

Draped over the wearer's shoulders, such a cloak creates a sensuously textured and colored abstract design, which in this example joins to create matching patterns of paired crescents on front and back. The cloak's foundation consisted of coconut fiber netting onto which were tied bundles of feathers—part of an annual tribute paid to the king by his subjects. The red, and especially the yellow feathers, were highly prized and came from several species of birds including the *i'iwi*, *apapane*, *'o'o*, and *mamo* (which is now extinct). In some cases, each bird yielded only seven or eight feathers, making the collecting of feathers very labor-intensive and increasing the value of the cloaks.

Cloaks were so closely associated with the spiritual power (*mana*) of the elite person that they could be made only by specialists trained in both the complicated technique of manufacture and the rituals attending their fabrication. Surrounded by protective objects, they created the cloak while reciting the chief's genealogy to imbue it with the power of his ancestors. As a result, the cloaks were seen as protective of the wearer, while also proclaiming his elite status and political and economic power.

Feathers were used for decorating not just cloaks, but also helmets, capes, blankets, and garlands (*leis*), all of which conferred status and prestige. The annual tribute paid to the king by his subjects included feathers, and tall feather pompons (*kahili*) mounted on long slender sticks were symbols of royalty. Even the effigies of gods that Hawaiian warriors carried into battle were made of light, basketlike structures covered with feathers.

MONUMENTAL MOAI ON RAPA NUI

Rapa Nui (Easter Island) is the most isolated inhabited locale in Oceania, located 2,300 miles west of the coast of South America and 1,200 miles from Pitcairn Island, the nearest Polynesian outpost. Three volcanoes, one at each corner, make up the small triangular island. Originally known to its native inhabitants as Te Pito o te Henúa (Navel of the World) and now known as Rapa Nui, it was named Easter Island by Captain Jacob Roggeveen, the Dutch explorer who first landed there on Easter Sunday in 1722. Rapa Nui became part of Chile in 1888.

MONUMENTAL MOAI Rapa Nui is the site of Polynesia's most impressive stone sculpture. Though many imaginative theories have been posited regarding the origins of its statues—from space aliens to Native Americans—they are most definitely part of an established Polynesian tradition. Sacred religious sites (*marae*) with stone altar platforms (*ahu*) are common throughout Polynesia. On

28-15 • FEATHER CLOAK, KNOWN AS THE KEARNY CLOAK
Hawaii. c. 1843. Red, yellow, and black feathers, olona cordage, and netting, length 55¾″ (143 cm). Bishop Museum, Honolulu.

King Kamehameha III (r. 1825–1854) presented this cloak to Commodore Lawrence Kearny, commander of the frigate USS *Constellation*.

Rapa Nui the Polynesians who arrived at the island in canoes between 800 and 1200 CE built most of the *ahu* near the coast, parallel to the shore, and began to erect stone figures on them, perhaps as memorials to deceased chiefs or ancestors. Nearly 1,000 of these figures, called **moai**, have been found on the island, including some 400 unfinished ones in the quarry at Rano Raraku where they were being carved. The statues themselves are made from yellowish-brown volcanic tuff. On their heads, *pukao* (topknots of hair) were rendered in red scoria, another volcanic stone. When the statues were in place, the insertion of white coral and stone "opened" the eyes. In 1978, several figures on Ahu Nau Nau (**FIG. 28-16**) were restored to their original condition. These are about 36 feet tall, but *moai* range in size from much smaller to a 65-foot statue that is still in the quarry, where the sculptures were produced before being transported up to 11 miles to the sites of the *anu*. A recent theory proposes that the completed *moai* were "walked" from the quarry to the *anu* as handlers rocked them from side to side using attached ropes. The fragmentary remains of statues, which line the road away from the quarry, indicate that not all *moai* completed the journey.

Like other Polynesian statues, the *moai* face frontally. Their large heads have deep-set eyes under a prominent brow ridge; a long, concave, pointed nose; a small mouth with pursed lips; and an angular chin. The extremely elongated earlobes have parallel engraved lines that suggest ear ornaments. The figures have schematically indicated breastbones and pectorals, and small arms with hands pressed close to the sides. Since their bodies emerge from the ground at just below waist level, they have no legs.

The island's indigenous population, which has been estimated at 3,000 people when the Dutch arrived in 1722, was nearly eradicated in 1877 when Peruvian slave traders precipitated an epidemic of smallpox and tuberculosis that left only 110 inhabitants alive. Today, a vibrant population of some 5,000 people is known especially for its energetic and athletic dance performances and thrives primarily on tourism.

SAMOA

***TAPA (SIAPO)* IN SAMOA** As they migrated across the Pacific, Polynesians brought with them the production of bark cloth. Known by various names throughout the Pacific, most commonly

28-16 • MOAI ANCESTOR FIGURES
Ahu Nau Nau, Rapa Nui (Easter Island). c. ?1000–1500 CE, restored 1978. Volcanic stone (tufa), average height approx. 36′ (11 m).

👁—⎾**Watch** a video about Easter Island on myartslab.com

as **tapa**, in Samoa bark cloth is called **siapo**. It is usually made by women, although sometimes men help obtain the bark or decorate the completed cloth. In Samoa, *siapo* is made by stripping the inner bark from branches of the paper mulberry tree (banyan and breadfruit are sometimes used in other archipelagos). The bark is beaten with a wooden mallet, then folded over and beaten again, to various degrees of softness. Larger pieces can be made by building up the cloth in a process of felting or using natural pastes as glue. The heavy wooden mallets used for beating the cloth are often incised with complex patterns, which leave impressions like watermarks in the cloth, viewable when held up to the light.

Plain and decorated *tapa* of various thicknesses and qualities was used throughout Polynesia for clothing, sails, mats, and ceremonial purposes, including wrapping the dead. *Tapa* was also used to cover wooden or wicker frames to make human effigies in the Marquesas and Rapa Nui, serving a purpose we still do not completely understand. In western Polynesia (Samoa and Tonga), very large pieces, 7–10 feet across and hundreds of feet long, were traditionally given in ceremonial exchanges of valuables and as gifts. Along with fine mats, *siapo* is still sometimes given on important ceremonial occasions. And *tapa* was widely used for clothing. Samoan men and women wore large pieces of *siapo* as wraparound skirts (*lavalava*) (see FIG. 28–19). Special chiefs, called talking chiefs, who spoke on behalf of the highest-ranking chief in the village council, wore special *tapa* skirts called *siapo vala* (**FIG. 28–17**).

Distinctive design styles for *tapa* evolved across the Pacific, even when the cloth used was essentially the same from one island to the next. It could be dyed bright yellow with turmeric or brown with dyes made from nuts. It could also be exposed to smoke to turn it black or darker brown. Today, contemporary fabric paint is often used. Decorative designs were made through a variety of means from freehand painting to printing with tiny bamboo stamps, or using stencils, as is done in Fiji. This Samoan *siapo vala* has designs that were produced by first placing the cloth over a wooden design tablet, an **upeti**, and then rubbing pigment over the cloth to pick up the carved pattern. Subsequently, this lighter rubbed pattern was overpainted by hand. The result is a boldly patterned, symmetrical design.

RECENT ART IN OCEANIA

In the late 1960s and early 1970s, a cultural resurgence swept across the Pacific. Growing independence and autonomy throughout the region, the model of civil rights and other movements in the United States, and dramatic increases in tourism, among other factors, brought a new awareness of the importance of indigenous cultures. Many of them had been fundamentally changed, if not nearly destroyed, by colonial rule and missionary efforts to eradicate local customs and beliefs.

FESTIVAL OF PACIFIC ARTS

In the early 1970s, the South Pacific Commission conceived the idea of an arts festival that would promote traditional song and dance. The first Festival of Pacific Arts was held in 1972 in Fiji; subsequent festivals, held every four years, have been hosted by New Zealand, Papua New Guinea, Tahiti, Australia, Cook Islands, Samoa, New Caledonia, Palau, and American Samoa.

Musicians from the highlands of Papua New Guinea (**FIG. 28–18**) were among the more than 2,000 participants from 27 countries at the tenth festival at Pago Pago, American Samoa, in 2008. Carrying traditional drums, they wore elaborate headdresses topped with bird of paradise feathers and neck ornaments made from kina shells, a once valuable medium of exchange in New Guinea.

In the 36 years since their founding, the festivals have had an enormous impact on the arts. Many Pacific cultures now have their own festivals; in the Marquesas Islands one is held every four years. In an age of globalization and the Internet, festivals are one of the main ways in which young people become involved in, and learn about, their culture and heritage. However, the festivals are not without controversy: Some people are critical of an increasing level of professionalism and commercialism.

CENTRAL DESERT PAINTING

In Australia, indigenous artists have adopted canvas and acrylic paint for rendering imagery traditionally associated with more ephemeral media like body and sand drawing. Sand drawing is an ancient ritual art form that involves creating large colored designs on bare earth. Made with red and yellow ochers, seeds, and feathers arranged on the ground in symbolic patterns, they are used to

28-17 • TAPA (SIAPO VALA)
Samoa. 20th century. 58⅝" × 57" (149 × 145 cm). Auckland Museum, New Zealand. (AM 46892)

28-18 • MUSICIANS FROM PAPUA NEW GUINEA AT THE FESTIVAL OF PACIFIC ARTS
Pago Pago, American Samoa, 2008.

convey tribal knowledge to initiates. In 1971, several indigenous Pintubi men who were trained and initiated in sacred knowledge, and were living in government-controlled Papunya Tula in the Central Desert of Australia, were encouraged by non-indigenous art teacher Geoffrey Bardon to transform their ephemeral art into a painted mural on the school wall. The success of the public mural encouraged community elders to allow others to try their hand at painting. In Utopia, a neighboring community, it was the women who began painting in 1988 after success in tie-dyeing with fabrics. Art galleries, originally located in Alice Springs, spread the art form, and "dot paintings" were a worldwide phenomenon by the late 1980s. Paintings also became an economic mainstay for many Aboriginal groups in the central and western Australia desert. Although they are creating work for sale, the artists can paint only stories to which they have rights, and must be careful to depict only what a non-initiated person is allowed to know.

Clifford Possum Tjapaltjarri (c. 1932–2002), a founder of the Papunya Tula Artists Cooperative in 1972, gained an international reputation after a 1988 exhibition of his paintings. He worked with his canvases on the floor, as in traditional sand painting, using ancient patterns and colors, principally red and yellow, as well as touches of blue. The superimposed layers of concentric circles and undulating lines and dots in a painting like *Man's Love Story* (see "A Closer Look," page 878) create an effect of shifting colors and lights that was highly valued in a global art world.

The painting seems entirely abstract, but it actually conveys a narrative involving two mythical ancestors. One of these ancestors—represented by the white U shape on the left, seated in front of a water hole with an ants' nest indicated by concentric circles—came to Papunya in search of honey ants. His digging stick lies to his right, and white sugary leaves lie to his left. The straight white "journey line" represents his trek from the west. The second ancestor—represented by the brown-and-white U-shaped form—came from the east, leaving footprints, and sat down by another water hole nearby. He began to spin a hair string on a spindle (the form leaning toward the upper right of the painting) but was distracted by thoughts of the woman he loved, who belonged to a kinship group into which he could not marry. When she approached, he let his hair string blow away (represented by the brown flecks below him) and lost all his work. Four women (the dotted U shapes) came at night and surrounded the camp to guard the lovers. Rich symbolism also fills other areas of the painting: the white footprints are those of another ancestral figure following a woman, and the wavy line at the top is the path of yet another ancestor. The black, dotted oval area indicates the site where young men were taught this story. The long horizontal bars are mirages, while the wiggly shapes represent caterpillars, a source of food. Possum Tjapaltjarri painted numerous variations of this Dreaming story.

The painting is effectively a map showing the ancestors' journeys. To begin the work Possum Tjapaltjarri first painted the

A CLOSER LOOK | *Man's Love Story*

by Clifford Possum Tjapaltjarri. 1978. Synthetic polymer paint on canvas.
6′11¾″ × 8′4¼″ (2.15 × 2.57 m). Art Gallery of South Australia, Adelaide.
Visual Arts Board of the Australia Council Contemporary Art Purchase Grant, 1980

Designs may have multiple meanings. A circle can represent a water hole or ant hole, as here, but also a hole where the ancestral Spirit Beings exited and entered the earth, a person as viewed from above, or a campfire.

Honey ants are a sweet delicacy. A digging stick is used to open up the nest, exposing the ant colony so that the ants can be removed and eaten.

Hair is spun into string using a spindle that is rotated across the thigh. The string is surprisingly strong and was used for utilitarian and ceremonial purposes, depending on the region.

Synthetic polymer, or acrylic, paint replaces the earth-toned ochers used in the original sand paintings that provide the model for paintings such as this.

Women are important figures in the Dreaming stories and are represented in several places in this painting. Indigenous women artists paint their own stories, too, which usually center on food and food gathering.

The dots are made using a stick with a round, flat end that is dipped into the paint. Several people can work at the same time to fill in dotted areas.

 View the Closer Look for *Man's Love Story* on myartslab.com

landscape features and the impressions left on the earth by the figures—their tracks, direction lines, and the U-shaped marks they left when sitting. Then, working carefully, dot by dot, he captured the vast expanse and shimmering light of the arid landscape. The painting's resemblance to modern Western painting styles such as Abstract Expressionism, gestural painting, pointillism, or color field painting (see Chapter 32) is accidental. Possum Tjapaltjarri's work is rooted in the mythic narratives of the Dreaming. He and other contemporary artists working in both age-old and new media continue to create arts that express the deepest meanings of their culture.

SHIGEYUKI KIHARA

Many contemporary Pacific artists live in urban settings, were trained at colleges and universities, and create artworks in modern media that deal with a range of political issues, including the colonial legacy, discrimination, misappropriation, cultural identity, and land rights. Shigeyuki Kihara is a multimedia and performance artist of Samoan and Japanese descent who lives in New Zealand. In **ULUGALI'I SAMOA: SAMOAN COUPLE** (**FIG. 28-19**), she explores issues of culture, identity, stereotypes, authenticity, representation, and gender roles through a reappropriation of nineteenth- and early twentieth-century colonial photographs. Made in studio settings, colonial photographs were often turned into postcards depicting Pacific island men and women, both alone and in couples, the women as bare-breasted and sexualized "dusky maidens" and the men as emasculated "noble savages." Kihara confronts these stereotyped images of the South Seas in carefully restaged, sepia-toned photographs that, through ironic twists, also directly challenge the viewer's understanding of gender and gender roles.

In this photograph of a male and female couple both figures are clothed as they might have been in the nineteenth century, wearing large pieces of Samoan bark cloth (see FIG. 28–17), and holding traditional Samoan status objects—a plaited fan and a fly-whisk. Kihara herself poses as the native woman, but has also superimposed her own face, with wig and mustache, onto the body of the male figure. *Ulugali'i Samoa: Samoan Couple* is part of a series of photographs called "Fa'a fafine: In a Manner of a Woman." *Fa'a fafine* is the Samoan term for a biological male who lives as a woman, the "third gender" socially accepted historically throughout much of Polynesia (as in the Americas, see FIG. 27–23). Kihara is, herself, *fa'a fafine*, a transgender woman who lives and identifies in that gender role. In this photograph and the others in the series, she blurs stereotyped notions of who or what is male or female, original or copy, reality or perception. This work was part of the exhibition "Shigeyuki Kihara: Living Photographs," the first solo exhibition by a Samoan in the Metropolitan Museum of Art in New York. Her work and that of other urban artists draws on the richness of Pacific cultures while addressing global issues of the twenty-first century.

28-19 • Shigeyuki Kihara ULUGALI'I SAMOA: SAMOAN COUPLE
2004–2005. C-type photograph, edition 5, 31½″ × 23⅗″ (80 × 60 cm). Metropolitan Museum of Art, New York. Gift of Shigeyuki Kihara, 2009

THINK ABOUT IT

28.1 Explain how differences in environment, including available resources, affect the nature of the visual arts in the Pacific. Include architectural forms and body adornment in your answer.

28.2 How is the human body adorned and/or depicted in art across the Pacific? How do these adornments and depictions define or enhance status, authority, and gender roles?

28.3 Assess the importance of ancestors and the different ways in which ancestors are engaged, honored, or invoked through various Pacific art forms. Focus your answer on two works from two different cultural and geographic settings.

28.4 Discuss the impact of contact with Western society on the arts and cultures of the peoples of the Pacific. How are contemporary indigenous artists throughout the Pacific addressing the issues of their own time and place?

CROSSCURRENTS

FIG. 27–9   FIG. 28–17

The production of fabric was an important aspect of the culture of both Peru and Samoa. Although there are compelling similarities in the designs of these two cloths, their style, media, and their context of production are distinct in significant ways. Discuss these differences and how they relate to the cultural values and distinctive environments of the artists who made them and the societies that valued them.

✓—Study and review on myartslab.com

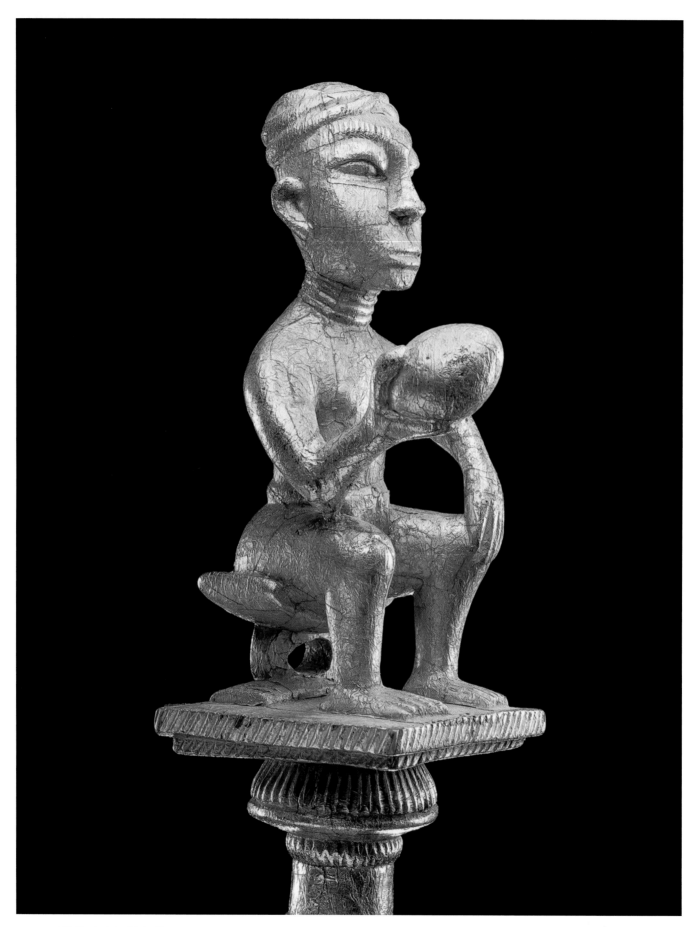

29–1 • Attributed to Kojo Bonsu **FINIAL OF A SPEAKER'S STAFF (OKYEAME POMA)**
Ghana. Ashanti culture, 1960s–1970s. Wood and gold, height 11¼″ (28.57 cm).
Gold of Africa Barbier-Mueller Museum.

Art of Africa in the Modern Era

Political power is like an egg, says an Ashanti proverb. Grasp it too tightly and it will shatter in your hand; hold it too loosely and it will slip from your fingers. Whenever the *okyeame* (spokesman) for one twentieth-century Ashanti ruler was conferring with that ruler or communicating the ruler's words to others, he held a staff with this symbolic caution on the use and abuse of power prominently displayed on the gold-leaf-covered finial (**FIG. 29–1**). Since about 1900 these advisors have carried staffs of office such as the one pictured here. The carved figure at the top illustrates a story that may have multiple meanings when told by a witty owner. This staff was probably carved in the 1960s or 1970s by Kojo Bonsu. The son of Osei Bonsu (1900–1976), a famous carver, Kojo Bonsu lives in the Ashanti city of Kumasi and continues to carve prolifically.

A staff or scepter is a nearly universal symbol of authority and leadership. Today in many colleges and universities a ceremonial mace is still carried by the leader of an academic procession, and it is often placed in front of the speaker's lectern, as a symbol of the speaker's authority. The Ashanti spokesmen who carry their image-topped staffs are part of this widespread tradition.

Since the fifteenth century, when the first Europeans explored Africa, objects such as this staff have been shipped back to Western collections and museums, where they were initially enjoyed as marvelous curiosities, and later catalogued as ethnographic artifacts of "primitive cultures." Toward the end of the nineteenth century, however, changes in Western thinking about African culture gradually led more and more people to appreciate the inherent aesthetic qualities of these unfamiliar objects and at last to embrace them fully as art. In recent years the appreciation of traditional African arts has been further enhanced through the exploration of their meaning from the point of view of the people who made and first experienced them.

If we are to understand African art such as this staff on its own terms, we must envision it out of the glass case of the museum where we usually encounter it, and playing its vital role in a human community. Indeed, this is true of any work of art produced anywhere in the world. When we recognize in an artwork the true expression of values and beliefs, our imaginations can allow us to cross a bridge to understanding.

LEARN ABOUT IT

29.1 Explore the variety of styles, media, and techniques used by artists across Africa during the nineteenth and twentieth centuries.

29.2 Understand the themes and symbols used in African societal rituals of leadership, initiation, divination, and death.

29.3 Evaluate the role of masquerade in African rites of passage such as initiation and funeral rituals.

29.4 Examine the relationship of African arts to the colonial experience.

((•—[**Listen** to the chapter audio on myartslab.com

TRADITIONAL AND CONTEMPORARY AFRICA

The second-largest continent in the world, Africa is a land of enormous diversity (**MAP 29-1**). Geographically, it ranges from vast deserts to tropical rainforest, from flat grasslands to spectacular mountains and dramatic rift valleys. Cultural diversity in Africa is equally impressive. More than 1,000 African languages have been identified and grouped into five major linguistic families. Various languages represent unique cultures, with their own history, customs, and art forms.

Before the nineteenth century, the most important outside influence to pervade Africa had been the religious culture of Islam, which spread gradually and largely peacefully through much of west Africa and along the east African coast (see "Foundations of African Cultures," page 885). The modern era, in contrast, begins with the European exploration during the nineteenth century and subsequent colonization of the African continent, developments that brought traditional African societies into sudden and traumatic contact with the "modern" world that Europe had largely created.

European ships first visited sub-Saharan Africa in the fifteenth century. For the next several hundred years, however, European contact with Africa was almost entirely limited to coastal areas, where trade, including the tragic slave trade, was carried out. Between the sixteenth and nineteenth centuries, over 10 million slaves were taken from Africa to colonies in North and South America and the Caribbean islands. Countries that participated in the Atlantic slave trade included Great Britain, Portugal, France, Spain, Denmark, Holland, and the United States.

During the nineteenth century, as the slave trade was gradually eliminated, European explorers began to investigate the unmapped African interior in earnest. They were soon followed by Christian missionaries, whose reports excited popular interest in the continent. Drawn by the potential wealth of Africa's natural resources, European governments began to seek territorial concessions from African rulers. Diplomacy soon gave way to force, and toward the end of the century competition among rival European powers fueled the so-called Scramble for Africa, during which England, France, Germany, Belgium, Italy, Spain, and Portugal raced to lay claim to whatever part of the continent they could. By 1914 virtually all of Africa had fallen under colonial rule.

Public and private collections of African art grew rapidly in size during this period. This was due not only to geographic exploration and colonial expansion, but also to the development of anthropology as a field of study. Artifacts from various African cultures became instruments through which university professors and museum curators could explain human development in purely evolutionary terms. Museums and collectors competed with one another to collect everywhere and as quickly as possible, believing that "traditional" African cultures were being rapidly altered by the colonial experience. As territory was subsumed under European control, vast quantities of art objects flowed into European city, state, and national collections.

Objects also entered Western collections through conflict. For example, when a British expedition headed by the newly appointed Acting Council-General, James Phillips, embarked on a mission to discuss the trade agreement with the *oba* of Benin City, he was told he could not meet with the king because he was engaged in an important annual ceremony honoring his ancestors. Phillips refused to postpone his visit and the expedition was attacked, without the king's knowledge, by a group headed by two chiefs; all but two expedition members were killed. A punitive expedition was launched in

29-2 • MEMBERS OF THE BRITISH PUNITIVE EXPEDITION IN THE BENIN PALACE IN 1897 WITH OBJECTS FROM THE ROYAL TREASURY

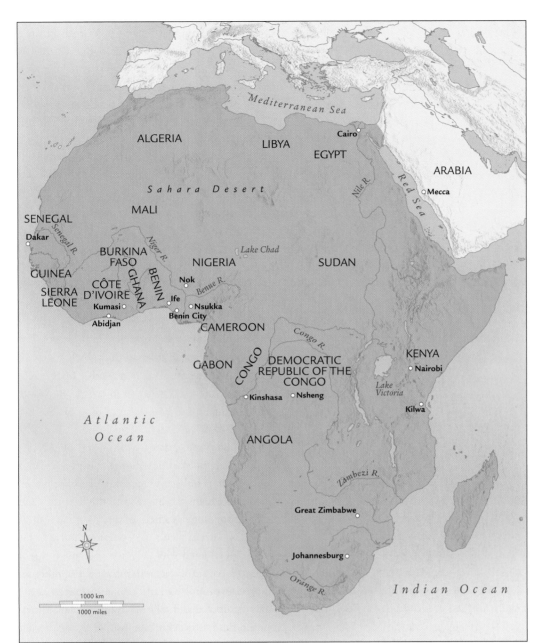

MAP 29-1 • PRESENT-DAY AFRICA

The vast continent of Africa is home to over 50 countries and innumerable cultures.

1897 by the British (**FIG. 29-2**) which resulted the destruction of much of the town, including the palace, and the seizing of over 2,000 antiquities—nearly the entire store of artifacts from the royal palace. The king was deposed and sent into exile, and his successor only assumed the throne in 1914. The antiquities were taken to Europe and auctioned to defray the costs of the expedition and provide pensions for those who had been ambushed or their survivors. These objects are now dispersed in museums and private collections throughout the world.

Changes in Western thinking about art gradually led people to appreciate the aesthetic qualities of African "artifacts" and finally to embrace them fully as art. The earliest collections of African art were, for the most part, acquired by museums of natural history or ethnography, which exhibited the works as curious artifacts of "primitive" cultures. By the latter half of the twentieth century, art museums, both in Africa and in the West, began to collect African art seriously and methodically. Today, these collections afford us a rich sampling of African art created for the most part in the nineteenth and twentieth centuries.

In the years following World War I, nationalistic movements resisting European incursion arose across Africa. Their leaders generally did not advocate a return to earlier forms of political organization but rather demanded the transformation of colonial divisions into modern nation-states governed by Africans. From the 1950s through the mid 1970s, one colony after another gained its independence, and the present-day map of Africa took shape. Today, the continent is composed of over 50 independent countries.

While African societies were profoundly disrupted during the colonial period, numerous tribal or ethnic-based societies persist, both within and across contemporary political borders, and art continues to play a vital role in the spiritual and social life of the community. This chapter explores African art in light of how

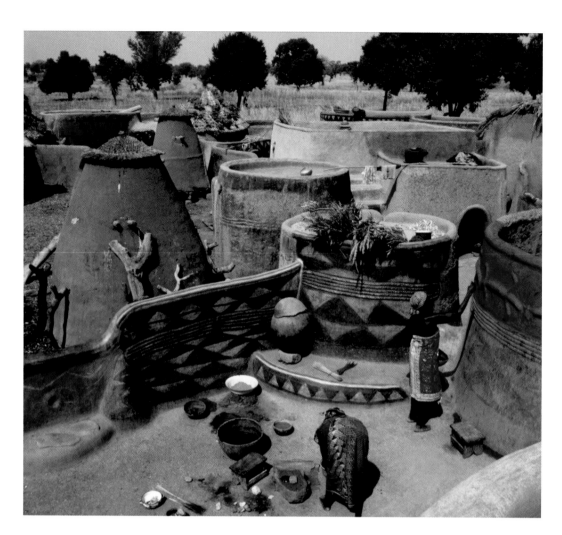

Among the Nankani people, creating living areas is a cooperative but gender-specific project. Men build the structures, women decorate the surfaces. The structures are also gendered. The round dwellings shown here are women's houses located in an interior courtyard; men occupy rectangular flat-roofed houses. The bisected lozenge design on the dwelling to the left is called *zalanga*, the name for the braided sling that holds a woman's gourds and most treasured possessions.

it addresses some of the fundamental concerns of human existence. Works of art are often directly related to the commemoration of significant rites of passage such as procreation and birth, initiation to adulthood, socialization in adult life, and death. While political leaders throughout the world use art to express their authority and status, in Africa community leaders are thought to connect the living community with the spirit world. In this regard, African art often especially idealizes the spirits of community leaders and deceased persons, who are expected to mediate between the temporal and supernatural worlds to help achieve well-being both for themselves and for the entire community. In these contexts, art is often intended to help mediate aid and support from a supernatural world of ancestors and other spirit forces. These concerns—rather than geographical region or time frame—form the backdrop against which we look at artworks in this chapter, as African art can be more fully understood within contexts of production and use.

Generally, the full meaning of traditional works of art can only be realized in the context of their use. For instance, when masked dancers perform within a specific ceremonial event, the mask itself—which we generally see isolated as an artwork in a museum—is only one part of a temporal process that most fully reveals its meaning in performance.

DOMESTIC ARCHITECTURE

Shelter is a basic human concern, yet, as we have seen, different cultures approach its design and construction in different ways, ways that often help us understand cultural values and priorities. The farming communities of the Nankani people in the border area between Burkina Faso and Ghana, in west Africa, have developed a distinctive painted architecture. The earthen buildings of their walled compounds are low and single-storied, with either conical roofs or flat roofs that form terraces. Each compound is surrounded by a defensive wall with a single entrance on the west side. Each building inside the enclosure is arranged so that it has a direct view of the entrance. Some buildings are used only by men, others only by women. For example, Nankani men are in charge of the ancestral shrine near the entrance of the compound, the corral for cattle, and the granary; they have rectangular houses. The inner courtyards, outdoor kitchen, and round houses are women's areas (**FIG. 29-3**). Men build the compound; women paint the buildings inside and out.

The women decorate the walls with horizontal molded ridges called *yidoor* ("rows in a cultivated field") and long eye ("long life"), to express good wishes for the family. They paint the walls with rectangles and squares divided diagonally to create triangular patterns that contrast with the curvature of the walls. The painted

Africa was the site of one of the great civilizations of the ancient world: Egypt developed along the fertile banks of the Nile River during the fourth millennium BCE and endured for 3,000 years. Egypt's rise coincided with the emergence of the Sahara—now the largest desert in the world—from the formerly lush grasslands of northern Africa. Some of the oldest-known African art, images inscribed and painted in the mountains of the central Sahara beginning around 8000 BCE, bear witness to this gradual transformation and how it affected the lives of the pastoral peoples who once lived in the region.

As the grassland dried up, its populations migrated in search of pasture and arable land. Many probably made their way to the Sudan, the broad band of savanna south of the Sahara. During the sixth century BCE, knowledge of iron smelting spread across the Sudan, enabling larger and more complex societies to emerge, including the ironworking Nok culture, which arose in present-day Nigeria around 500 BCE and lasted until about 200 CE. Terra-cotta figures created by Nok artists are the earliest-known sculpture from sub-Saharan Africa.

Farther south, in present-day Nigeria, a remarkable culture developed in the city of Ife, which rose to prominence around 800 CE. There, from roughly 1000 to 1400, a tradition of naturalistic sculpture in bronze and terra cotta flourished. Ife was, and remains, the sacred city of the Yoruba people. According to legend, Ife artists brought the techniques of bronze casting to the kingdom of Benin, and from 1170 to the present century, Benin artists in the service of the court created numerous works in bronze, at first in the naturalistic style of Ife, then in an increasingly stylized and elaborate manner.

With the Arab conquest of North Africa during the seventh and eighth centuries, Islamic travelers and merchants became regular visitors to the Sudan. Largely through their writings, we know of the powerful west African empires of Ghana and Mali, which flourished successively from the fourth through the sixteenth centuries along the great bend in the Niger River. Both grew wealthy by controlling the flow of African gold and forest products into the lucrative trans-Sahara trade. The city of Jenné, in Mali, served not only as a commercial hub but also as a prominent center of Islam.

Meanwhile, since before the Common Era, peoples along the coast of east Africa had participated in a maritime trade network that ringed the Indian Ocean and extended east to the islands of Indonesia. Over time, trading centers arose along the coastline, settled by Arab, Persian, and Indian merchants as well as Africans. By the thirteenth century these settlements were important port cities, and a new language, Swahili, had developed from the longtime mingling of Arabic with local African languages. Peoples of the interior organized extensive trade networks to funnel goods to these ports. From 1000 to 1500 many of these interior routes were controlled by the Shona people from Great Zimbabwe. The extensive stone palace compound there stood in the center of a city of 10,000 people at its height. Numerous cities and kingdoms, often of great wealth and opulence, greeted the astonished eyes of the first European visitors to Africa at the end of the fifteenth century.

---

patterns are called braided sling, broken pottery, broken gourd, and sometimes, since the triangular motifs can be seen as pointing up or down, they are called filed teeth. The same geometric motifs are used on pottery and baskets, and for scarification of the skin. When people decorate themselves, their homes, and their possessions with the same patterns, art serves to enhance cultural identity.

CHILDREN AND THE CONTINUITY OF LIFE

Among the most fundamental of human concerns is the continuation of life from one generation to the next. In some African societies children are especially important: Not only do they represent the future of the family and the community, but they also provide a form of "social security," guaranteeing that parents will have someone to care for them when they are old.

In the often harsh and unpredictable climates of Africa, human life can be fragile. In some areas half of all infants die before the age of 5, and the average life expectancy may be as low as 40 years. In these areas women bear many children in hopes that at least a few will survive into adulthood, and failure to have children is a disaster for a wife, her husband, and her husband's lineage. Women who have had difficulty bearing children appeal for help with special offerings or prayers, often involving the use of art.

YORUBA TWIN FIGURES The Yoruba people of southwestern Nigeria have one of the highest rates of twin births in the world. The birth of twins is a joyful occasion, yet it is troubling as well, for twins are more delicate than single babies, and one or both may well die. Many African peoples believe that a dead child continues its life in a spirit world and that the parents' care and affection may reach it there, often through the medium of art. When a Yoruba twin dies, parents often consult a diviner, a specialist in ritual and spiritual practices, who may tell them that an image of a twin (ere ibeji) must be carved to serve as a dwelling place for the deceased twin's spirit (FIG. 29–4).

When the image is finished, the mother brings the artist gifts. Then, carrying the figure as she would a living child, she dances home accompanied by the singing of neighborhood women. She places the figure in a shrine in her bedroom and lavishes care upon it, feeding it, dressing it with beautiful textiles and jewelry, anointing it with cosmetic oils. The Yoruba believe that the spirit of a dead twin, thus honored, is appeased and will look with favor on the surviving family members.

The twins here are female. They may be the work of the Yoruba artist Akiode, who died in 1936. Like most objects that Africans produce to encourage the birth and growth of children, the figures emphasize health and well-being. They have beautiful, glossy surfaces to suggest that they are well fed, as well as marks of

29-4 • TWIN FIGURES (ERE IBEJI)
Nigeria. Yoruba culture, 20th century. Wood, height 7⅞" (20 cm). The University of Iowa Museum of Art, Iowa City. The Stanley Collection (x1986.489 and x1986.488)

As with other African sculpture, patterns of use result in particular signs of wear. The facial features of *ere ibeji* are often worn down or even obliterated by repeated feedings and washings. Camwood powder applied as a cosmetic builds to a thick crust in areas that are rarely handled, and the blue indigo dye regularly applied to the hair eventually builds to a thin layer of color.

adulthood, such as elaborate hairstyles and scarification patterns, that will one day be achieved. They represent hope for the future, for survival, and for prosperity.

CHILDREN, ART, AND PERFORMANCE In sub-Saharan Africa, as elsewhere, children from an early age are intensely interested in adult roles and activities, including art making and the performative arts. In many societies a child's link to a particular artistic or craft activity is fixed. For example, in Africa, wood carving is universally a male-dominated activity, while women are most often involved in pottery production, and individual children may be apprenticed to a wood carver or potter according to their gender. But, even beyond such formal apprenticeships, children are especially interested in the festive activities of community life, such as masquerade. While mask making and masquerade performance are usually controlled by adult associations, children are given space at the edges of events to experiment with their home-made masks and costumes. Yoruba masquerades such as Gelede or Egungun are often organized so that children perform first (**FIG.**

29-5). Some families even purchase or make elaborate costuming for their children in a similar style to that worn by adults. Adults view these early forays into masquerade as a training ground. As children perform, they are encouraged and gently corrected from the sidelines by family members. The Yoruba of Nigeria, especially, place a significant value on the training of children in adult performance and aesthetic forms, and children are encouraged to perform from an early age.

INITIATION

In contemporary North America, initiation into the adult world is extended over several years and punctuated by numerous rites, such as being confirmed in a religion, earning a driver's license, and graduating from high school. These steps all involve acquiring the knowledge society deems appropriate and accepting the corresponding responsibilities. In other cultures, initiation can take other forms. The acquisition of knowledge can be supplemented

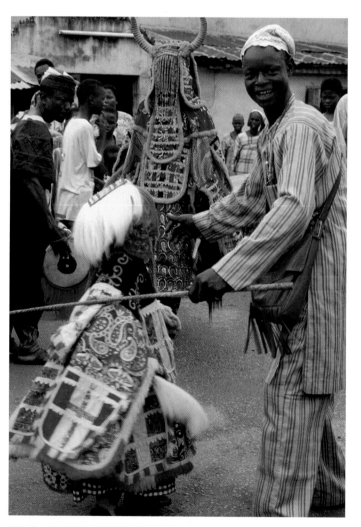

29-5 • ELDER GUIDING SMALL BOY IN EGUNGUN PERFORMANCE WHILE ADULT EGUNGUN PERFORMER LOOKS ON
Nigeria. Yoruba culture, 1986. National Museum of African Art, Smithsonian Institution, Washington, DC. Eliot Elisofon Photographic Archive, Henry John Drewal and Margaret Thompson Drewal Collection (1992-028-02691)

by trials of endurance to prove that candidates are equal to the responsibilities of adult life.

MASKS OF BWA INITIATION The Bwa people of central Burkina Faso initiate young men and women into adulthood following the onset of puberty. The initiates are first separated from younger playmates by being "kidnapped" by older relatives, though their disappearance is explained in the community by saying that they have been devoured by wild beasts. The initiates remove their clothing and sleep on the ground without blankets. Isolated from the community, they are instructed about the world of nature spirits and about the masks that represent them. They learn of the spirit each mask represents, and they memorize the story of each spirit's encounter with the founding ancestors of the clan. They also learn how to construct costumes from hemp to be worn with the masks, and they learn the songs and instruments that accompany the masks in performance. Only boys wear each mask in turn and learn the dance steps that express the character and personality each mask represents. Returning to the community, the initiates display their new knowledge in a public ceremony. Each boy performs with one of the masks, while the girls sing the accompanying songs. At the end of the mask ceremony the young men and young women rejoin their families as adults, ready to marry, to start farms, and to begin families of their own.

Most Bwa masks depict spirits that have taken an animal form, such as crocodile, hyena, hawk, or serpent. Others represent spirits in human form. Among the most spectacular masks, however, are those that represent spirits that have taken neither human nor animal form. Crowned with tall, narrow planks (**FIG. 29-6**), these masks are covered in abstract patterns that are easily recognized by the initiated. The white crescent at the top represents the quarter moon, under which the initiation is held. The white triangles below represent bull roarers—sacred sound-makers that are swung around the head on a long cord to recreate spirit voices. The large central X represents the scar that every initiated Bwa bears as a mark of devotion. The horizontal zigzags at the bottom represent the path of the ancestors and symbolize adherence to ancestral ways. That the path is difficult to follow is clearly conveyed. The curving red hook that projects in front of the face is said to represent the beak of the hornbill, a bird associated with the supernatural world and believed to be an intermediary between the living and the dead. The mask thus proudly announces the initiate's passage to adulthood while encoding secrets of initiation in abstract symbols of proper moral conduct.

29-6 • FIVE MASKS IN PERFORMANCE
Dossi, Burkina Faso. Bwa culture, 1984. Wood, mineral pigments, and fiber, height approx. 7′ (2.13 m).

The Bwa have been making and using such masks since well before Burkina Faso achieved its independence in 1960. We might assume their use is centuries old, but in this case, the masks are a comparatively recent innovation. The elders of the Bwa family who own these masks state that they, like all Bwa, once followed the cult of the spirit of Do, who is represented by masks made of leaves. In the last quarter of the nineteenth century, the Bwa were the targets of slave raiders from the north and east. Their response to this new danger was to acquire wooden masks from their neighbors, for such masks seemed a more effective and powerful way of communicating with spirits who could help them. Thus, faced with a new form of adversity, the Bwa sought a new tradition to cope with it.

👁— **Watch** a video of the Bwa masks in a performance on myartslab.com

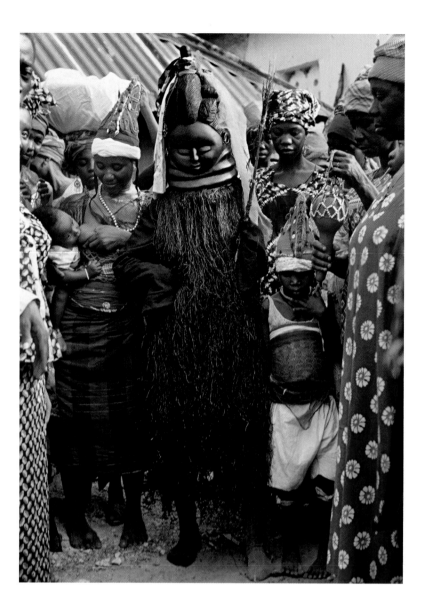

INITIATION TO WOMANHOOD IN WEST AFRICA
Among the Mende, Temne, Vai, and Kpelle peoples of Sierra Leone, the initiation of girls into adulthood is organized by a society of older women called Sande or Bondo. The initiation culminates with a ritual bath in a river, after which the initiated return to the village. At the ceremony, the Sande women wear black gloves and stockings, black costumes of shredded raffia fibers that cover the entire body, and black masks called *nowo* or *sowei* (**FIG. 29-7**).

With its glossy black surface, high forehead, elaborately plaited hairstyle decorated with combs, and refined facial features, the mask represents ideal female beauty. The mask is worn by a senior member of the women's Sande society whose responsibility it is to prepare Sande girls for their adult roles in society, including marriage and child rearing. The meanings of the mask are complex. It has been related to the chrysalis of a certain African butterfly, with the creases at the base of the mask representing its body segments. Thus, the young woman entering adulthood is like a butterfly emerging from its cocoon. The comparison extends even further, for just as the butterfly feeds on the toxic sap of

the milkweed to make itself poisonous to predatory birds, so the medicinal powers of the Sande society are believed to protect the young women from danger. The creases may additionally refer to the concentric waves that radiate outward as the initiate emerges from the river to take her place as a member of the adult community.

***BWAMI* ASSOCIATION AMONG THE LEGA** A ceremony of initiation may also accompany the achievement of other types of membership. Among the Lega people, who live in the dense forests between the headwaters of the Congo River and the great lakes of east Africa, the political system is based on a voluntary association called *bwami*, which comprises six levels or grades. Some 80 percent of Lega men belong to *bwami*, and all aspire to the highest grade. Women can also belong to *bwami*, although not at a higher grade than their husbands.

Promotion from one grade of *bwami* to the next takes many years. It is based not only on a candidate's character but also on his or her ability to pay the initiation fees, which increase dramatically with each grade. No candidate for any level of *bwami* can pay the fees without assistance and must enlist the help of relatives to provide the necessary payment, which may include cowrie shells, goats, wild game, palm oil, clothing, and trade goods. Thus, the ambition to move from one level of *bwami* to the next encourages a harmonious community, for all must stay on good terms with other members of the community if they are to advance.

Bwami initiations into advanced grades are held in the plaza at the center of the community in the presence of all members.

29-8 • BWAMI MASK (LUKWAKONGO)
Democratic Republic of Congo. 20th century. Wood, plant fiber, and pigment, height 22¾″ (57.5 cm). Fowler Museum of Cultural History, University of California in Los Angeles.

Dances and songs are performed, and the values and ideals of the appropriate grade are explained through proverbs and sayings. These standards are illustrated by natural or crafted objects, which are presented to the initiate as signs of membership. At the highest two levels of *bwami*, such objects include exquisitely made small masks and sculpted figures.

The mask in **FIGURE 29-8** is associated with *yananio*, the second-highest grade of *bwami*. Typical of Lega masks, the head is fashioned as an oval into which is carved a concave, heart-shaped face with narrow, raised features. The masks are often colored white with clay and fitted with a long beard made of plant fibers. Too small to cover the face, they are displayed in other ways—held in the palm of a hand, for example, or attached to a thigh. Each means of display recalls a different value or saying, so that one mask may convey a variety of meanings. Generally, the masks symbolize continuity between the ancestors and the living community and are thought to be direct links to deceased relatives and past members of *bwami*.

***KIKAKU* OF THE NKANU PEOPLES** During the late nineteenth and early twentieth century, Nkanu peoples residing in the Democratic Republic of Congo and Angola celebrated the completion of coming-of-age initiation rites (*nkanda*) by creating brightly painted figurative sculpture and decorated wall panels adorned with human and animal figures, displayed in a *kikaku*—a three-sided roofed enclosure built at a crossroads near the initiation campground. These displays reinforced the values taught during *nkanda* and announced to the community that initiation was coming to a close—that their children would soon be home.

The *kikaku* resembled a stage. Wall panels were carved, painted, and attached to its back and sides, and sculpted figures were placed in front of the wall panels on the floor of the structure. The *kikaku* wall panels were brightly colored with symbolically charged patterns that conveyed specific meanings associated with the initiation ritual (**FIG. 29-9**). European colonial officials were a favorite subject. Their depictions were considered "portraits" of specific individuals, included distinguishing characteristics such as costume and hairstyle—often ridiculing officials who were despised for their cruelty or because of their dalliances with Nkanu women. These caricatures became a means of confronting colonial domination without openly attacking colonial officials, which would have undoubtedly led to severe repercussions.

The wall panels here depict a central colonial administrator flanked by two figures representing Congolese men who served in the Force Publique, the Belgian colonial military force. One soldier wears an ammunition belt, while the other assumes the awkward stance of an initiate, required to balance on one leg. Both the stance and the painted patterns on the panels symbolize the virility and procreative capacity of the initiate upon the successful completion of *nkanda*. After the initiation sequence, the *kikaku* and its contents were left to decay. A few individual pieces—but no entire *kikaku*—have been acquired by Western museums.

29-9 • INITIATION WALL PANELS
Democratic Republic of Congo. Nkanu peoples, Kimvula region, early 20th century. Wood, pigment, height 33⅜" (84.8 cm). National Museum of African Art, Smithsonian Institution, Washington, DC. Museum purchase (99-2-1)

THE SPIRIT WORLD

While African religious beliefs have been influenced by Christianity and Islam for hundreds of years, many African peoples still rely on local customs and belief systems to find the answers to universal human problems. Why does one child fall ill and die while another remains healthy? Why does one year bring rain and a bountiful crop, while the next brings drought and famine? People everywhere confront these fundamental and troubling questions. In many African belief systems, a supreme creator god is not thought to be fundamentally involved in the daily lives of humans. Instead, numerous subordinate spirit forces are believed to be ever-present and involved in human affairs. For instance, such spirits may inhabit agricultural fields, the river that provides fish, the forest that is home to game, or the land that must be cleared in order to build a new village. Families, too, may acknowledge the existence of ancestral spirits. These spirits control success and failure in life, and if a proper relationship is not maintained with them, harm in the form of illness or misfortune can befall an individual, a family, or an entire community.

***NKISI NKONDE* OF THE KONGO** To communicate with these all-important spirits, many African societies rely on a specialist, such as a diviner who serves as a link between the supernatural and human worlds, opening the lines of communication through such techniques as prayer, sacrifice, offerings, ritual performance, and divination. Sometimes art plays a role in the diviner's dealings with the spirit world, giving visible identity and personality to what is imaginary and intangible (see "Divination Among the Chokwe," page 893). *Minkisi* (the plural of *Nkisi*, a Kikongo word meaning "container") are objects harnessing spirit forces or powers, and were made by the Kongo and Songye peoples of the Democratic Republic of Congo, primarily during the nineteenth and early to mid twentieth centuries, to alleviate illness, protect vulnerable individuals, and bring success in hunting, trade, and other endeavors. The more specialized *Nkisi Nkonde* object served a divinatory and judicial function to seek out wrongdoers and punish them for their misdeeds (see "A Closer Look," page 894). A *Nkisi Nkonde* began as an unadorned wooden figure, often in human or animal form. It was commissioned by a diviner or chief on behalf of his society if it had encountered some adversity. The diviner prescribed medicinal ingredients (*bilongo*) from the plant, animal, and mineral worlds, which activated the object with potent earthly and supernatural powers. A *Nkisi Nkonde* served an important public function as an impartial arbiter of justice in smaller villages where European colonial rule had removed local judicial authorities to the capital cities. Two warring rural communities, for example, might agree to end their conflict by swearing an oath of peace and then driving a nail into the *Nkisi Nkonde* to seal the agreement. Should either party break the oath, it was believed that the *Nkisi Nkonde* would avenge the wronged party by meting out an appropriate punishment to the offender.

29-10 • SPIRIT SPOUSE (BLOLO BLA)
Ivory Coast. Baule culture, early–mid 20th century. Wood, glass beads, gold hollow beads, plant fiber, white pigment, encrustation, height 19¼" (48.9 cm). National Museum of African Art, Smithsonian Institution, Washington, DC. Museum purchase (85-15-2)

SPIRIT SPOUSE OF THE BAULE Some African peoples conceive of the spirit world as a parallel realm in which spirits may have families, live in villages, attend markets, and possess personalities, complete with faults and virtues. The Baule people in the Ivory Coast believe that each of us lived in the spirit world before we were born. While there, we had a spirit spouse, whom we left behind when we entered this life. A person who has difficulty assuming his or her gender-specific role as an adult Baule—a man who has not married or achieved his expected status in life, for example, or a woman who has not borne children—may dream of his or her spirit spouse.

For such a person, the diviner may prescribe the carving of an image of the **SPIRIT SPOUSE** (**FIG. 29-10**)—a *blolo bla* (otherworld wife) for a man, or a *blolo bian* (otherworld husband) for a woman. The figures display the most admired and desirable marks of beauty so that the spirit spouses may be encouraged to enter and inhabit them. Spirit spouse figures are broadly naturalistic, with swelling, fully rounded musculature and careful attention to details of hairstyle, jewelry, and scarification patterns. They may be carved standing in a quiet, dignified pose or seated on a stool. The owner keeps the figure in his or her room, dressing it in beautiful textiles and jewelry, washing it, anointing it with oil, feeding it, and caressing it. Over time, the surface of the figure softens as it takes on a glossy sheen indicating the attention it has been given. The Baule hope that by caring for and pleasing his or her spirit spouse a balance may be restored that will free the individual's human life to unfold smoothly.

YORUBA DIVINATION While spirit beings are often portrayed in African art, major deities are generally considered to be far removed from the everyday lives of humans and are thus rarely depicted. Such is the case with Olodumare, the creator god of the Yoruba people of Nigeria.

The Yoruba have a sizable pantheon of lesser, but still important, gods (*orisha*). Two *orisha* are principal mediators: Orunmila who represents certainty, fate, order, and equilibrium; and his counterpart Eshu who represents uncertainty, disorder, and chance. Commonly represented in art, Eshu is a capricious and mischievous trickster who loves nothing better than to disrupt things that appear to be going well. The opposing forces of order and disorder are mediated through the agency of a diviner (*babalawo*) who employs a divination board (*opon ifa*) and its paraphernalia to reveal the causes of a client's problems (**FIG. 29-11**). The divination board is sprinkled with a white wood dust and the *orisha* Orunmila and Eshu are called to the divination by tapping the board with a special tapper. The *babalawo* throws 16 palm nuts and after each toss records the way the palm nuts have landed in the white wood dust on the divination board. Each configuration of the palm nuts relates to particular verses from a complex oral tradition also known as Ifa. As the selected verses are recited by the diviner, the client relates the verses to his or her own particular problems or concerns.

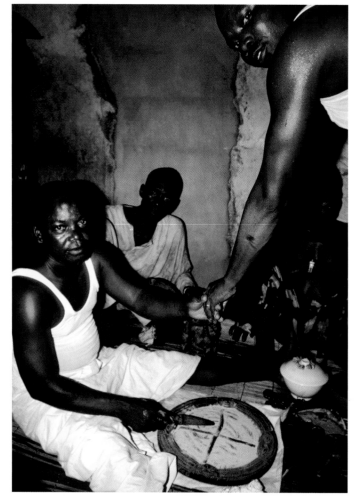

29-11 • IFA DIVINATION SESSION
Yoruba culture, Nigeria, 1982. National Museum of African Art, Smithsonian Institution, Washington, DC. Henry John Drewal and Margaret Thompson Drewal Collection (EEPA 1992-028-02016)

Eshu's image often appears on divination objects and in shrines employed by his worshipers. His image always appears at the top of the divination board, while other images along the edge of the board relate symbolically to the world of Ifa divination. Eshu is associated with two eternal sources of human conflict—sex and money—and is usually portrayed with a long hairstyle: The Yoruba consider long hair to represent excess libidinous energy and unrestrained sexuality. Figures of Eshu are usually adorned with long strands of cowrie shells, a traditional African currency. Shrines to him are erected wherever there is the potential for encounters that lead to conflict, especially at crossroads, in markets, or in front of banks. Eshu's followers hope their offerings will persuade the god to spare them the pitfalls he places in front of others.

LEADERSHIP

As in societies throughout the world, art in Africa is used to identify those who hold power, to validate their right to their authority as representatives of the family or community, and to communicate the rules for moral behavior that must be obeyed by all members

of the society. This chapter opened with one example—a gold-and-wood spokesman's staff (see FIG. 29-1) from the culture of the Ashanti of Ghana, in west Africa. The Ashanti greatly admire fine language—one of their adages is, "We speak to the wise man in proverbs, not in plain speech"—and consequently their governing system includes the special post of spokesman to the ruler.

The Ashanti use gold not only for objects, such as the staff, that are reserved for the use of rulers, but also for jewelry, as do other peoples of the region. But for the Ashanti, who live in the middle of the richest goldfields of west Africa, gold was long a major source of power; for centuries they traded it, first via intermediaries across the Sahara to the Mediterranean world, then later directly to Europeans on the west African coast.

KENTE CLOTH The Ashanti are also renowned for the beauty of their woven textiles (**kente**) (**FIG. 29-13**). Weaving was introduced in Ghana sometime during the seventeenth century from neighboring regions of west Africa. Ashanti weavers—traditionally men—work on small, light, horizontal looms that produce long, narrow strips of cloth that are subsequently sewn together to form large rectangles of finished *kente* cloth. Weavers begin by laying out the long warp threads in brightly colored stripes. Today the threads are likely to be rayon. Formerly, however, they were cotton and later silk, which the Ashanti first procured in the seventeenth century by unraveling silk cloth obtained through European trade. Weft threads are woven through the warp to produce complex patterns. The example shown belongs to a type known as *faprenu*, with a dense double weave consisting of twice as many weft threads as warp threads.

Kente cloth was originally associated with royalty and produced under royal control. A man wore a single piece, about 6–7 feet by 12–13 feet, wrapped like a toga, with no belt and the right shoulder bare. Women wore two pieces—a skirt and a shawl. Even though its use is now more widespread, *kente* cloth is primarily reserved for festive attire worn at special occasions. The pattern in FIGURE 29-13 is known as *Oyokoman Adweneasa*, characterized by wide gold and green stripes set on deep red grounds. *Oyokoman* refers to the powerful Oyoka clan, and *Adweneasa* means "my skill is exhausted," a reference to the way the artist has woven elaborate patterns into every available area to the very edge of the fabric, until running out of space.

THE KUBA NYIM The Kuba people of the Democratic Republic of Congo also relate art and leadership. At the pinnacle of the political hierarchy sits the Kuba paramount ruler (*nyim*) whose residence was located approximately in the center of the Kuba region. The current *nyim* can trace his predecessors back to the founding of the kingdom in the seventeenth century. At the installation of a new monarch, a new capital city (*Nsheng*) is built that includes the residence of the *nyim* and his wives and children, as well as areas for other governmental functions, all surrounded by a high palisade.

Chokwe peoples of the Democratic Republic of Congo and Angola consult diviners (*nganga*) about problems such as death, illness, impotence, sterility, and theft. As the mediator between this world and the supernatural, the diviner's role is to ascertain the true meaning and underlying cause of an affliction or misfortune, and whether it is due to a conflict with human protagonists or with spirit forces. The diviner's ability to uncover the cause of a client's problems comes through the agency of powerful spirit forces and the efficacy of divinatory paraphernalia. A Chokwe *nganga*, utilizing a rattle to call the spirits to the divination, begins to shake a shallow covered basket (*ngombo ya kuse*kula) (**FIG. 29–12**) containing a variety of natural objects including small antelope horns, seeds, and minerals. The basket also contains a number of carved wooden objects representing humans (in various symbolic poses), animals, and other objects such as small models of masks and masked figures. The objects in the basket are tossed about as the basket is shaken and when finished the cover is removed to reveal the arrangement of the objects as they came to rest inside. The *nganga* interprets the results of multiple tosses to disclose the underlying cause of the client's problem and suggests what steps need to be taken to remedy the situation.

29–12 • DIVINATION BASKET (NGOMBO)
Democratic Republic of Congo and Angola. Chokwe peoples, mid 19th–early 20th century. Plant fiber, seed, stone, horn, shell, bone, metal, feather, and camwood, depth 12¹⁄₁₆″ (30.7 cm). National Museum of African Art, Smithsonian Institution, Washington, DC. Museum purchase (86-12-17.1)

29–13 • KENTE CLOTH
Ghana. Ashanti culture, c. 1980. Rayon, 10′3½″ × 7′1½″ (3.14 × 2.17 m). Fowler Museum of Cultural History, University of California in Los Angeles.

Power Figure (*Nkisi Nkonde*).
From the Democratic Republic of Congo. Kongo culture, 19th century. Wood, nails, pins, blades, and other materials, height 44″ (111.7 cm). The Field Museum, Chicago.

The *bilongo* (medicinal ingredients) may be placed on the head of the figure, thought to be an especially appropriate site to communicate with spirit forces.

Clients drive a nail, blade, or other pointed object into the figure to capture the *Nkonde*'s attention and prick it into action. The large number of objects driven into this *Nkonde* suggests that its powers were both formidable and efficacious.

This *Nkonde* stands in a pose called *pakalala*, a stance of alertness like that of a wrestler challenging an opponent. Other *Nkonde* figures hold a knife or spear in an upraised hand, ready to strike or attack.

Bilongo may also be suspended in a packet from the figure's neck or waist or even placed into the figure's beard. The beard is associated with the powers that come with age and seniority.

Additional *bilongo* are inserted into a body cavity such as the figure's belly, as this is thought to be the seat of a person's life or soul. The term *mooyo* means both "belly" and "life."

 View the Closer Look for the Kongo *Nkisi Nkonde* on myartslab.com

Powerful individuals often lavish elaborate surface decoration on objects that belong to them to indicate their rank and prestige within the political and social hierarchy. In Kuba culture this happens with geometric decoration—woven on the walls of royal buildings (**FIG. 29-14**) and intricately carved on wooden drums, boxes, and other objects. It is also seen on the lavishly embroidered textiles for men and women and on regalia such as headdresses and jewelry that serve as prestige and festive attire for celebratory occasions. An eagle feather chief (*kum apoong*) displays sumptuous adornment at his investiture. Each element of regalia signifies a prerogative of an individual's titled position relative to the position of others within a complicated system of titleholding. Naturally the most extravagant adornment is worn by the paramount ruler, as can be seen in a photograph of the Kuba *nyim* taken in 1971 (**FIG. 29-15**). Textile display is also an essential aspect of funeral rituals where textiles are worn at celebratory dances and displayed on the body of the deceased. The textiles are subsequently buried in the deceased's grave, where the Kuba believe an individual remains for a period of time before being reborn.

29-14 • DECORATED BUILDING (SLEEPING ROOM FOR NYIM) IN THE ROYAL COMPOUND OF THE KUBA NYIM
Nsheng, Democratic Republic of Congo. 1980.

◉ **Watch** an architectural simulation about Kuba woven decoration on walls on myartslab.com

YORUBA PALACE ART The kings of the Yoruba people of Nigeria also manifested their authority and power through the large palaces in which they lived. In a typical palace plan, the principal rooms opened onto a veranda with elaborately carved posts facing a courtyard (**FIG. 29-16**). Elaborate carving also covered the palace doors. Among the most important Yoruba artists of the early twentieth century was Olowe of Ise (d. 1938), who carved doors and veranda posts for the rulers of the Ekiti-Yoruba kingdoms in southwestern Nigeria.

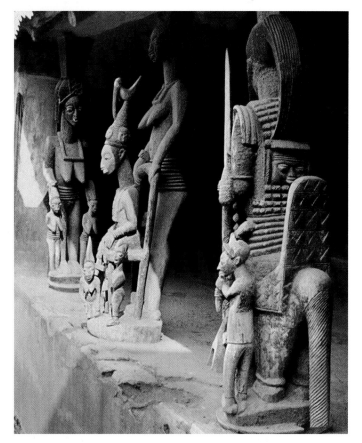

29-16 • Olowe of Ise VERANDA POSTS INSTALLED IN THE COURTYARD OF THE PALACE OF THE OGAGA OF IKERE
Nigeria. Yoruba culture, c. 1910–1914. Wood and pigment. Photograph 1964.

▭◉ **Read** the document related to Olowe of Ise on myartslab.com

29-15 • KOT AMBWEEK IN CEREMONIAL DRESS
Democratic Republic of Congo. Photograph 1971. National Museum of African Art, Smithsonian Institution, Washington, DC. (EEPA EECL 2145)

The Kuba people of the Democratic Republic of Congo perform funerary masquerades to honor deceased members of the men's initiation society and high-ranking individuals who belonged to the community council of elders.

In the southern Kuba region, funeral rites for initiated men are often accompanied by the appearance of one or more masquerade figures on the day of interment of the deceased. On these occasions, initiation society members and family and friends of the deceased celebrate the departed's life while mourning his death. In part, funeral rites are elaborate because of the belief that the spirit of the recently deceased (*mwendu*) may bring harm to his family or community if his achievements and status in life are not acknowledged at the funeral. The *mwendu* may be angered for a variety of reasons. Perhaps outstanding debts were not paid and money or other goods were kept back by a family member. Or the deceased had asked for something to be buried with him and this request was not honored. Disrespect is most often shown if the deceased is not given a proper burial, one equal to his rank in life. For an initiated man, a funeral masquerade is mandatory in this region, and members of the community-based men's initiation society show their solidarity with the deceased and his spirit by performing a masquerade at his funeral.

Among the most spectacular masquerades performed in the Kuba region is that of *Ngady mwaash*—the name means literally "female mask" (FIG. 29-17). The mask is carved from wood, and attached to a framework covered with cloth and decorated with beads and shells that forms the top, sides, and back of the head.

Wooden ears, carved separately, are attached to the sides of the head. The face of the mask presents an exuberant blend of bold geometric patterns composed of contrasting areas of triangles and parallel lines. A triangular-shaped hat, identical to that worn by female diviners, is attached to the mask. The hat signifies that *Ngady mwaash* is invested with the power of nature spirits (*ngesh*) to whom Kuba diviners attribute their extraordinary powers.

The costume for *Ngady mwaash* is composed of a shirt and leggings made from animal hide or cloth, often extensively decorated with painted black-and-white triangles. Small wooden dowels attached to the front of the shirt represent breasts. Although wearing a woman's long embroidered skirt under a short decorated skirt affixed with a belt, *Ngady mwaash* is always performed by a man. Costume accessories include strands of beaded and shell-laden bandoliers that crisscross the chest and decorated arm- and legbands. The mask, costume, and accessories, as well as the fly-whisk that *Ngady mwaash* carries, represent wealth and high status.

29-17 • NGADY MWAASH MASK
Democratic Republic of Congo. Kuba peoples, late 19th–mid 20th century. Wood, pigment, glass beads, cowrie shells, fabric, and thread, height 12½″ (31.8 cm). The Art Institute of Chicago. (1982.1505)

29–18 • BWOOM MASKED DANCER AT THE FUNERAL OF AN INITIATED MAN

Democratic Republic of Congo. Southern Kuba peoples, 1982.

The funeral masquerade performance is held near the residence of the man who has died, just prior to burial. The perimeter of the dance ground is lined with family, friends, and onlookers who have come to bid a final farewell to the deceased and witness the performance. *Ngady mwaash* takes turns performing with another masked figure designated as male, such as the masked figure *Bwoom*.

The individual character or persona of male and female masked figures is fully realized during performance. *Bwoom*, who carries a short sword, exudes power and restrained aggression. The dancer employs lunging movements and quick short jabs with his sword, causing onlookers to suspect that he may suddenly lose control and harm someone. This feeling of apprehension is a constituent part of the performance style of *Bwoom*, and is a principal reason why community members look forward to masquerade with such anticipation. In contrast, the performance style of *Ngady mwaash* is decidedly nonthreatening, with graceful movements as the dancer's body, legs, arms, and hands move in fluid gestures. The differences in the performance styles of male and female masquerade figures parallel the difference in the dance styles of men and women in Kuba culture. The men's initiation society, which organizes funeral masquerades, expresses its control and dominance of ritual affairs in part through the contrasting performance styles of *Bwoom* and *Ngady mwaash* (FIGS. 29–18, 29–19).

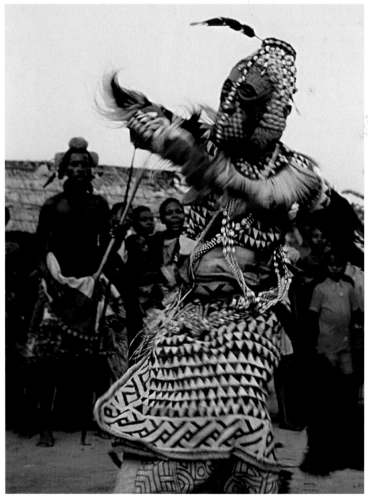

29–19 • NGADY MWAASH MASKED DANCER AT THE FUNERAL OF AN INITIATED MAN

Democratic Republic of Congo. Southern Kuba peoples, 1982.

figures. The relief is so high that the figures' upper portions are actually carved in the round. The energetic movement of the figures is set against an underlying decorative pattern. The entire surface of the doors was originally painted, but only traces of the original colors remain.

This door panel commemorates the *arinjale* (king) of Ise's reception of Major W.R. Reeve-Tucker, the first British traveling commissioner for the province, and his entourage. A separate door panel, in a private collection, presents the European entourage. In the second register of this panel, the *arinjale* appears on horseback wearing a conical crown and accompanied by court messengers. Other registers contain other members of the court—royal wives lifting their breasts (a gesture of generosity and affection performed by elder women), men carrying kegs of gunpowder, royal guards, and priests. The bottom register portrays a human sacrifice, with birds pecking at the corpse, and the two rows of heads on the left side of the panel may represent either ancestors of the *arinjale* or enemies taken in battle.

Olowe seems to have worked from the early 1900s until his death in 1938. Although he was famous throughout Yorubaland and called upon by patrons as distant as 60 miles from his home, few records of his activities remain, and only one European, Philip Allison, wrote of meeting him and watching him work. Allison described Olowe carving the iron-hard African oak "as easily as [he would] a calabash [gourd]."

DEATH AND ANCESTORS

In the view of many African peoples, death is not an end but a transition—the leaving behind of one phase of life and the beginning of another. Just as ceremonies mark the initiation of young men and women into the community of adults, so too they mark the initiation of the newly dead into the community of spirits. Like the rites of initiation into adulthood, death begins with a separation from the community, in this case the community of the living. A period of isolation and trial follows, during which the newly dead spirit may, for example, journey to the land of ancestors. Finally, the deceased is reintegrated into a community, this time the community of ancestral spirits. The living who preserve the memory of the deceased may appeal to his or her spirit to intercede on their behalf with nature spirits or to prevent the spirits of the dead from using their powers to harm (see "Kuba Funerary Mask," page 896).

29–20 • Olowe of Ise PALACE DOOR
From the palace at Ise, Nigeria, Yoruba culture, c. 1904–1910. Wood and pigment, height 81½″ × width 34⅝″ × depth 6¼″ (207 × 88 × 15.9 cm). National Museum of African Art, Smithsonian Institution, Washington, DC. Gift of Dr. and Mrs Robert Kuhn (88-13-1)

Olowe carved the door panel for the royal palace at Ise (**FIG. 29-20**) as an asymmetrical composition, combining narrative and symbolic scenes in horizontal rectangular panels. Tall figures with bodies in profile turn their heads outward to confront the viewer. Their long necks and elaborate hairstyles make them appear even taller, unlike typical Yoruba sculpture which uses short, static

DOGON FUNERARY *DAMA* Among the Dogon people of Mali, in west Africa, a collective funeral rite called *dama*, is held every 12 to 13 years (**FIG. 29-21**). During *dama*, a variety of different masks perform to the sound of gunfire to drive the souls of the deceased from the village. Among the most common masks to perform is the *kanaga*, whose rectangular face supports a superstructure of planks that depict a woman, bird, or lizard with splayed legs.

For a deceased man, men from the community later engage in a mock battle on the roof of his home and participate in ritual hunts; for a deceased woman, the women of the community smash her cooking vessels on the threshold of her home. These portions of *dama* are reminders of human activities the deceased will no longer engage in. The *dama* may last as long as six days and include the performance of hundreds of masks. Because a *dama* is so costly, it is performed for several deceased elders at the same time. However, in certain Dogon communities frequented by tourists, *dama* performances have become more frequent as new masked characters are invented, including masks representing tourists holding wooden cameras or anthropologists holding notebooks in their hands. Dogon mask-makers produce additional masks that are offered for sale to tourists at the conclusion of the performance.

FANG ANCESTOR GUARDIAN The Fang, along with other peoples who live near the Atlantic coast from southern Cameroon through Rio Muni and into Gabon, shared a number of similar institutions and beliefs in which the skulls, bones, and relics of ancestors who had performed great deeds during their lifetimes were collected after burial and placed in a cylindrical bark container (*nsek-bieri*), which was preserved by the family. Deeds thus honored included victory in warfare, killing an elephant, being the first to trade with Europeans, bearing an especially large number of children, or founding a particular lineage or community. The bones and relics of deceased family members were thought to have special powers that could be drawn upon to aid the living with problems that confronted or threatened the family. Before colonial officials banned many ritual practices, ancestral spirits

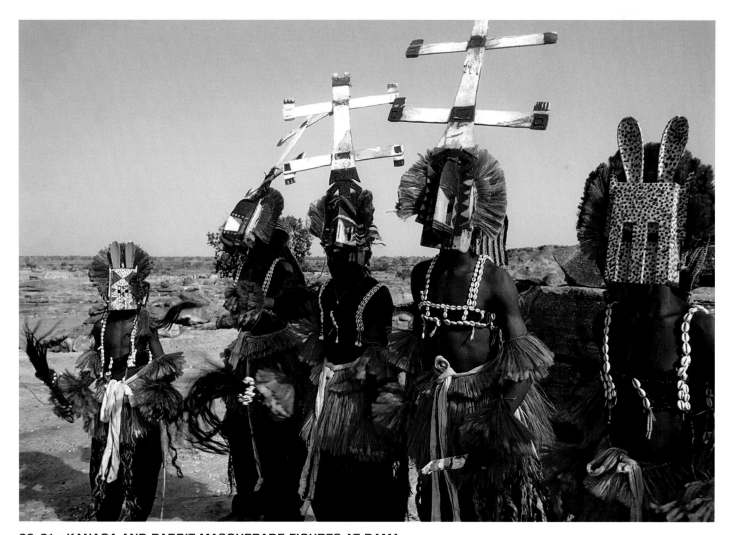

29-21 • KANAGA AND RABBIT MASQUERADE FIGURES AT DAMA
Mali. Dogon culture, 1959. National Museum of African Art, Smithsonian Institution, Washington, DC. (EEPA 3502)

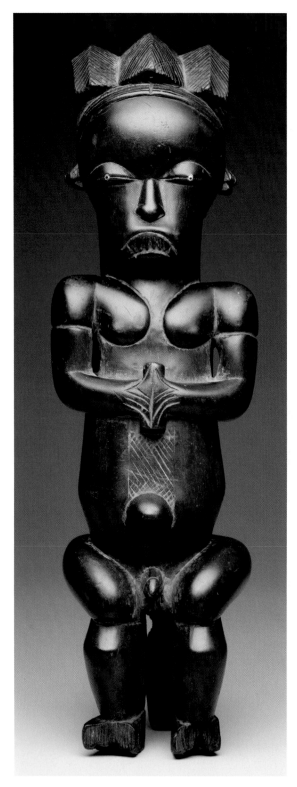

29-22 • RELIQUARY GUARDIAN (EYEMA BIERI)
Gabon. Fang people, Mvai group, mid–late 19th century. Wood, metal, and shell, height 21¼″ (53.97 cm). Dallas Museum of Art. The Eugene and Margaret McDermott Art Fund, Inc. (2000.3.MCD)

One authority on Fang culture suggests that *bieri* aim to achieve a balance between the opposing forces of chaos and order, male and female, pure and impure, powerful and weak. The Fang value an attitude of quiet composure, of reflection and tranquility—qualities embodied in the symmetry of the *bieri*, which communicates the calm and wisdom of the ancestor while also instilling awe and fear in those not initiated into the Fang religion.

represented by the reliquaries were regularly consulted on problems with fertility—failure in conceiving and bringing to term children—or with hunting and farming, or before embarking on a commercial venture.

As a point of focus for mediation between the ancestors and the living, the Fang placed a wooden sculpture called an *eyema bieri* on top of the container holding the relics. These sculptures functioned as points of contact for ancestral support and veneration and also as guardians to protect the relics from malevolent spirit forces (**FIG. 29-22**).

Bieri were carved in a number of different forms and styles. Some are large heads with long necks that are secured into the lid of the container, which represents the ancestral body. Other *bieri* were created as full figures with carefully arranged hairstyles, fully rounded torsos, and heavily muscled legs and arms. Here, the figure's firmly set jaw and powerfully built, muscular body exudes a sense of authority and confidence. These powerfully realized sculptures were often enhanced by the frequent application of cleansing and purifying palm oil over an extended period of time, producing a rich, glossy black surface that may literally exude oil.

CONTEMPORARY ART

The photographs of rituals and ceremonies in this chapter show ways in which African traditional arts have continued during the modern era. All of the photographs are somewhat dated, yet even today performances are staged in which the traditional types of masks appear. But Africa is ever-changing, and, as new experiences pose new challenges and offer new opportunities, African art moves with the times.

Perhaps the most obvious modern development in African art has been the adaptation of new materials to traditional forms. Some Yoruba, for example, have used photographs and children's brightly colored, imported plastic dolls in place of the traditional *ere ibeji*, images of twins, shown in FIGURE 29-4. The Guro people of Ivory Coast continue to commission delicate masks dressed with costly textiles and other materials, but they enliven them with brilliantly colored oil-based enamel paints. The Baule create brightly painted versions of spirit-spouse figures dressed as businessmen or soccer players.

Throughout the colonial period and especially during the years following World War II, many African artists trained in the techniques of European art. In the postcolonial era, numerous African artists have studied in Europe and the United States, and many have become internationally renowned through exhibitions of their work in galleries and museums around the world. Yet the diversity of influences on contemporary Africa makes it impossible to render a homogeneous view of what constitutes contemporary African art. As the art historian and curator Salah Hassan writes: "The development of a modern idiom in African art is closely linked to modern Africa's search for identity. Most contemporary works have apparent ties to traditional African folklore, belief

29-23 • Seydou Keïta UNTITLED
1952–1955. Gelatin-silver print, 24″ × 20″ (61 × 50.8 cm). Edition of ten.

Seydou Keïta said about his work, "It's easy to take a photo, but what really made a difference was that I always knew how to find the right position, and I never was wrong. Their head slightly turned, a serious face, the position of the hands … I was capable of making someone look really good. The photos were always very good. That's why I always say that it's a real art."

he specialized as a portraitist, taking unidealized and engaging photographs of the proud people of this newly independent nation. He was among the first to portray his own nation and people as prosperous and urban rather than objectified as ethnographic subjects, as seen in magazines such as *National Geographic*. In the image shown here (**FIG. 29-23**), the sitters occupy a visually luxurious space but are not confined by it. The heavy, strong patterns of the wife's clothing contrast with the stark white worn by her husband and child. Keïta's elegant composition monumentalizes individuals whose power and pride are communicated through their commanding poses and relaxed gestures. The sitters look out of the photograph with disarming frankness, inviting and returning our gaze, demanding that we see them as real people, as equals, with identities as multivalent and as complex as our own. While Keïta made his photographs for domestic consumption (his studio archive comprised over 10,000 negatives), he was "discovered" by the Western art world during the 1990s and is frequently exhibited in Europe and the United States.

EL ANATSUI OF GHANA The complex, multimedia work of El Anatsui affirms Africa's rich legacy with unexpected materials. Born in Ghana in 1944, Anatsui studied art in Kumasi where he took course work he describes as predominantly Western in orientation, while Ghana's own rich legacy was ignored. Following his own inclinations, he began to study Ghanaian surface design traditions as produced by Ewe and Ashanti textile artists. In 1975, Anatsui took a position in the Fine Arts Department of the University of Nigeria at Nsukka. There he found a like-minded spirit in Uche Okeke, who was intensely interested in revitalizing *uli*, an important Igbo surface design system. Anatsui began to create what would become a large body of work inspired by *uli* and other graphic systems using tools such as chain saws and blowtorches. More recently, while still concerned with the survival and transmission of inherited traditions, Anatsui began to appropriate cast-off objects he found in and around Nsukka, including broken and discarded mortars, large coconut graters, liquor-bottle caps, and aluminum labels from whiskey bottles to create revelatory art forms in a variety of media. These include immense wall sculptures that fold and undulate like textiles but are made from metal sewn together with copper wire (**FIG. 29-24**).

Although he lives in Nigeria, El Anatsui, like many contemporary African artists, also participates in international art events—including workshops, symposia, biennial exhibitions, and art festivals that dramatically invigorate our global visual culture. On the other hand, many other African artists have moved

systems and imagery. The only way to interpret or understand these works is in the light of the dual experience of colonialism and assimilation into Western culture in Africa. They reflect the search for a new identity."

SEYDOU KEÏTA OF MALI Photography was among earliest modern art media to be embraced broadly in Africa, and Seydou Keïta (c. 1921–2001) has become one of the best-known photographers. Trained as a carpenter, Keïta's interest in photography was serendipitously sparked by his uncle's gift of a Kodak Brownie Flash camera in 1935, and after using this unassuming equipment to hone his craft, he acquired a large-format camera and in 1948 opened his own studio in his hometown of Bamako, Mali. There permanently to major European and American cities, which offer them increased opportunities for exposure to art dealers, museum curators, art critics, and the expanding base of public and private collectors of African contemporary art.

AFRICAN ARTISTS IN DIASPORA While many African artists are primarily influenced by their own culture and traditions, others—especially some who no longer live on the continent—seem entirely removed from African stylistic influences and yet still express the search for a new African identity in revelatory ways. Their experiences of movement, accommodation, and change often become important elements in their art making and form an additional basis for the interpretation of their work.

Julie Mehretu (**FIG. 29-25**) is an eminent example of this kind of artist. Born in Ethiopia in 1970, but having lived in Senegal and the United States, and now in New York City, Mehretu

makes intensely energetic large-scale paintings and wall drawings. Her works speak not only to her own history of movement and change, but also to the transnational movement of myriad others uprooted by choice or by force as they create new identities in this increasingly turbulent period of globalization and change.

The underpinnings of her intricately layered canvases are architectural plans of airports, passenger terminals, and other places where people congregate and pass through during their lives. Layered and at times obscuring these architectural elements is an immense inventory of signs and markings influenced by cartography, weather maps, Japanese and Chinese calligraphy, tattooing, graffiti, and various stylized forms suggesting smoke and explosions borrowed from cartoons, comic books, and anime. The ambiguous reading of the paintings as either implosion and chaos or explosion and regeneration gives the works visual and conceptual complexity. Mehretu explains that she is not interested in

29-25 • Julie Mehretu DISPERSION
2002. Ink and acrylic on canvas, 90″ × 144″ (228.6 × 365.8 cm). Collection of Nicolas and Jeanne Greenberg Rohatyn, New York.

👁—❙**Watch** a video about Julie Mehretu on myartslab.com

describing or mapping specific locations but "in the multi-faceted layers of place, space, and time that impact the formation of personal and communal identity." Mehretu's concerns echo those of other contemporary African artists whose identification with the continent becomes increasingly complex as they move from Africa and enter a global arena.

THINK ABOUT IT

29.1 Compare the representation of the human figure in FIGURES 29–10 and 29–22. How could the differences in style be related to the function of these two works and their origin in distinct cultures?

29.2 Explain the use of art during African divination rituals and discuss one work from the chapter that is used in the practice.

29.3 Explain the role of masquerade in African art by analyzing the rite-of-passage ceremony of the Bwa culture in Burkina Faso.

29.4 Analyze the initiation wall panels shown in FIGURE 29–9 and discuss how the artist addresses the experience of colonialism.

CROSSCURRENTS

FIG. 28–19

FIG. 29–23

How do these two photographers from Samoa and Mali—whose work has received attention and acclaim within a contemporary global art world—address the specific concerns of their own cultural situation and at the same time evoke concerns shared by people around the world?

✓—❙**Study** and review on myartslab.com

Glossary

abacus (p. 108) The flat slab at the top of a **capital**, directly under the **entablature**.

abbey church (p. 239) An abbey is a monastic religious community headed by an abbot or abbess. An abbey church often has an especially large **choir** to provide space for the monks or nuns.

absolute dating (p. 12) A method, especially in archaeology, of assigning a precise historical date at which, or span of years during which, an object was made. Based on known and recorded events in the region, as well as technically extracted physical evidence (such as carbon-14 disintegration). See also **radiometric dating**, **relative dating**.

abstract (p. 7) Of art that does not attempt to describe the appearance of visible forms but rather to transform them into stylized patterns or to alter them in conformity to ideals.

academy (p. 926) An institution established for the training of artists. Academies date from the Renaissance and after; they were particularly powerful, state-run institutions in the seventeenth and eighteenth centuries. In general, academies replaced **guild**s as the venues where students learned the craft of art and were educated in art theory. Academies helped the recognition of artists as trained specialists, rather than craftsmakers, and promoted their social status. An academician is an academy-trained artist.

acanthus (p. 110) A Mediterranean plant whose leaves are reproduced in Classical architectural ornament used on **molding**s, **frieze**s, and **capital**s.

acroterion (*pl.* **acroteria**) (p. 110) An ornament at the corner or peak of a roof.

Action painting (p. 1074) Using broad gestures to drip or pour paint onto a pictorial surface. Associated with mid-twentieth-century American Abstract Expressionists, such as Jackson Pollock.

adobe (p. 399) Sun-baked blocks made of clay mixed with straw. Also: buildings made with this material.

aedicula (p. 609) A decorative architectural frame, usually found around a niche, door, or window. An aedicula is made up of a **pediment** and **entablature** supported by **column**s or **pilaster**s.

aerial perspective (p. 626) See under **perspective**.

agora (p. 137) An open space in a Greek town used as a central gathering place or market. Compare **forum**.

aisle (p. 225) Passage or open corridor of a church, hall, or other building that parallels the main space, usually on both sides, and is delineated by a row, or **arcade**, of **column**s or **pier**s. Called side aisles when they flank the **nave** of a church.

akropolis (p. 128) The citadel of an ancient Greek city, located at its highest point and housing temples, a treasury, and sometimes a royal palace. The most famous is the Akropolis in Athens.

album (p. 796) A book consisting of a series of paintings or prints (album leaves) mounted into book form.

allegory (p. 627) In a work of art, an image (or images) that symbolizes an idea, concept, or principle, often moral or religious.

alloy (p. 23) A mixture of metals; different metals melted together.

altarpiece (p. xl) A painted or carved panel or ensemble of panels placed at the back of or behind and above an altar. Contains religious imagery (often specific to the place of worship for which it was made) that viewers can look at during liturgical ceremonies (especially the **Eucharist**) or personal devotions.

amalaka (p. 302) In Hindu architecture, the circular or square-shaped element on top of a spire (**shikhara**), often crowned with a **finial**, symbolizing the cosmos.

ambulatory (p. 224) The passage (walkway) around the **apse** in a church, especially a **basilica**, or around the central space in a **central-plan building**.

amphora (*pl.* **amphorae**) (p. 101) An ancient Greek or Roman jar for storing oil or wine, with an egg-shaped body and two curved handles.

animal style or **interlace** (p. 433) Decoration made of interwoven animals or serpents, often found in early medieval Northern European art.

ankh (p. 51) A looped cross signifying life, used by ancient Egyptians.

appropriation (p. xxviii) The practice of some Postmodern artists of adopting images in their entirety from other works of art or from visual culture for use in their own art. The act of recontextualizing the appropriated image allows the artist to critique both it and the time and place in which it was created.

apse (p. 192) A large semicircular or polygonal (and usually **vaulted**) recess on an end wall of a building. In a Christian church, it often contains the altar. "Apsidal" is the adjective describing the condition of having such a space.

arabesque (p. 267) European term for a type of linear surface decoration based on foliage and calligraphic forms, thought by Europeans to be typical of Islamic art and usually characterized by flowing lines and swirling shapes.

arcade (p. 170) A series of **arch**es, carried by **column**s or **pier**s and supporting a common wall or **lintel**. In a **blind arcade**, the arches and supports are **engaged** and have a purely decorative function.

arch (p. 95) In architecture, a curved structural element that spans an open space. Built from wedge-shaped stone blocks called **voussoir**s placed together and held at the top by a trapezoidal **keystone**. It forms an effective space-spanning and weight-bearing unit, but requires **buttress**es at each side to contain the outward **thrust** caused by the weight of the structure. *Corbeled arch*: an arch or **vault** formed by **course**s of stones, each of which projects beyond the lower course until the space is enclosed; usually finished with a **capstone**. *Horseshoe arch*: an arch of more than a half-circle; typical of western Islamic architecture. *Round arch*: an arch that displaces most of its weight, or downward thrust along its curving sides, transmitting that weight to adjacent supporting uprights (door or window **jamb**s, **column**s, or **pier**s). *Ogival arch*: a sharply pointed arch created by S-curves. *Relieving arch*: an arch built into a heavy wall just above a **post-and-lintel** structure (such as a gate, door, or window) to help support the wall above by transferring the load to the side walls. *Transverse arch*: an arch that connects the wall **pier**s on both sides of an interior space, up and over a stone **vault**.

Archaic smile (p. 114) The curved lips of an ancient Greek statues in the period c. 600–480 BCE, usually interpreted as a way of animating facial features.

architrave (p. 107) The bottom element in an **entablature**, beneath the **frieze** and the **cornice**.

archivolt (p. 478) A band of **molding** framing an **arch**, or a series of stone blocks that form an arch resting directly on flanking **column**s or **pier**s.

ashlar (p. 99) A highly finished, precisely cut block of stone. When laid in even **course**s, ashlar masonry creates a uniform face with fine joints. Often used as a facing on the visible exterior of a building, especially as a veneer for the **façade**. Also called **dressed stone**.

assemblage (p. 1026) Artwork created by gathering and manipulating two- and/or three-dimensional found objects.

astragal (p. 110) A thin convex decorative **molding**, often found on a Classical **entablature**, and usually decorated with a continuous row of beadlike circles.

atelier (p. 946) The studio or workshop of a master artist or craftsmaker, often including junior associates and apprentices.

atmospheric perspective (p. 183) See under **perspective**.

atrial cross (p. 943) A cross placed in the **atrium** of a church. In Colonial America, used to mark a gathering and teaching place.

atrium (p. 158) An unroofed interior courtyard or room in a Roman house, sometimes having a pool or garden, sometimes surrounded by **column**s. Also: the open courtyard in front of a Christian church; or an entrance area in modern architecture.

automatism (p. 1057) A technique in which artists abandon the usual intellectual control over their brushes or pencils to allow the subconscious to create the artwork without rational interference.

avant-garde (p. 972) Term derived from the French military word meaning "before the group," or "vanguard." Avant-garde denotes those artists or concepts of a strikingly new, experimental, or radical nature for their time.

axis (p. xxxii) In pictures, an implied line around which elements are composed or arranged. In buildings, a dominant line around which parts of the structure are organized and along which human movement or attention is concentrated.

axis mundi (p. 300) A concept of an "axis of the world," which marks sacred sites and denotes a link between the human and celestial realms. For example, in Buddhist art, the axis mundi can be marked by monumental free-standing decorative pillars.

baldachin (p. 472) A canopy (whether suspended from the ceiling, projecting from a wall, or supported by columns) placed over an honorific or sacred space such as a throne or church altar.

bar tracery (p. 510) See under **tracery**.

barbarian (p. 149) A term used by the ancient Greeks and Romans to label all foreigners outside their cultural orbit (e.g., Celts, Goths, Vikings). The word derives from an imitation of what the "barblings" of their language sounded like to those who could not understand it.

barrel vault (p. 187) See under **vault**.

bas-relief (p. 325) Another term for low relief ("bas" is the French word for "low"). See under **relief sculpture**.

basilica (p. 191) A large rectangular building. Often built with a **clerestory**, side **aisles** separated from the center **nave** by **colonnades**, and an **apse** at one or both ends. Originally Roman centers for administration, later adapted to Christian church use.

bay (p. 170) A unit of space defined by architectural elements such as **columns**, **piers**, and walls.

beehive tomb (p. 98) A **corbel-vaulted** tomb, conical in shape like a beehive, and covered by an earthen mound.

Benday dots (p. 1095) In modern printing and typesetting, the individual dots that, together with many others, make up lettering and images. Often machine- or computer-generated, the dots are very small and closely spaced to give the effect of density and richness of tone.

bilum (p. 865) Netted bags made mainly by women throughout the central highlands of New Guinea. The bags can be used for everyday purposes or even to carry the bones of the recently deceased as a sign of mourning.

biomorphic (p. 1058) Denoting the biologically or organically inspired shapes and forms that were routinely included in abstracted Modern art in the early twentieth century.

black-figure (p. 105) A technique of ancient Greek **ceramic** decoration in which black figures are painted on a red clay ground. Compare **red-figure**.

blackware (p. 855) A **ceramic** technique that produces pottery with a primarily black surface with **matte** and glossy patterns on the surface.

blind arcade (p. 780) See under **arcade**.

bodhisattva (p. 311) In Buddhism, a being who has attained enlightenment but chooses to remain in this world in order to help others advance spiritually. Also defined as a potential Buddha.

Book of Hours (p. 549) A prayer book for private use, containing a calendar, services for the canonical hours, and sometimes special prayers.

boss (p. 556) A decorative knoblike element that can be found in many places, e.g. at the intersection of a Gothic **rib vault** or as a buttonlike projection on metalwork.

bracket, bracketing (p. 341) An architectural element that projects from a wall to support a horizontal part of a building, such as beams or the eaves of a roof.

buon fresco (p. 87) See under **fresco**.

burin (p. 592) A metal instrument used in **engraving** to cut lines into the metal plate. The sharp end of the burin is trimmed to give a diamond-shaped cutting point, while the other end is finished with a wooden handle that fits into the engraver's palm.

buttress, buttressing (p. 170) A projecting support built against an external wall, usually to counteract the lateral **thrust** of a **vault** or **arch** within. In Gothic church architecture, a **flying buttress** is an arched bridge above the **aisle** roof that extends from the upper **nave** wall, where the lateral thrust of the main vault is greatest, down to a solid **pier**.

cairn (p. 17) A pile of stones or earth and stones that served both as a prehistoric burial site and as a marker for underground tombs.

calligraphy (p. 275) Handwriting as an art form.

calyx krater (p. 119) See under **krater**.

calotype (p. 969) The first photographic process utilizing negatives and paper positives; invented by William Henry Fox Talbot in the late 1830s.

came (*pl.* **cames**) (p. 501) A lead strip used in the making of leaded or **stained-glass** windows. Cames have an indented groove on the sides into which individual pieces of glass are fitted to make the overall design.

cameo (p. 172) Gemstone, clay, glass, or shell having layers of color, carved in low relief (see under **relief sculpture**) to create an image and ground of different colors.

camera obscura (p. 750) An early cameralike device used in the Renaissance and later for recording images from the real world. It consists of a dark box (or room) with a hole in one side (sometimes fitted with a lens). The camera obscura operates when bright light shines through the hole, casting an upside-down image of an object outside onto the inside wall of the box.

canon of proportions (p. 64) A set of ideal mathematical ratios in art based on measurements, as in the proportional relationships between the basic elements of the human body.

canopic jar (p. 53) In ancient Egyptian culture, a special jar used to store the major organs of a body before embalming.

capital (p. 110) The sculpted block that tops a **column**. According to the **convention**s of the orders, capitals include different decorative elements (see **order**). A *historiated* capital is one displaying a figural composition and/or narrative scenes.

capriccio (*pl.* *capricci*) (p. 915) A painting or print of a fantastic, imaginary landscape, usually with architecture.

capstone (p. 17) The final, topmost stone in a **corbeled arch** or vault, which joins the sides and completes the structure.

cartoon (p. 501) A full-scale drawing of a design that will be executed in another **medium**, such as wall painting, **tapestry**, or **stained glass**.

cartouche (p. 187) A frame for a **hieroglyphic** inscription formed by a rope design surrounding an oval space. Used to signify a sacred or honored name. Also: in architecture, a decorative device or plaque, usually with a plain center used for inscriptions or epitaphs.

caryatid (p. 107) A sculpture of a draped female figure acting as a **column** supporting an **entablature**.

cassone (*pl.* *cassoni*) (p. 616) An Italian dowry chest often highly decorated with carvings, paintings, inlaid designs, and gilt embellishments.

catacomb (p. 215) An underground cemetery consisting of tunnels on different levels, having niches for urns and **sarcophagi** and often incorporating rooms (**cubicula**).

cathedral (p. 220) The principal Christian church in a diocese, the bishop's administrative center and housing his throne (*cathedra*).

celadon (p. 358) A high-fired, transparent **glaze** of pale bluish-green hue whose principal coloring agent is an oxide of iron. In China and Korea, such glazes were typically applied over a pale gray **stoneware** body, though Chinese potters sometimes applied them over **porcelain** bodies during the Ming (1368–1644) and Qing (1644–1911) dynasties. Chinese potters invented celadon glazes and initiated the continuous production of celadon-glazed wares as early as the third century CE.

cella (p. 108) The principal interior room at the center of a Greek or Roman temple within which the cult statue was usually housed. Also called the **naos**.

celt (p. 383) A smooth, oblong stone or metal object, shaped like an axe-head.

cenotaph (p. 771) A funerary monument commemorating an individual or group buried elsewhere.

centering (p. 170) A temporary structure that supports a masonry **arch**, **vault**, or **dome** during construction until the mortar is fully dried and the masonry is self-sustaining.

central-plan building (p. 225) Any structure designed with a primary central space surrounded by symmetrical areas on each side, e.g., a **rotunda**.

ceramics (p. 20) A general term covering all types of wares made from fired clay.

chacmool (p. 396) In Maya sculpture, a half-reclining figure probably representing an offering bearer.

chaitya (p. 305) A type of Buddhist temple found in India. Built in the form of a hall or **basilica**, a *chaitya* hall is highly decorated with sculpture and usually is carved from a cave or natural rock location. It houses a sacred shrine or **stupa** for worship.

chamfer (p. 780) The slanted surface produced when an angle is trimmed or beveled, common in building and metalwork.

chasing (p. 432) Ornamentation made on metal by incising or hammering the surface.

château (*pl.* **châteaux**) (p. 693) A French country house or residential castle. A *château fort* is a military castle incorporating defensive works such as towers and battlements.

chattri (p. 780) In Indian architecture, a decorative pavilion with an umbrella-shaped **dome**.

chevron (p. 357) A decorative or heraldic motif of repeated Vs; a zigzag pattern.

chiaroscuro (p. 636) An Italian word designating the contrast of dark and light in a painting, drawing, or print. *Chiaroscuro* creates spatial depth and volumetric forms through gradations in the intensity of light and shadow.

choir (p. 225) The part of a church reserved for the clergy, monks, or nuns, either between the **transept** crossing and the **apse** or extending farther into the **nave**; separated from the rest of the church by screens or walls and fitted with stalls (seats).

cista (*pl.* *cistae*) (p. 157) Cylindrical containers used in antiquity by wealthy women as a case for toiletry articles such as a mirror.

clerestory (p. 57) In a **basilica**, the topmost zone of a wall with windows, extending above the **aisle** roofs. Provides direct light into the **nave**.

cloisonné (p. 257) An **enamel**ing technique in which artists affix wires or strips to a metal surface to delineate designs and create compartments (*cloisons*) that they subsequently fill with enamel.

cloister (p. 448) An enclosed space, open to the sky, especially within a monastery, surrounded by an **arcade**d walkway, often having a fountain and garden. Since the most important monastic buildings (e.g., dormitory, refectory, church) open off the cloister, it represents the center of the monastic world.

codex (*pl.* **codices**) (p. 245) A book, or a group of **manuscript** pages (folios), held together by stitching or other binding along one edge.

coffer (p. 197) A recessed decorative panel used to decorate ceilings or **vaults**. The use of coffers is called coffering.

coiling (p. 848) A technique in basketry. In coiled baskets a spiraling coil, braid, or rope of material is held in place by stitching or interweaving to create a permanent shape.

collage (p. 1025) A composition made of cut and pasted scraps of materials, sometimes with lines or forms added by the artist.

colonnade (p. 69) A row of **column**s, supporting a straight **lintel** (as in a **porch** or **portico**) or a series of **arch**es (an **arcade**).

colophon (p. 438) The data placed at the end of a book listing the book's author, publisher, illuminator, and other information related to its production. In East Asian **handscroll**s, the inscriptions which follow the painting are also called colophons.

column (p. 110) An architectural element used for support and/or decoration. Consists of a rounded or polygonal vertical **shaft** placed on a **base** and topped by a decorative **capital**. In Classical architecture, columns are built in accordance with the rules of one of the architectural **order**s. They can be free-standing or attached to a background wall (**engaged**).

combine (p. 1087) Combination of painting and sculpture using nontraditional art materials.

complementary color (p. 995) The primary and secondary colors across from each other on the color wheel (red and green, blue and orange, yellow and purple). When juxtaposed, the intensity of both colors increases. When mixed together, they negate each other to make a neutral gray-brown.

Composite order (p. 161) See under **order**.

composite pose or **image** (p. 10) Combining different viewpoints within a single representation.

composition (p. xxix) The overall arrangement, organizing design, or structure of a work of art.

conch (p. 236) A halfdome.

connoisseur (p. 289) A French word meaning "an expert," and signifying the study and evaluation of art based primarily on formal, visual, and stylistic analysis. A connoisseur studies the style and technique of an object to assess its relative quality and identify its maker through visual comparison with other works of secure authorship. See also **Formalism**.

continuous narrative (p. 245) See under **narrative image**.

contrapposto (p. 120) Italian term meaning "set against," used to describe the Classical convention of representing human figures with opposing alternations of tension and relaxation on either side of a central **axis** to imbue figures with a sense of the potential for movement.

convention (p. 31) A traditional way of representing forms.

corbel, corbeling (p. 19) An early roofing and arching technique in which each **course** of stone projects slightly beyond the previous layer (a corbel) until the uppermost corbels meet; see also under **arch**. Also: **bracket**s that project from a wall.

corbeled vault (p. 99) See under **vault**.

Corinthian order (p. 108) See under **order**.

cornice (p. 110) The uppermost section of a Classical **entablature**. More generally, a horizontally projecting element found at the top of a building wall or **pedestal**. A *raking cornice* is formed by the junction of two slanted cornices, most often found in **pediment**s.

course (p. 99) A horizontal layer of stone used in building.

crenellation, crenellated (p. 44) Alternating high and low sections of a wall, giving a notched appearance and creating permanent defensive shields on top of fortified buildings.

crocket (p. 587) A stylized leaf used as decoration along the outer angle of spires, pinnacles, gables, and around **capital**s in Gothic architecture.

cruciform (p. 228) Of anything that is cross-shaped, as in the cruciform plan of a church.

cubiculum (*pl.* **cubicula**) (p. 220) A small private room for burials in a **catacomb**.

cuneiform (p. 28) An early form of writing with wedge-shaped marks impressed into wet clay with a **stylus**, primarily used by ancient Mesopotamians.

curtain wall (p. 1045) A wall in a building that does not support any of the weight of the structure.

cyclopean (p. 93) A method of construction using huge blocks of rough-hewn stone. Any large-scale, monumental building project that impresses by sheer size. Named after the Cyclopes (sing. Cyclops), one-eyed giants of legendary strength in Greek myths.

cylinder seal (p. 35) A small cylindrical stone decorated with **incised** patterns. When rolled across soft clay or wax, the resulting raised pattern or design served in Mesopotamian and Indus Valley cultures as an identifying signature.

dado (*pl.* **dadoes**) (p. 161) The lower part of a wall, differentiated in some way (by a **molding** or different coloring or paneling) from the upper section.

daguerreotype (p. 969) An early photographic process that makes a positive print on a light-sensitized copperplate; invented and marketed in 1839 by Louis-Jacques-Mandé Daguerre.

dendrochronology (p. xxxvi) The dating of wood based on the patterns of the tree's growth rings.

dentils (p. 110) A row of projecting rectangular blocks forming a **molding** or running beneath a **cornice** in Classical architecture.

desert varnish (p. 406) A naturally occurring coating that turns rock faces into dark surfaces. Artists would draw images by scraping through the dark surface and revealing the color of the underlying rock. Extensively used in southwest North America.

diptych (p. 212) Two panels of equal size (usually decorated with paintings or reliefs) hinged together.

dogu (p. 362) Small human figurines made in Japan during the Jomon period. Shaped from clay, the figures have exaggerated expressions and are in contorted poses. They were probably used in religious rituals.

dolmen (p. 17) A prehistoric structure made up of two or more large upright stones supporting a large, flat, horizontal slab or slabs.

dome (p. 187) A rounded **vault**, usually over a circular space. Consists of curved masonry and can vary in shape from hemispherical to bulbous to ovoidal. May use a supporting vertical wall (**drum**), from which the vault springs, and may be crowned by an open space (**oculus**) and/or an exterior **lantern**. When a dome is built over a square space, an intermediate element is required to make the transition to a circular drum. There are two systems. A dome on **pendentives** incorporates arched, sloping intermediate sections of wall that carry the weight and **thrust** of the dome to heavily **buttress**ed supporting **pier**s. A dome on **squinch**es uses an arch built into the wall (squinch) in the upper corners of the space to carry the weight of the dome across the corners of the square space below. A halfdome or **conch** may cover a semicircular space.

domino construction (p. 1045) System of building construction introduced by the architect Le Corbusier in which reinforced concrete floor slabs are floated on six free-standing posts placed as if at the positions of the six dots on a domino playing piece.

Doric order (p. 108) See **order**.

dressed stone (p. 84) Another term for **ashlar**.

drillwork (p. 188) The technique of using a drill for the creation of certain effects in sculpture.

drum (p. 110) The circular wall that supports a **dome**. Also: a segment of the circular **shaft** of a **column**.

drypoint (p. 748) An **intaglio** printmaking process by which a metal (usually copper) plate is directly inscribed with a pointed instrument (**stylus**). The resulting design of scratched lines is inked, wiped, and printed. Also: the print made by this process.

earthenware (p. 20) A low-fired, opaque **ceramic** ware, employing humble clays that are naturally heat-resistant and remain porous after firing unless **glaze**d. Earthenware occurs in a range of earth-toned colors, from white and tan to gray and black, with tan predominating.

earthwork (p. 1102) Usually very large-scale, outdoor artwork that is produced by altering the natural environment.

echinus (p. 110) A cushionlike circular element found below the **abacus** of a Doric **capital**. Also: a similarly shaped **molding** (usually with egg-and-dart motifs) underneath the **volute**s of an Ionic capital.

electronic spin resonance (p. 12) Method that uses magnetic field and microwave irradiation to date material such as tooth enamel and its surrounding soil.

elevation (p. 108) The arrangement, proportions, and details of any vertical side or face of a building. Also: an architectural drawing showing an exterior or interior wall of a building.

embroidery (p. 397) Stitches applied in a decorative pattern on top of an already-woven fabric ground.

en plein air (p. 987) French term (meaning "in the open air") describing the Impressionist practice of painting outdoors so artists could have direct access to the fleeting effects of light and atmosphere while working.

enamel (p. 255) Powdered, then molten, glass applied to a metal surface, and used by artists to create designs. After firing, the glass forms an opaque or transparent substance that fuses to the metal background. Also: an object created by the enameling technique. See also *cloisonné*.

encaustic (p. 246) A painting **medium** using pigments mixed with hot wax.

engaged (p. 171) Of an architectural feature, usually a **column**, attached to a wall.

engraving (p. 592) An **intaglio** printmaking process of inscribing an image, design, or letters onto a metal or wood surface from which a print is made. An engraving is usually drawn with a sharp implement (**burin**) directly onto the surface of the plate. Also: the print made from this process.

entablature (p. 107) In the Classical **order**s, the horizontal elements above the **column**s and **capital**s. The entablature consists of, from bottom to top, an **architrave**, a **frieze**, and a **cornice**.

entasis (p. 108) A slight swelling of the **shaft** of a Greek **column**. The optical illusion of entasis makes the column appear from afar to be straight.

esquisse (p. 946) French for "sketch." A quickly executed drawing or painting conveying the overall idea for a finished painting.

etching (p. 748) An **intaglio** printmaking process in which a metal plate is coated with acid-resistant resin and then inscribed with a **stylus** in a design, revealing the plate below. The plate is then immersed in acid, and the exposed metal of the design is eaten away by the acid. The resin is removed, leaving the design etched permanently into the metal and the plate ready to be inked, wiped, and printed.

Eucharist (p. 220) The central rite of the Christian Church, from the Greek word for "thanksgiving." Also known as the Mass or Holy Communion, it reenacts Christ's sacrifice on the cross and commemorates the Last Supper. According to traditional Catholic Christian belief, consecrated bread and wine become the body and blood of Christ; in Protestant belief, bread and wine symbolize the body and blood.

exedra (*pl.* **exedrae**) (p. 197) In architecture, a semicircular niche. On a small scale, often used as decoration, whereas larger exedrae can form interior spaces (such as an **apse**).

expressionism (p. 149) Artistic styles in which aspects of works of art are exaggerated to evoke subjective emotions rather than to portray objective reality or elicit a rational response.

façade (p. 52) The face or front wall of a building.

faience (p. 88) Type of **ceramic** covered with colorful, opaque glazes that form a smooth, impermeable surface. First developed in ancient Egypt.

fang ding (p. 334) A square or rectangular bronze vessel with four legs. The *fang ding* was used for ritual offerings in ancient China during the Shang dynasty.

fête galante (p. 910) A subject in painting depicting well-dressed people at leisure in a park or country setting. It is most often associated with eighteenth-century French Rococo painting.

filigree (p. 90) Delicate, lacelike ornamental work.

fillet (p. 110) The flat ridge between the carved-out **flutes** of a **column shaft**.

finial (p. 780) A knoblike architectural decoration usually found at the top point of a spire, pinnacle, canopy, or gable. Also found on furniture. Also the ornamental top of a staff.

flutes (p. 110) In architecture, evenly spaced, rounded parallel vertical grooves incised on **shaft**s of **column**s or on columnar elements such as **pilaster**s.

flying buttress (p. 503) See under **buttress**.

flying gallop (p. 88) A non-naturalistic pose in which animals are depicted hovering above the ground with legs fully extended backwards and forwards to signify that they are running.

foreshortening (p. xxxi) The illusion created on a flat surface by which figures and objects appear to recede or project sharply into space. Accomplished according to the rules of **perspective**.

formal analysis (p. xxix) An exploration of the visual character that artists bring to their works through the expressive use of elements such as line, form, color, and light, and through its overall structure or composition.

Formalism (p. 1073) An approach to the understanding, appreciation, and valuation of art based almost solely on considerations of form. The Formalist's approach tends to regard an artwork as independent of its time and place of making.

forum (p. 176) A Roman town center; site of temples and administrative buildings and used as a market or gathering area for the citizens.

fresco (p. 81) A painting technique in which water-based pigments are applied to a plaster surface. If the plaster is painted when wet, the color is absorbed by the plaster, becoming a permanent part of the wall (*buon fresco*). *Fresco secco* is created by painting on dried plaster, and the color may eventually flake off. Murals made by both these techniques are called frescos.

frieze (p. 107) The middle element of an **entablature**, between the **architrave** and the **cornice**. Usually decorated with sculpture, painting, or **molding**s. Also: any continuous flat band with **relief sculpture** or painted decoration.

frottage (p. 1057) A design produced by laying a piece of paper over a textured surface and rubbing with charcoal or other soft **medium**.

fusuma (p. 820) Sliding doors covered with paper, used in traditional Japanese construction. *Fusuma* are often highly decorated with paintings and colored backgrounds.

gallery (p. 236) A roofed passageway with one or both of its long sides open to the air. In church architecture, the story found above the side **aisle**s of a church or across the width at the end of the **nave** or **transept**s, usually open to and overlooking the area below. Also: a building or hall in which art is displayed or sold.

garbhagriha (p. 302) From the Sanskrit word meaning "womb chamber," a small room or shrine in a Hindu temple containing a holy image.

genre painting (p. 714) A term used to loosely categorize paintings depicting scenes of everyday life, including (among others) domestic interiors, parties, inn scenes, and street scenes.

geoglyph (p. 399) Earthen design on a colossal scale, often created in a landscape as if to be seen from an aerial viewpoint.

gesso (p. 546) A ground made from glue, gypsum, and/or chalk, used as the ground of a wood panel or the priming layer of a canvas. Provides a smooth surface for painting.

gilding (p. 90) The application of paper-thin gold leaf or gold pigment to an object made from another **medium** (for example, a sculpture or painting). Usually used as a decorative finishing detail.

giornata (*pl.* **giornate**) (p. 539) Adopted from the Italian term meaning "a day's work," a *giornata* is the section of a **fresco** plastered and painted in a single day.

glazing (p. 600) In **ceramics**, an outermost layer of vitreous liquid (**glaze**) that, upon firing, renders the ware waterproof and forms a decorative surface. In painting, a technique used with oil **media** in which a transparent layer of paint (glaze) is laid over another, usually lighter, painted or glazed area. In architecture, the process of filling openings in a building with windows of clear or **stained glass**.

gold leaf (p. 47) Paper-thin sheets of hammered gold that are used in **gilding**. In some cases (such as Byzantine **icon**s), also used as a ground for paintings.

gopura (p. 775) The towering gateway to an Indian Hindu temple complex.

Grand Manner (p. 923) An elevated style of painting popular in the eighteenth century in which the artist looked to the ancients and to the Renaissance for inspiration; for portraits as well as history painting, the artist would adopt the poses, compositions, and attitudes of Renaissance and antique models.

Grand Tour (p. 913) Popular during the eighteenth and nineteenth centuries, an extended tour of cultural sites in France and Italy intended to finish the education of a young upper-class person primarily from Britain or North America.

granulation (p. 90) A technique of decoration in which metal granules, or tiny metal balls, are fused onto a metal surface.

graphic arts (p. 698) A term referring to those arts that are drawn or printed and that utilize paper as the primary support.

grattage (p. 1057) A pattern created by scraping off layers of paint from a canvas laid over a textured surface. Compare **frottage**.

grid (p. 65) A system of regularly spaced horizontally and vertically crossed lines that gives regularity to an architectural plan or in the composition of a work of art. Also: in painting, a grid is used to allow designs to be enlarged or transferred easily.

grisaille (p. 540) A style of monochromatic painting in shades of gray. Also: a painting made in this style.

groin vault (p. 187) See under **vault**.

grozing (p. 501) Chipping away at the edges of a piece of glass to achieve the precise shape needed for inclusion in the composition of a **stained-glass** window.

guild (p. 419) An association of artists or craftsmakers. Medieval and Renaissance guilds had great economic power, as they controlled the marketing of their members' products and provided economic protection, political solidarity, and training in the craft to its members. The painters' guild was usually dedicated to St. Luke, their patron saint.

hall church (p. 521) A church with **nave** and **aisle**s of the same height, giving the impression of a large, open hall.

halo (p. 215) A circle of light that surrounds and frames the heads of emperors and holy figures to signify their power and/or sanctity. Also known as a nimbus.

handscroll (p. 343) A long, narrow, horizontal painting or text (or combination thereof) common in Chinese and Japanese art and of a size intended for individual use. A handscroll is stored wrapped tightly around a wooden pin and is unrolled for viewing or reading.

hanging scroll (p. 796) In Chinese and Japanese art, a vertical painting or text mounted within sections of silk. At the top is a semicircular rod; at the bottom is a round dowel. Hanging scrolls are kept rolled and tied except for special occasions, when they are hung for display, contemplation, or commemoration.

haniwa (p. 362) Pottery forms, including cylinders, buildings, and human figures, that were placed on top of Japanese tombs or burial mounds during the Kofun period (300–552 CE).

Happening (p. 1087) An art form developed by Allan Kaprow in the 1960s, incorporating performance, theater, and visual images. A Happening was organized without a specific narrative or intent; with audience participation, the event proceeded according to chance and individual improvisation.

hemicycle (p. 512) A semicircular interior space or structure.

henge (p. 17) A circular area enclosed by stones or wood posts set up by Neolithic peoples. It is usually bounded by a ditch and raised embankment.

hierarchic scale (p. 27) The use of differences in size to indicate relative importance. For example, with human figures, the larger the figure, the greater her or his importance.

hieratic (p. 484) Highly stylized, severe, and detached, often in relation to a strict religious tradition.

hieroglyph (p. 52) Picture writing; words and ideas rendered in the form of pictorial symbols.

high relief (p. 307) See under **relief sculpture**.

historiated capital (p. 484) See under **capital**.

historicism (p. 965) The strong consciousness of and attention to the institutions, themes, styles, and forms of the past, made accessible by historical research, textual study, and archaeology.

history paintings (p. 926) Paintings based on historical, mythological, or biblical narratives. Once considered the noblest form of art, history paintings generally convey a high moral or intellectual idea and are often painted in a grand pictorial style.

horizon line (p. 569) A horizontal "line" formed by the implied meeting point of earth and sky. In **linear perspective**, the **vanishing point** or points are located on this "line."

horseshoe arch (p. 272) See under **arch**.

hue (p. 77) Pure color. The saturation or intensity of the hue depends on the purity of the color. Its value depends on its lightness or darkness.

hydria (p. 139) A large ancient Greek or Roman jar with three handles (horizontal ones at both sides and one vertical at the back), used for storing water.

hypostyle hall (p. 66) A large interior room characterized by many closely spaced **column**s that support its roof.

icon (p. 246) An image representing a sacred figure or event in the Byzantine (later the Orthodox) Church. Icons are venerated by the faithful, who believe their prayers are transmitted through them to God.

iconic image (p. 215) A picture that expresses or embodies an intangible concept or idea.

iconoclasm (p. 248) The banning and/or destruction of images, especially **icon**s and religious art. Iconoclasm in eighth- and ninth-century Byzantium and sixteenth- and seventeenth-century Protestant territories arose from differing beliefs about the power, meaning, function, and purpose of imagery in religion.

iconography (p. xxxiii) Identifying and studying the subject matter and **conventional** symbols in works of art.

iconology (p. xxxv) Interpreting works of art as embodiments of cultural situation by placing them within broad social, political, religious, and intellectual contexts.

iconophile (p. 247) From the Greek for "lover of images." In periods of **iconoclasm**, iconophiles advocate the continued use of sacred images.

idealization (p. 134) A process in art through which artists strive to make their forms and figures attain perfection, based on pervading cultural values and/or their own personal ideals.

illumination (p. 431) A painting on paper or parchment used as an illustration and/or decoration in a **manuscript** or **album**. Usually richly colored, often supplemented by gold and other precious materials. The artists are referred to as illuminators. Also: the technique of decorating manuscripts with such paintings.

impasto (p. 749) Thick applications of pigment that give a painting a palpable surface texture.

impluvium (p. 178) A pool under a roof opening that collected rainwater in the **atrium** of a Roman house.

impost block (p. 170) A block of masonry imposed between the top of a **pier** or above the **capital** of a **column** in order to provide extra support at the springing of an **arch**.

incising (p. 118) A technique in which a design or inscription is cut into a hard surface with a sharp instrument. Such a surface is said to be incised.

ink painting (p. 812) A monochromatic style of painting developed in China, using black ink with gray washes.

inlay (p. 30) To set pieces of a material or materials into a surface to form a design. Also: material used in or decoration formed by this technique.

installation, installation art (p. 1051) Contemporary art created for a specific site, especially a gallery or outdoor area, that creates a complete and controlled environment.

intaglio (p. 592) A technique in which the design is carved out of the surface of an object, such as an engraved seal stone. In the **graphic arts**, intaglio includes **engraving**, **etching**, and **drypoint**—all processes in which ink transfers to paper from incised, ink-filled lines cut into a metal plate.

intarsia (p. 618) Technique of **inlay** decoration using variously colored woods.

intuitive perspective (p. 182) See under **perspective**.

Ionic order (p. 107) See under **order**.

iwan (p. 277) In Islamic architecture, a large, vaulted chamber with a monumental arched opening on one side.

jamb (p. 478) In architecture, the vertical element found on both sides of an opening in a wall, and supporting an **arch** or **lintel**.

Japonisme (p. 996) A style in French and American nineteenth-century art that was highly influenced by Japanese art, especially prints.

jasperware (p. 919) A fine-grained, unglazed, white **ceramic** developed in the eighteenth century by Josiah Wedgwood, often with raised designs remaining white above a background surface colored by metallic oxides.

Jataka **tales** (p. 303) In Buddhism, stories associated with the previous lives of Shakyamuni, the historical Buddha.

joggled voussoirs (p. 268) Interlocking **voussoir**s in an **arch** or **lintel**, often of contrasting materials for colorful effect.

joined-block sculpture (p. 373) Large-scale wooden sculpture constructed by a method developed in Japan. The entire work is made from smaller hollow blocks, each individually carved, and assembled when complete. The joined-block technique allowed production of larger sculpture, as the multiple joints alleviate the problems of drying and cracking found with sculpture carved from a single block.

kantharos (p. 117) A type of ancient Greek goblet with two large handles and a wide mouth.

keep (p. 477) The innermost and strongest structure or central tower of a medieval castle, sometimes used as living quarters, as well as for defense. Also called a donjon.

kente (p. 892) A woven cloth made by the Ashanti peoples of West Africa. *Kente* cloth is woven in long, narrow pieces featuring complex and colorful patterns, which are then sewn together.

key block (p. 828) The master block in the production of a colored **woodblock print**, which requires different blocks for each color. The key block is a flat piece of wood upon which the outlines for the entire design of the print were first drawn on its surface and then all but these outlines were carved away with a knife. These outlines serve as a guide for the accurate **registration** or alignment of the other blocks needed to add colors to specific parts of a print.

keystone (p. 170) The topmost **voussoir** at the center of an **arch**, and the last block to be placed. The pressure of this block holds the arch together. Often of a larger size and/or decorated.

kiln (p. 20) An oven designed to produce enough heat for the baking, or firing, of clay, for the melting of the glass used in **enamel** work, and for the fixing of vitreous paint on **stained glass**.

kiva (p. 405) A subterranean, circular room used as a ceremonial center in some Native American cultures.

kondo (p. 366) The main hall inside a Japanese Buddhist temple where the images of Buddha are housed.

korambo (p. 865) A ceremonial or spirit house in Pacific cultures, reserved for the men of a village and used as a meeting place as well as to hide religious artifacts from the uninitiated.

kore (*pl.* **korai**) (p. 114) An Archaic Greek statue of a young woman.

koru (p. 872) A design depicting a curling stalk with a bulb at the end that resembles a young tree fern; often found in Maori art.

kouros (*pl.* **kouroi**) (p. 114) An Archaic Greek statue of a young man or boy.

kowhaiwhai (p. 872) Painted curvilinear patterns often found in Maori art.

krater (p. 99) An ancient Greek vessel for mixing wine and water, with many subtypes that each have a distinctive shape. *Calyx krater*: a bell-shaped vessel with handles near the base that resembles a flower calyx. *Volute krater*: a krater with handles shaped like scrolls.

Kufic (p. 275) An ornamental, angular Arabic script.

kylix (p. 120) A shallow ancient Greek cup, used for drinking, with a wide mouth and small handles near the rim.

lacquer (p. 824) A type of hard, glossy surface varnish, originally developed for use on objects in East Asian cultures, made from the sap of the Asian sumac or from shellac, a resinous secretion from the lac insect. Lacquer can be layered and manipulated or combined with pigments and other materials for various decorative effects.

lakshana (p. 306) The 32 marks of the historical Buddha. The *lakshana* include, among others, the Buddha's golden body, his long arms, the wheel impressed on his palms and the soles of his feet, and his elongated earlobes.

lamassu (p. 42) Supernatural guardian-protector of ancient Near Eastern palaces and throne rooms, often represented sculpturally as a combination of the bearded head of a man, powerful body of a lion or bull, wings of an eagle, and the horned headdress of a god, usually possessing five legs.

lancet (p. 505) A tall, narrow window crowned by a sharply pointed arch, typically found in Gothic architecture.

lantern (p. 464) A turretlike structure situated on a roof, vault, or dome, with windows that allow light into the space below.

lekythos (*pl.* **lekythoi**) (p. 141) A slim ancient Greek oil vase with one handle and a narrow mouth.

linear perspective (p. 595) See under **perspective**.

linga shrine (p. 315) A place of worship centered on an object or representation in the form of a phallus (the lingam), which symbolizes the power of the Hindu god Shiva.

lintel (p. 18) A horizontal element of any material carried by two or more vertical supports to form an opening.

literati painting (p. 793) A style of painting that reflects the taste of the educated class of East Asian intellectuals and scholars. Characteristics include an appreciation for the antique, small scale, and an intimate connection between maker and audience.

lithography (p. 953) Process of making a print (lithograph) from a design drawn on a flat stone block with greasy crayon. Ink is applied to the wet stone and adheres only to the greasy areas of the design.

loggia (p. 534) Italian term for a **gallery**. Often used as a corridor between buildings or around a courtyard, a loggia usually features an **arcade** or **colonnade**.

longitudinal-plan building (p. 225) Any structure designed with a rectangular shape and a longitudinal axis. In a cross-shaped building, the main arm of the building would be longer than any arms that cross it. For example, a **basilica**.

lost-wax casting (p. 36) A method of casting metal, such as bronze. A wax mold is covered with clay and plaster, then fired, thus melting the wax and leaving a hollow form. Molten metal is then poured into the hollow space and slowly cooled. When the hardened clay and plaster exterior shell is removed, a solid metal form remains to be smoothed and polished.

low relief (p. 40) See under **relief sculpture**.

lunette (p. 221) A semicircular wall area, framed by an **arch** over a door or window. Can be either plain or decorated.

lusterware (p. 277) Pottery decorated with metallic **glaze**s.

madrasa (p. 277) An Islamic institution of higher learning, where teaching is focused on theology and law.

maenad (p. 104) In ancient Greece, a female devotee of the wine god Dionysos who participated in orgiastic rituals. Often depicted with swirling drapery to indicate wild movement or dance. Also called a Bacchante, after Bacchus, the Roman equivalent of Dionysos.

majolica (p. 573) Pottery painted with a tin **glaze** that, when fired, gives a lustrous and colorful surface.

mandala (p. 302) An image of the cosmos represented by an arrangement of circles or concentric geometric shapes containing diagrams or images. Used for meditation and contemplation by Buddhists.

mandapa (p. 302) In a Hindu temple, an open hall dedicated to ritual worship.

mandorla (p. 479) Light encircling, or emanating from, the entire figure of a sacred person.

manuscript (p. 244) A hand-written book or document.

maqsura (p. 272) An enclosure in a Muslim **mosque**, near the *mihrab*, designated for dignitaries.

martyrium (*pl.* **martyria**) (p. 238) A church, chapel, or shrine built over the grave of a Christian martyr.

mastaba (p. 53) A flat-topped, one-story structure with slanted walls built over an ancient Egyptian underground tomb.

matte (p. 573) Of a smooth surface that is without shine or luster.

mausoleum (p. 175) A monumental building used as a tomb. Named after the tomb of King Mausolos erected at Halikarnassos around 350 BCE.

medallion (p. 222) Any round ornament or decoration. Also: a large medal.

medium (*pl.* **media**) (p. xxix) The material from which a work of art is made.

megalith (*adj.* **megalithic**) (p. 16) A large stone used in some prehistoric architecture.

megaron (p. 93) The main hall of a Mycenaean palace or grand house.

memento mori (p. 909) From Latin for "remember that you must die." An object, such as a skull or extinguished candle, typically found in a *vanitas* image, symbolizing the transience of life.

menorah (p. 186) A Jewish lampstand with seven or nine branches; the nine-branched menorah is used during the celebration of Hanukkah. Representations of the seven-branched menorah, once used in the Temple of Jerusalem, became a symbol of Judaism.

metope (p. 110) The carved or painted rectangular panel between the **triglyph**s of a Doric **frieze**.

mihrab (p. 265) A recess or niche that distinguishes the wall oriented toward Mecca (*qibla*) in a **mosque**.

millefiori (p. 434) A glassmaking technique in which rods of differently colored glass are fused in a long bundle that is subsequently sliced to produce disks or beads with small-scale, multicolor patterns. The term derives from the Italian for "a thousand flowers."

minaret (p. 274) A tower on or near a **mosque** from which Muslims are called to prayer five times a day.

minbar (p. 265) A high platform or pulpit in a **mosque**.

miniature (p. 245) Anything small. In painting, miniatures may be illustrations within **album**s or **manuscript**s or intimate portraits.

mirador (p. 280) In Spanish and Islamic palace architecture, a very large window or room with windows, and sometimes balconies, providing views to interior courtyards or the exterior landscape.

mithuna (p. 305) The amorous male and female couples in Buddhist sculpture, usually found at the entrance to a sacred building. The *mithuna* symbolizes the harmony and fertility of life.

moai (p. 875) Statues found in Polynesia, carved from tufa, a yellowish brown volcanic stone, and depicting the human form. Nearly 1,000 of these statues have been found on the island of Rapa Nui but their significance has been a matter of speculation.

modeling (p. xxix) In painting, the process of creating the illusion of three-dimensionality on a two-dimensional surface by use of light and shade. In sculpture, the process of molding a three-dimensional form out of a malleable substance.

module (p. 346) A segment or portion of a repeated design. Also: a basic building block.

molding (p. 319) A shaped or sculpted strip with varying contours and patterns. Used as decoration on architecture, furniture, frames, and other objects.

mortise-and-tenon (p. 18) A method of joining two elements. A projecting pin (tenon) on one element fits snugly into a hole designed for it (mortise) on the other.

mosaic (p. 145) Image formed by arranging small colored stone or glass pieces (**tesserae**) and affixing them to a hard, stable surface.

mosque (p. 265) A building used for communal Islamic worship.

Mozarabic (p. 439) Of an eclectic style practiced in Christian medieval Spain when much of the Iberian peninsula was ruled by Islamic dynasties.

mudra (p. 307) A symbolic hand gesture in Buddhist art that denotes certain behaviors, actions, or feelings.

mullion (p. 510) A slender straight or curving bar that divides a window into subsidiary sections to create **tracery**.

muqarna (p. 280) In Islamic architecture, one of the nichelike components, often stacked in tiers to mark the transition between flat and rounded surfaces and often found on the **vault** of a **dome**.

naos (p. 236) The principal room in a temple or church. In ancient architecture, the **cella**. In a Byzantine church, the **nave** and **sanctuary**.

narrative image (p. 215) A picture that recounts an event drawn from a story, either factual (e.g. biographical) or fictional. In **continuous narrative**, multiple scenes from the same story appear within a single compositional frame.

narthex (p. 220) The vestibule or entrance porch of a church.

nave (p. 191) The central space of a church, two or three stories high and usually flanked by **aisle**s.

necropolis (p. 53) A large cemetery or burial area; literally a "city of the dead."

nemes headdress (p. 51) The royal headdress of ancient Egypt.

niello (p. 90) A metal technique in which a black sulfur **alloy** is rubbed into fine lines engraved into metal (usually gold or silver). When heated, the alloy becomes fused with the surrounding metal and provides contrasting detail.

oculus (*pl.* **oculi**) (p. 187) In architecture, a circular opening. Usually found either as windows or at the apex of a **dome**. When at the top of a dome, an oculus is either open to the sky or covered by a decorative exterior **lantern**.

odalisque (p. 952) Turkish word for "harem slave girl" or "concubine."

oil painting (p. 575) Any painting executed with pigments suspended in a **medium** of oil. Oil paint has particular properties that allow for greater ease of working: among others, a slow drying time (which allows for corrections), and a great range of relative opaqueness of paint layers (which permits a high degree of detail and luminescence).

oinochoe (p. 126) An ancient Greek jug used for wine.

olpe (p. 105) Any ancient Greek vessel without a spout.

one-point perspective (p. 259) See under **perspective**.

orant (p. 220) Of a standing figure represented praying with outstretched and upraised arms.

oratory (p. 228) A small chapel.

order (p. 110) A system of proportions in Classical architecture that includes every aspect of the building's plan, elevation, and decorative system. *Composite*: a combination of the Ionic and the Corinthian orders. The **capital** combines **acanthus** leaves with **volute** scrolls. *Corinthian*: the most ornate of the orders, the Corinthian includes a **base**, a **fluted column shaft** with a capital elaborately decorated with acanthus leaf carvings. Its **entablature** consists of an **architrave** decorated with **moldings**, a **frieze** often containing **relief sculpture**, and a **cornice** with **dentils**. *Doric*: the column shaft of the Doric order can be fluted or smooth-surfaced and has no base. The Doric capital consists of an undecorated **echinus** and **abacus**. The Doric entablature has a plain architrave, a frieze with **metope**s and **triglyph**s, and a simple cornice. *Ionic*: the column of the Ionic order has a base, a fluted shaft, and a capital decorated with volutes. The Ionic entablature consists of an architrave of three panels and moldings,

a frieze usually containing sculpted relief ornament, and a cornice with dentils. *Tuscan*: a variation of Doric characterized by a smooth-surfaced column shaft with a base, a plain architrave, and an undecorated frieze. *Colossal* or *giant*: any of the above built on a large scale, rising through two or more stories in height and often raised from the ground on a **pedestal**.

Orientalism (p. 968) A fascination with Middle Eastern cultures that inspired eclectic nineteenth-century European fantasies of exotic life that often formed the subject of paintings.

orthogonal (p. 138) Any line running back into the represented space of a picture perpendicular to the imagined **picture plane**. In **linear perspective**, all orthogonals converge at a single **vanishing point** in the picture and are the basis for a **grid** that maps out the internal space of the image. An orthogonal plan is any plan for a building or city that is based exclusively on right angles, such as the grid plan of many major cities.

pagoda (p. 347) An East Asian **reliquary** tower built with successively smaller, repeated stories. Each story is usually marked by an elaborate projecting roof.

painterly (p. 253) A style of painting which emphasizes the techniques and surface effects of brushwork (also color, light, and shade).

palace complex (p. 41) A group of buildings used for living and governing by a ruler and his or her supporters, usually fortified.

palazzo (p. 602) Italian term for palace, used for any large urban dwelling.

palette (p. 183) A hand-held support used by artists for arranging colors and mixing paint during the process of painting. Also: the choice of a range of colors used by an artist in a particular work, as typical of his or her style. In ancient Egypt, a flat stone used to grind and prepare makeup.

panel painting (p. xli) Any painting executed on a wood support, usually planed to provide a smooth surface. A panel can consist of several boards joined together.

parchment (p. 245) A writing surface made from treated skins of animals. Very fine parchment is known as **vellum**.

parterre (p. 761) An ornamental, highly regimented flowerbed; especially as an element of the ornate gardens of a seventeenth-century palace or **château**.

passage grave (p. 17) A prehistoric tomb under a **cairn**, reached by a long, narrow, slab-lined access passageway or passageways.

pastel (p. 914) Dry pigment, chalk, and gum in stick or crayon form. Also: a work of art made with pastels.

pedestal (p. 107) A platform or base supporting a sculpture or other monument. Also: the block found below the base of a Classical **column** (or **colonnade**), serving to raise the entire element off the ground.

pediment (p. 107) A triangular gable found over major architectural elements such as Classical Greek **portico**s, windows, or doors. Formed by an **entablature** and the ends of a sloping roof or a raking **cornice**. A similar architectural element is often used decoratively above a door or window, sometimes with a curved upper **molding**. A *broken pediment* is a variation on the traditional pediment, with an open space at the center of the topmost angle and/or the horizontal cornice.

pendant (also **pendent**) (p. 640) One of a pair of artworks meant to be seen in relation to each other as a set.

pendentive (p. 236) The concave triangular section of a **vault** that forms the transition between a square or polygonal space and the circular base of a **dome**.

Performance art (p. 1087) A contemporary artwork based on a live, sometimes theatrical performance by the artist.

peristyle (p. 66) In Greek architecture, a surrounding **colonnade**. A peristyle building is surrounded on the exterior by a colonnade. Also: a peristyle court is an open colonnaded courtyard, often having a pool and garden.

perspective (p. xxvii) A system for representing three-dimensional space on a two-dimensional surface. *Atmospheric* or *aerial perspective*: a method of rendering the effect of spatial distance by subtle variations in color and clarity of representation. *Intuitive perspective*: a method of giving the impression of recession by visual instinct, not by the use of an overall system or program. *Oblique perspective*: an intuitive spatial system in which a building or room is placed with one corner in the **picture plane**, and the other parts of the structure recede to an imaginary **vanishing point** on its other side. Oblique perspective is not a comprehensive, mathematical system. *One-point* and multiple-point perspective (also called linear, scientific, or mathematical perspective): a method of creating the illusion of three-dimensional space on a two-dimensional surface by delineating a **horizon line** and multiple **orthogonal** lines. These recede to meet at one or more points on the horizon (vanishing point), giving the appearance of spatial depth. Called scientific or mathematical because its use requires some knowledge of geometry and mathematics, as well as optics. *Reverse perspective*: a Byzantine perspective theory in which the orthogonals or rays of sight do not converge on a vanishing point in the picture, but are thought to originate in the viewer's eye in front of the picture. Thus, in reverse perspective the image is constructed with orthogonals that diverge, giving a slightly tipped aspect to objects.

photomontage (p. 1039) A photographic work created from many smaller photographs arranged (and often overlapping) in a composition, which is then rephotographed.

pictograph (p. 337) A highly stylized depiction serving as a symbol for a person or object. Also: a type of writing utilizing such symbols.

picture plane (p. 575) The theoretical plane corresponding to the actual surface of a painting, separating the spatial world evoked in the painting from the spatial world occupied by the viewer.

picturesque (p. 919) Of the taste for the familiar, the pleasant, and the agreeable, popular in the eighteenth and nineteenth centuries in Europe. Originally used to describe the "picturelike" qualities of some landscape scenes. When contrasted with the **sublime**, the picturesque stood for the interesting but ordinary domestic landscape.

piece-mold casting (p. 334) A casting technique in which the mold consists of several sections that are connected during the pouring of molten metal, usually bronze. After the cast form has hardened, the pieces of the mold are disassembled, leaving the completed object.

pier (p. 270) A masonry support made up of many stones, or rubble and concrete (in contrast to a column **shaft** which is formed from a single stone or a series of **drums**), often square or rectangular in plan, and capable of carrying very heavy architectural loads.

pietà (p. 230) A devotional subject in Christian religious art. After the Crucifixion the body of Jesus was laid across the lap of his grieving mother, Mary. When other mourners are present, the subject is called the Lamentation.

pietra serena (p. 602) A gray Tuscan sandstone used in Florentine architecture.

pilaster (p. 158) An **engaged** columnlike element that is rectangular in format and used for decoration in architecture.

pilgrimage church (p. 239) A church that attracts visitors wishing to venerate **relic**s as well as attend religious services.

pinnacle (p. 503) In Gothic architecture, a steep pyramid decorating the top of another element such as a **buttress**. Also: the highest point.

plate tracery (p. 505) See under **tracery**.

plein air (p. 989) See under *en plein air*.

plinth (p. 161) The slablike base or **pedestal** of a **column**, statue, wall, building, or piece of furniture.

pluralism (p. 1107) A social structure or goal that allows members of diverse ethnic, racial, or other groups to exist peacefully within the society while continuing to practice the customs of their own divergent cultures. Also: an adjective describing the state of having a variety of valid contemporary styles available at the same time to artists.

podium (p. 138) A raised platform that acts as the foundation for a building, or as a platform for a speaker.

poesia (*pl.* **poesie**) (p. 656) Italian Renaissance paintings based on Classical themes, often with erotic overtones, notably in the mid-sixteenth-century works of the Venetian painter Titian.

polychromy (p. 524) Multicolored decoration applied to any part of a building, sculpture, or piece of furniture. This can be accomplished with paint or by the use of multicolored materials.

polyptych (p. 566) An **altarpiece** constructed from multiple panels, sometimes with hinges to allow for movable wings.

porcelain (p. 20) A type of extremely hard and fine white **ceramic** first made by Chinese potters in the eighth century CE. Made from a mixture of kaolin and petuntse, porcelain is fired at a very high temperature, and the final product has a translucent surface.

porch (p. 108) The covered entrance on the exterior of a building. With a row of **column**s or **colonnade**, also called a **portico**.

portal (p. 40) A grand entrance, door, or gate, usually to an important public building, and often decorated with sculpture.

portico (p. 63) In architecture, a projecting roof or porch supported by **column**s, often marking an entrance. See also **porch**.

post-and-lintel (p. 19) An architectural system of construction with two or more vertical elements (posts) supporting a horizontal element (**lintel**).

potassium-argon dating (p. 12) Archaeological method of **radiometric dating** that measures the decay of a radioactive potassium isotope into a stable isotope of argon, and inert gas.

potsherd (p. 20) A broken piece of **ceramic** ware.

poupou (p. 873) In Pacific cultures, a house panel, often carved with designs.

Prairie Style (p. 1046) Style developed by a group of Midwestern architects who worked together using the aesthetic of the prairie and indigenous prairie plants for landscape design to create mostly domestic homes and small public buildings.

predella (p. 550) The base of an **altarpiece**, often decorated with small scenes that are related in subject to that of the main panel or panels.

primitivism (p. 1022) The borrowing of subjects or forms, usually from non-European or prehistoric sources by Western artists, in an attempt to infuse their work with the expressive qualities they attributed to other cultures, especially colonized cultures.

pronaos (p. 108) The enclosed vestibule of a Greek or Roman temple, found in front of the **cella** and marked by a row of **column**s at the entrance.

proscenium (p. 148) The stage of an ancient Greek or Roman theater. In a modern theater, the area of the stage in front of the curtain. Also: the framing **arch** that separates a stage from the audience.

psalter (p. 256) In Jewish and Christian scripture, a book of the Psalms (songs) attributed to King David.

psykter (p. 126) An ancient Greek vessel with an extended base to allow it to float in a larger **krater**; used to chill wine.

putto (*pl.* **putti**) (p. 224) A plump, naked little boy, often winged. In Classical art, called a cupid; in Christian art, a cherub.

pylon (p. 66) A massive gateway formed by a pair of tapering walls of oblong shape. Erected by ancient Egyptians to mark the entrance to a temple complex.

qibla (p. 274) The **mosque** wall oriented toward Mecca; indicated by the *mihrab*.

quatrefoil (p. 508) A four-lobed decorative pattern common in Gothic art and architecture.

quillwork (p. 847) A Native American technique in which the quills of porcupines and bird feathers are dyed and attached to materials in patterns.

radiometric dating (p. 12) Archaeological method of **absolute dating** by measuring the degree to which radioactive materials have degenerated over time. For dating organic (plant or animal) materials, one radiometric method measures a carbon isotope called radiocarbon, or carbon-14.

raigo (p. 378) A painted image that depicts the Amida Buddha and other Buddhist deities welcoming the soul of a dying believer to paradise.

raku (p. 823) A type of **ceramic** made by hand, coated with a thick, dark **glaze**, and fired at a low heat. The resulting vessels are irregularly shaped and glazed and are highly prized for use in the Japanese tea ceremony.

readymade (p. 1038) An object from popular or material culture presented without further manipulation as an artwork by the artist.

red-figure (p. 119) A technique of ancient Greek **ceramic** decoration characterized by red clay-colored figures on a black background. The figures are reserved against a painted ground and details are drawn, not engraved; compare **black-figure**.

register (p. 30) A device used in systems of spatial definition. In painting, a register indicates the use of differing groundlines to differentiate layers of space within an image. In **relief sculpture**, the placement of self-contained bands of reliefs in a vertical arrangement.

registration marks (p. 828) In Japanese **woodblock prints**, two marks carved on the blocks to indicate proper alignment of the paper during the printing process. In multicolor printing, which used a separate block for each color, these marks were essential for achieving the proper position or registration of the colors.

relative dating (p. 12) Archaeological process of determining relative chronological relationships among excavated objects. Compare **absolute dating**.

relic (p. 239) Venerated object or body part associated with a holy figure, such as a saint, and usually housed in a **reliquary**.

relief sculpture (p. 5) A three-dimensional image or design whose flat background surface is carved away to a certain depth, setting off the figure. Called *high* or *low (bas-) relief* depending upon the extent of projection of the image from the background. Called *sunken relief* when the image is carved below the original surface of the background, which is not cut away.

reliquary (p. 366) A container, often elaborate and made of precious materials, used as a repository for sacred relics.

repoussé (p. 90) A technique of pushing or hammering metal from the back to create a protruding image. Elaborate reliefs are created by pressing or hammering metal sheets against carved wooden forms.

rhyton (p. 88) A vessel in the shape of a figure or an animal, used for drinking or pouring liquids on special occasions.

rib vault (p. 499) See under **vault**.

ridgepole (p. 16) A longitudinal timber at the apex of a roof that supports the upper ends of the rafters.

roof comb (p. 392) In a Maya building, a masonry wall along the apex of a roof that is built above the level of the roof proper. Roof combs support the highly decorated false **façade**s that rise above the height of the building at the front.

rose window (p. 505) A round window, often filled with stained glass set into tracery patterns in the form of wheel spokes, found in the **façade**s of the **nave**s and **transept**s of large Gothic churches.

rosette (p. 105) A round or oval ornament resembling a rose.

rotunda (p. 195) Any building (or part thereof) constructed in a circular (or sometimes polygonal) shape, usually producing a large open space crowned by a **dome**.

round arch (p. 170) See under **arch**.

roundel (p. 158) Any ornamental element with a circular format, often placed as a decoration on the exterior of a building.

rune stone (p. 442) In early medieval northern Europe, a stone used as a commemorative monument and carved or inscribed with runes, a writing system used by early Germanic peoples.

rustication (p. 602) In architecture, the rough, irregular, and unfinished effect deliberately given to the exterior facing of a stone edifice. Rusticated stones are often large and used for decorative emphasis around doors or windows, or across the entire lower floors of a building.

sacra conversazione (p. 630) Italian for "holy conversation." Refers to a type of religious painting developed in fifteenth-century Florence in which a central image of the Virgin and Child is flanked by standing saints of comparable size who stand within the same spatial setting and often acknowledge each other's presence.

salon (p. 907) A large room for entertaining guests or a periodic social or intellectual gathering, often of prominent people, held in such a room. Also: a hall or **gallery** for exhibiting works of art.

sanctuary (p. 102) A sacred or holy enclosure used for worship. In ancient Greece and Rome, consisted of one or more temples and an altar. In Christian architecture, the space around the altar in a church called the chancel or presbytery.

sarcophagus (*pl.* **sarcophagi**) (p. 49) A stone coffin. Often rectangular and decorated with **relief sculpture**.

scarab (p. 51) In ancient Egypt, a stylized dung beetle associated with the sun and the god Amun.

scarification (p. 409) Ornamental decoration applied to the surface of the body by cutting the skin for cultural and/or aesthetic reasons.

school of artists or **painting** (p. 285) An art-historical term describing a group of artists, usually working at the same time and sharing similar styles, influences, and ideals. The artists in a particular school may not necessarily be directly associated with one another, unlike those in a workshop or **atelier**.

scriptorium (*pl.* **scriptoria**) (p. 244) A room in a monastery for writing or copying **manuscript**s.

scroll painting (p. 347) A painting executed on a flexible support with rollers at each end. The rollers permit the horizontal scroll to be unrolled as it is studied or the vertical scroll to be hung for contemplation or decoration.

sculpture in the round (p. 5) Three-dimensional sculpture that is carved free of any background or block. Compare **relief sculpture**.

serdab (p. 53) In ancient Egyptian tombs, the small room in which the *ka* statue was placed.

sfumato (p. 636) Italian term meaning "smoky," soft, and mellow. In painting, the effect of haze in an image. Resembling the color of the atmosphere at dusk, *sfumato* gives a smoky effect.

sgraffito (p. 604) Decoration made by incising or cutting away a surface layer of material to reveal a different color beneath.

shaft (p. 110) The main vertical section of a **column** between the **capital** and the base, usually circular in cross section.

shaft grave (p. 97) A deep pit used for burial.

shikhara (p. 302) In the architecture of northern India, a conical (or pyramidal) spire found atop a Hindu temple and often crowned with an *amalaka*.

shoin (p. 821) A term used to describe the various features found in the most formal room of upper-class Japanese residential architecture.

shoji (p. 821) A standing Japanese screen covered in translucent rice paper and used in interiors.

siapo (p. 876) A type of **tapa** cloth found in Samoa and still used as an important gift for ceremonial occasions.

silkscreen printing (p. 1092) A technique of printing in which paint or ink is pressed through a stencil and specially prepared cloth to reproduce a design in multiple copies.

sinopia (*pl.* **sinopie**) (p. 539) Italian word taken from Sinope, the ancient city in Asia Minor that was famous for its red-brick pigment. In **fresco** paintings, a full-sized, preliminary sketch done in this color on the first rough coat of plaster or *arriccio*.

site-specific (p. 1102) Of a work commissioned and/or designed for a particular location.

slip (p. 118) A mixture of clay and water applied to a **ceramic** object as a final decorative coat. Also: a solution that binds different parts of a vessel together, such as the handle and the main body.

spandrel (p. 170) The area of wall adjoining the exterior curve of an **arch** between its **springing** and the **keystone**, or the area between two arches, as in an **arcade**.

spolia (p. 471) Fragments of older architecture or sculpture reused in a secondary context. Latin for "hide stripped from an animal."

springing (p. 170) The point at which the curve of an **arch** or **vault** meets with and rises from its support.

squinch (p. 238) An **arch** or **lintel** built across the upper corners of a square space, allowing a circular or polygonal **dome** to be securely set above the walls.

stained glass (p. 287) Glass stained with color while molten, using metallic oxides. Stained glass is most often used in windows, for which small pieces of different colors are precisely cut and assembled into a design, held together by lead **came**s. Additional details may be added with vitreous paint.

stave church (p. 443) A Scandinavian wooden structure with four huge timbers (staves) at its core.

stele (*pl.* **stelai**), also **stela** (*pl.* **stelae**) (p. 27) A stone slab placed vertically and decorated with inscriptions or reliefs. Used as a grave marker or commemorative monument.

stereobate (p. 110) In Classical architecture, the foundation upon which a temple stands.

still life (*pl.* **still lifes**) (p. xxxv) A type of painting that has as its subject inanimate objects (such as food and dishes) or fruit and flowers taken out of their natural contexts.

stoa (p. 107) In Greek architecture, a long roofed walkway, usually having **column**s on one long side and a wall on the other.

stoneware (p. 20) A high-fired, vitrified, but opaque **ceramic** ware that is fired in the range of 1,100 to 1,200 degrees Celsius. At that temperature, particles of silica in the clay bodies fuse together so that the finished vessels are impervious to liquids, even without glaze. Stoneware pieces are glazed to enhance their aesthetic appeal and to aid in keeping them clean. Stoneware occurs in a range of earth-toned colors, from white and tan to gray and black, with light gray predominating. Chinese potters were the first in the world to produce stoneware, which they were able to make as early as the Shang dynasty.

stringcourse (p. 503) A continuous horizontal band, such as a **molding**, decorating the face of a wall.

stucco (p. 72) A mixture of lime, sand, and other ingredients made into a material that can easily be molded or modeled. When dry, it produces a durable surface used for covering walls or for architectural sculpture and decoration.

stupa (p. 302) In Buddhist architecture, a bell-shaped or pyramidal religious monument, made of piled earth or stone, and containing sacred **relic**s.

style (p. xxxvi) A particular manner, form, or character of representation, construction, or expression that is typical of an individual artist or of a certain place or period.

stylobate (p. 110) In Classical architecture, the stone foundation on which a temple **colonnade** stands.

stylus (p. 28) An instrument with a pointed end (used for writing and printmaking), which makes a delicate line or scratch. Also: a special writing tool for **cuneiform** writing with one pointed end and one triangular.

sublime (p. 955) Of a concept, thing, or state of greatness or vastness with high spiritual, moral, intellectual, or emotional value; or something awe-inspiring. The sublime was a goal to which many nineteenth-century artists aspired in their artworks.

sunken relief (p. 71) See under **relief sculpture**.

symposium (p. 119) An elite gathering of wealthy and powerful men in ancient Greece that focused principally on wine, music, poetry, conversation, games, and love making.

syncretism (p. 220) A process whereby artists assimilate and combine images and ideas from different cultural traditions, beliefs, and practices, giving them new meanings.

taotie (p. 334) A mask with a dragon or animal-like face common as a decorative motif in Chinese art.

tapa (p. 876) A type of cloth used for various purposes in Pacific cultures, made from tree bark stripped and beaten, and often bearing subtle designs from the mallets used to work the bark.

tapestry (p. 292) Multicolored decorative weaving to be hung on a wall or placed on furniture. Pictorial or decorative motifs are woven directly into the supporting fabric, completely concealing it.

tatami (p. 821) Mats of woven straw used in Japanese houses as a floor covering.

temenos (p. 108) An enclosed sacred area reserved for worship in ancient Greece.

tempera (p. 141) A painting **medium** made by blending egg yolks with water, pigments, and occasionally other materials, such as glue.

tenebrism (p. 723) The use of strong *chiaroscuro* and artificially illuminated areas to create a dramatic contrast of light and dark in a painting.

terra cotta (p. 114) A **medium** made from clay fired over a low heat and sometimes left unglazed. Also: the orange-brown color typical of this medium.

tessera (*pl.* **tesserae**) (p. 145) A small piece of stone, glass, or other object that is pieced together with many others to create a **mosaic**.

thatch (p. 16) Plant material such as reeds or straw tied over a framework of poles to make a roof, shelter, or small building.

thermo-luminescence dating (p. 12) A method of **radiometric dating** that measures the irradiation of the crystal structure of material such as flint or pottery and the soil in which it is found, determined by luminescence produced when a sample is heated.

tholos (p. 98) A small, round building. Sometimes built underground, e.g. as a Mycenaean tomb.

thrust (p. 170) The outward pressure caused by the weight of a **vault** and supported by **buttressing**. See also under **arch**.

tondo (*pl.* **tondi**) (p. 126) A painting or **relief sculpture** of circular shape.

torana (p. 302) In Indian architecture, an ornamental gateway arch in a temple, usually leading to the **stupa**.

torc (p. 149) A circular neck ring worn by Celtic warriors.

toron (p. 422) In West African **mosque** architecture, the wooden beams that project from the walls. Torons are used as support for the scaffolding erected annually for the replastering of the building.

tracery (p. 503) Stonework or woodwork forming a pattern in the open space of windows or applied to wall surfaces. In *plate tracery*, a series of openings are cut through the wall. In *bar tracery*, **mullion**s divide the space into segments to form decorative patterns.

transept (p. 225) The arm of a **cruciform** church perpendicular to the **nave**. The point where the nave and transept intersect is called the crossing. Beyond the crossing lies the **sanctuary**, whether **apse**, **choir**, or chevet.

transverse arch (p. 463) See under **arch**.

trefoil (p. 298) An ornamental design made up of three rounded lobes placed adjacent to one another.

triforium (p. 505) The element of the interior elevation of a church found directly below the **clerestory** and consisting of a series of arched openings in front of a passageway within the thickness of the wall.

triglyph (p. 110) Rectangular block between the **metope**s of a Doric frieze. Identified by the three carved vertical grooves, which approximate the appearance of the end of wooden beams.

triptych (p. 566) An artwork made up of three panels. The panels may be hinged together in such a way that the side segments (wings) fold over the central area.

trompe l'oeil (p. 618) A manner of representation in which artists faithfully describe the appearance of natural space and forms with the express intention of fooling the eye of the viewer, who may be convinced momentarily that the subject actually exists as three-dimensional reality.

trumeau (p. 478) A **column**, **pier**, or post found at the center of a large **portal** or doorway, supporting the **lintel**.

tugra (p. 288) A calligraphic imperial monogram used in Ottoman courts.

tukutuku (p. 872) Lattice panels created by women from the Maori culture and used in architecture.

Tuscan order (p. 158) See under **order**.

twining (p. 848) A basketry technique in which short rods are sewn together vertically. The panels are then joined together to form a container or other object.

tympanum (p. 478) In medieval and later architecture, the area over a door enclosed by an **arch** and a **lintel**, often decorated with sculpture or mosaic.

ukiyo-e (p. 828) A Japanese term for a type of popular art that was favored from the sixteenth century, particularly in the form of color **woodblock print**s. *Ukiyo-e* prints often depicted the world of the common people in Japan, such as courtesans and actors, as well as landscapes and myths.

undercutting (p. 212) A technique in sculpture by which the material is cut back under the edges so that the remaining form projects strongly forward, casting deep shadows.

underglaze (p. 800) Color or decoration applied to a **ceramic** piece before glazing.

upeti (p. 876) In Pacific cultures, a carved wooden design tablet, used to create patterns in cloth by dragging the fabric across it.

uranium-thorium dating (p. 12) Technique used to date prehistoric cave paintings by measuring the decay of uranium into thorium in the deposits of calcium carbinate that cover the surfaces of cave walls, to determine the minimum age of the paintings under the crust.

urna (p. 306) In Buddhist art, the curl of hair on the forehead that is a characteristic mark of a buddha. The *urna* is a symbol of divine wisdom.

ushnisha (p. 306) In Asian art, a round turban or tiara symbolizing royalty and, when worn by a buddha, enlightenment.

vanishing point (p. 610) In a **perspective** system, the point on the **horizon line** at which **orthogonals** meet. A complex system can have multiple vanishing points.

vanitas (p. xxxvi) An image, especially popular in Europe during the seventeenth century, in which all the objects symbolize the transience of life. *Vanitas* paintings are usually of **still lifes** or genre subjects.

vault (p. 17) An arched masonry structure that spans an interior space. *Barrel* or *tunnel vault*: an elongated or continuous semicircular vault, shaped like a half-cylinder. *Corbeled vault*: a vault made by projecting **course**s of stone; see also under **corbel**. *Groin* or *cross vault*: a vault created by the intersection of two barrel vaults of equal size which creates four side compartments of identical size and shape. *Quadrant vault*: a half-barrel vault. *Rib vault*: a groin vault with ribs (extra masonry) demarcating the junctions. Ribs may function to reinforce the groins or may be purely decorative.

veduta (*pl.* **vedute**) (p. 915) Italian for "vista" or "view." Paintings, drawings, or prints, often of expansive city scenes or of harbors.

vellum (p. 245) A fine animal skin prepared for writing and painting. See also **parchment**.

verism (p. 168) Style in which artists concern themselves with describing the exterior likeness of an object or person, usually by rendering its visible details in a finely executed, meticulous manner.

vihara (p. 305) From the Sanskrit term meaning "for wanderers." A *vihara* is, in general, a Buddhist monastery in India. It also signifies monks' cells and gathering places in such a monastery.

volute (p. 110) A spiral scroll, as seen on an Ionic **capital**.

votive figure (p. 31) An image created as a devotional offering to a deity.

voussoir (p. 170) Wedge-shaped stone block used to build an **arch**. The topmost voussoir is called a **keystone**. See also **joggled voussoirs**.

warp (p. 292) The vertical threads in a weaver's loom. Warp threads make up a fixed framework that provides the structure for the entire piece of cloth, and are thus often thicker than **weft** threads.

wattle and daub (p. 16) A wall construction method combining upright branches, woven with twigs (wattles) and plastered or filled with clay or mud (daub).

weft (p. 292) The horizontal threads in a woven piece of cloth. Weft threads are woven at right angles to and through the **warp** threads to make up the bulk of the decorative pattern. In carpets, the weft is often completely covered or formed by the rows of trimmed knots that form the carpet's soft surface.

westwork (p. 446) The monumental, west-facing entrance section of a Carolingian, Ottonian, or Romanesque church. The exterior consists of multiple stories between two towers; the interior includes an entrance vestibule, a chapel, and a series of **galleries** overlooking the **nave**.

white-ground (p. 141) A type of ancient Greek pottery in which the background color of the object was painted with a **slip** that turns white in the firing process. Figures and details were added by painting on or incising into this slip. White-ground wares were popular in the Classical period as funerary objects.

woodblock print (p. 591) A print made from one or more carved wooden blocks. In Japan, woodblock prints were made using multiple blocks carved in relief, usually with a block for each color in the finished print. See also **woodcut**.

woodcut (p. 592) A type of print made by carving a design into a wooden block. The ink is applied to the block with a roller. As the ink touches only on the surface areas and lines remaining between the carved-away parts of the block, it is these areas that make the print when paper is pressed against the inked block, leaving the carved-away parts of the design to appear blank. Also: the process by which the woodcut is made.

yaksha, yakshi (p. 301) The male (*yaksha*) and female (*yakshi*) nature spirits that act as agents of the Hindu gods. Their sculpted images are often found on Hindu temples and other sacred places, particularly at the entrances.

yamato-e (p. 374) A native style of Japanese painting developed during the twelfth and thirteenth centuries, distinguished from Japanese painting styles that emulate Chinese traditions.

ziggurat (p. 28) In ancient Mesopotamia, a tall stepped tower of earthen materials, often supporting a shrine.

Bibliography

Susan V. Craig, updated by Carrie L. McDade

This bibliography is composed of books in English that are suggested "further reading" titles. Most are available in good libraries, whether college, university, or public. Recently published works have been emphasized so that the research information would be current. There are three classifications of listings: general surveys and art history reference tools, including journals and Internet directories; surveys of large periods that encompass multiple chapters (ancient art in the Western tradition, European medieval art, European Renaissance through eighteenth-century art, modern art in the West, Asian art, and African and Oceanic art, and art of the Americas); and books for individual Chapters 1 through 33.

General Art History Surveys and Reference Tools

Adams, Laurie Schneider. *Art Across Time*. 4th ed. New York: McGraw-Hill, 2011.

Barnet, Sylvan. *A Short Guide to Writing about Art*. 10th ed. Upper Saddle River, NJ: Pearson/Prentice Hall, 2010.

Bony, Anne. *Design: History, Main Trends, Main Figures*. Edinburgh: Chambers, 2005.

Boström, Antonia. *Encyclopedia of Sculpture*. 3 vols. New York: Fitzroy Dearborn, 2004.

Broude, Norma, and Mary D. Garrard, eds. *Feminism and Art History: Questioning the Litany*. Icon Editions. New York: Harper & Row, 1982.

Chadwick, Whitney. *Women, Art, and Society*. 4th ed. New York: Thames & Hudson, 2007.

Chilvers, Ian, ed. *The Oxford Dictionary of Art*. 4th ed. New York: Oxford Univ. Press, 2009.

Curl, James Stevens. *A Dictionary of Architecture and Landscape Architecture*. 2nd ed. Oxford: Oxford Univ. Press, 2006.

Davies, Penelope J.E., et al. *Janson's History of Art: The Western Tradition*. 8th ed. Upper Saddle River, NJ: Prentice Hall, 2010.

The Dictionary of Art. Ed. Jane Turner. 34 vols. New York: Grove's Dictionaries, 1996.

Frank, Patrick, Duane Preble, and Sarah Preble. *Prebles' Artforms*. 10th ed. Upper Saddle River, NJ: Pearson/Prentice Hall, 2011.

Gaze, Delia, ed. *Dictionary of Women Artists*. 2 vols. London: Fitzroy Dearborn, 1997.

Griffiths, Antony. *Prints and Printmaking: An Introduction to the History and Techniques*. 2nd ed. London: British Museum Press, 1996.

Hadden, Peggy. *The Quotable Artist*. New York: Allworth Press, 2002.

Hall, James. *Dictionary of Subjects and Symbols in Art*. 2nd ed. Boulder, CO: Westview Press, 2008.

Holt, Elizabeth Gilmore, ed. *A Documentary History of Art*. 3 vols. New Haven: Yale Univ. Press, 1986.

Honour, Hugh, and John Fleming. *The Visual Arts: A History*. 7th ed. rev. Upper Saddle River, NJ: Pearson/Prentice Hall, 2010.

Johnson, Paul. *Art: A New History*. New York: HarperCollins, 2003.

Kemp, Martin, ed. *The Oxford History of Western Art*. Oxford: Oxford Univ. Press, 2000.

Kleiner, Fred S. *Gardner's Art through the Ages*. Enhanced 13th ed. Belmont, CA: Thomson/Wadsworth, 2011.

Kostof, Spiro. *A History of Architecture: Settings and Rituals*. 2nd ed. Revised Greg Castillo. New York: Oxford Univ. Press, 1995.

Mackenzie, Lynn. *Non-Western Art: A Brief Guide*. 2nd ed. Upper Saddle River, NJ: Pearson/Prentice Hall, 2001.

Marmor, Max, and Alex Ross, eds. *Guide to the Literature of Art History 2*. Chicago: American Library Association, 2005.

Onians, John, ed. *Atlas of World Art*. New York: Oxford Univ. Press, 2004.

Sayre, Henry M. *Writing about Art*. 6th ed. Upper Saddle River, NJ: Pearson/Prentice Hall, 2009.

Sed-Rajna, Gabrielle. *Jewish Art*. Trans. Sara Friedman and Mira Reich. New York: Abrams, 1997.

Slatkin, Wendy. *Women Artists in History: From Antiquity to the Present*. 4th ed. Upper Saddle River, NJ: Pearson/Prentice Hall, 2001.

Sutton, Ian. *Western Architecture: From Ancient Greece to the Present*. World of Art. New York: Thames & Hudson, 1999.

Trachtenberg, Marvin, and Isabelle Hyman. *Architecture, from Prehistory to Postmodernity*. 2nd ed. Upper Saddle River, NJ: Pearson/Prentice Hall, 2002.

Watkin, David. *A History of Western Architecture*. 4th ed. New York: Watson-Guptill, 2005.

Art History Journals: A Select List of Current Titles

African Arts. Quarterly. Los Angeles: Univ. of California at Los Angeles, James S. Coleman African Studies Center, 1967–.

American Art: The Journal of the Smithsonian American Art Museum. 3/year. Chicago: Univ. of Chicago Press, 1987–.

American Indian Art Magazine. Quarterly. Scottsdale, AZ: American Indian Art Inc., 1975–.

American Journal of Archaeology. Quarterly. Boston: Archaeological Institute of America, 1885–.

Antiquity: A Periodical of Archaeology. Quarterly. Cambridge: Antiquity Publications Ltd., 1927–.

Apollo: The International Magazine of the Arts. Monthly. London: Apollo Magazine Ltd., 1925–.

Architectural History. Annually. Farnham, UK: Society of Architectural Historians of Great Britain, 1958–.

Archives of American Art Journal. Quarterly. Washington, DC: Archives of American Art, Smithsonian Institution, 1960–.

Archives of Asian Art. Annually. New York: Asia Society, 1945–.

Ars Orientalis: The Arts of Asia, Southeast Asia, and Islam. Annually. Ann Arbor: Univ. of Michigan Dept. of Art History, 1954–.

Art Bulletin. Quarterly. New York: College Art Association, 1913–.

Art History: Journal of the Association of Art Historians. 5/year. Oxford: Blackwell Publishing Ltd., 1978–.

Art in America. Monthly. New York: Brant Publications Inc., 1913–.

Art Journal. Quarterly. New York: College Art Association, 1960–.

Art Nexus. Quarterly. Bogota, Colombia: Arte en Colombia Ltda, 1976–.

Art Papers Magazine. Bimonthly. Atlanta: Atlanta Art Papers Inc., 1976–.

Artforum International. 10/year. New York: Artforum International Magazine Inc., 1962–.

Artnews. 11/year. New York: Artnews LLC, 1902–.

Bulletin of the Metropolitan Museum of Art. Quarterly. New York: Metropolitan Museum of Art, 1905–.

Burlington Magazine. Monthly. London: Burlington Magazine Publications Ltd., 1903–.

Dumbarton Oaks Papers. Annually. Locust Valley, NY: J.J. Augustin Inc., 1940–.

Flash Art International. Bimonthly. Trevi, Italy: Giancarlo Politi Editore, 1980–.

Gesta. Semiannually. New York: International Center of Medieval Art, 1963–.

History of Photography. Quarterly. Abingdon, UK: Taylor & Francis Ltd., 1976–.

International Review of African American Art. Quarterly. Hampton, VA: International Review of African American Art, 1976–.

Journal of Design History. Quarterly. Oxford: Oxford Univ. Press, 1988–.

Journal of Egyptian Archaeology. Annually. London: Egypt Exploration Society, 1914–.

Journal of Hellenic Studies. Annually. London: Society for the Promotion of Hellenic Studies, 1880–.

Journal of Roman Archaeology. Annually. Portsmouth, RI: Journal of Roman Archaeology LLC, 1988–.

Journal of the Society of Architectural Historians. Quarterly. Chicago: Society of Architectural Historians, 1940–.

Journal of the Warburg and Courtauld Institutes. Annually. London: Warburg Institute, 1937–.

Leonardo: Art, Science, and Technology. 6/year. Cambridge, MA: MIT Press, 1968–.

Marg. Quarterly. Mumbai, India: Scientific Publishers, 1946–.

Master Drawings. Quarterly. New York: Master Drawings Association, 1963–.

October. Cambridge, MA: MIT Press, 1976–.

Oxford Art Journal. 3/year. Oxford: Oxford Univ. Press, 1978–.

Parkett. 3/year. Zürich, Switzerland: Parkett Verlag AG, 1984–.

Print Quarterly. Quarterly. London: Print Quarterly Publications, 1984–.

Simiolus: Netherlands Quarterly for the History of Art. Quarterly. Apeldoorn, Netherlands: Stichting voor Nederlandse Kunsthistorische Publicaties, 1966–.

Woman's Art Journal. Semiannually. Philadelphia: Old City Publishing Inc., 1980–.

Internet Directories for Art History Information: A Selected List

ARCHITECTURE AND BUILDING,
http://www.library.unlv.edu/arch/rsrce/webresources/
A directory of architecture websites collected by Jeanne Brown at the Univ. of Nevada at Las Vegas. Topical lists include architecture, building and construction, design, history, housing, planning, preservation, and landscape architecture. Most entries include a brief annotation and the last date the link was accessed by the compiler.

ART HISTORY RESOURCES ON THE WEB,
http://witcombe.sbc.edu/ARTHLinks.html
Authored by Professor Christopher L.C.E. Witcombe of Sweet Briar College in Virginia, since 1995, the site includes an impressive number of links for various art-historical eras as well as links to research resources, museums, and galleries. The content is frequently updated.

ART IN FLUX: A DIRECTORY OF RESOURCES FOR RESEARCH IN CONTEMPORARY ART,
http://www.boisestate.edu/art/artinflux/intro.html
Cheryl K. Shurtleff of Boise State Univ. in Idaho has authored this directory, which includes sites selected according to their relevance to the study of national or international contemporary art and artists. The subsections include artists, museums, theory, reference, and links.

ARTCYCLOPEDIA: THE GUIDE TO GREAT ART ON THE INTERNET,
http://www.artcyclopedia.com
With more than 2,100 art sites and 75,000 links, this is one of the most comprehensive Web directories for artists and art topics. The primary search is by artist's name but access is also available by title of artwork, artistic movement, museums and galleries, nationality, period, and medium.

MOTHER OF ALL ART AND ART HISTORY LINKS PAGES,
http://umich.edu/~motherha
Maintained by the Dept. of the History of Art at the Univ. of Michigan, this directory covers art history departments, art museums, fine arts schools and departments, as well as links to research resources. Each entry includes annotations.

VOICE OF THE SHUTTLE,
http://vos.ucsb.edu
Sponsored by Univ. of California, Santa Barbara, this directory includes more than 70 pages of links to humanities and humanities-related resources on the Internet. The structured guide includes specific subsections on architecture, on art (modern and contemporary), and on art history. Links usually include a one-sentence explanation and the resource is frequently updated with new information.

ARTBABBLE,
http://www.artbabble.org/
An online community created by staff at the Indianapolis Museum of Art to showcase art-based video content, including interviews with artists and curators, original documentaries, and art installation videos. Partners and contributors to the project include Art21, Los Angeles County Museum of Art, The Museum of Modern Art, The New York Public Library, San Francisco Museum of Modern Art, and Smithsonian American Art Museum.

YAHOO! ARTS>ART HISTORY,
http://dir.yahoo.com/Arts/Art_History/
Another extensive directory of art links organized into subdivisions with one of the most extensive being "Periods and Movements." Links include the name of the site as well as a few words of explanation.

Asian Art, General

Addiss, Stephen, Gerald Groemer, and J. Thomas Rimer, eds. *Traditional Japanese Arts and Culture: An Illustrated Sourcebook*. Honolulu: Univ. of Hawai'i Press, 2006.

Barnhart, Richard M. *Three Thousand Years of Chinese Painting*. New Haven: Yale Univ. Press, 1997.

Blunden, Caroline, and Mark Elvin. *Cultural Atlas of China*. 2nd ed. New York: Checkmark Books, 1998.

Brown, Kerry, ed. *Sikh Art and Literature*. New York: Routledge in collaboration with the Sikh Foundation, 1999.

Chang, Léon Long-Yien, and Peter Miller. *Four Thousand Years of Chinese Calligraphy*. Chicago: Univ. of Chicago Press, 1990.

Chang, Yang-mo. *Arts of Korea*. Ed. Judith G. Smith. New York: Metropolitan Museum of Art, 1998.

Clark, John. *Modern Asian Art*. Honolulu: Univ. of Hawai'i Press, 1998.

Clunas, Craig. *Art in China*. 2nd ed. Oxford History of Art. Oxford: Oxford Univ. Press, 2009.

Coaldrake, William H. *Architecture and Authority in Japan*. London: Routledge, 1996.

Collcutt, Martin, Marius Jansen, and Isao Kumakura. *Cultural Atlas of Japan*. New York: Facts on File, 1988.

Craven, Roy C. *Indian Art: A Concise History*. Rev. ed. World of Art. New York: Thames & Hudson, 1997.

Dehejia, Vidya. *Indian Art*. Art & Ideas. London: Phaidon Press, 1997.

Fisher, Robert E. *Buddhist Art and Architecture*. World of Art. New York: Thames & Hudson, 1993.

Fu, Xinian. *Chinese Architecture*. Ed. & exp., Nancy S. Steinhardt. New Haven: Yale Univ. Press, 2002.

Hearn, Maxwell K., and Judith G. Smith, eds. *Arts of the Sung and Yüan: Papers Prepared for an International Symposium*. New York: Dept. of Asian Art, Metropolitan Museum of Art, 1996.

Heibonsha Survey of Japanese Art. 31 vols. New York: Weatherhill, 1972–80.

Hertz, Betti-Sue. *Past in Reverse: Contemporary Art of East Asia*. San Diego: San Diego Museum of Art, 2004.

Japanese Arts Library. 15 vols. New York: Kodansha International, 1977–87.

Kerlogue, Fiona. *Arts of Southeast Asia*. World of Art. New York: Thames & Hudson, 2004.

Khanna, Balraj, and George Michell. *Human and Divine: 2000 Years of Indian Sculpture*. London: Hayward Gallery, 2000.

Lee, Sherman E. *A History of Far Eastern Art*. 5th ed. Ed. Naomi Noble Richards. New York: Abrams, 1994.

———. *China, 5000 Years: Innovation and Transformation in the Arts*. New York: Solomon R. Guggenheim Museum, 1998.

Liu, Cary Y., and Dora C.Y. Ching, eds. *Arts of the Sung and Yüan: Ritual, Ethnicity, and Style in Painting*. Princeton, NJ: Art Museum, Princeton Univ., 1999.

McArthur, Meher. *The Arts of Asia: Materials, Techniques, Styles*. New York: Thames & Hudson, 2005.

———. *Reading Buddhist Art: An Illustrated Guide to Buddhist Signs and Symbols*. New York: Thames & Hudson, 2002.

Mason, Penelope. *History of Japanese Art*. 2nd ed. Upper Saddle River, NJ: Pearson/Prentice Hall, 2005.

Michell, George. *Hindu Art and Architecture*. World of Art. London: Thames & Hudson, 2000.

———. *The Penguin Guide to the Monuments of India*. 2 vols. New York: Viking, 1989.

Mitter, Partha. *Indian Art*. Oxford History of Art. Oxford: Oxford Univ. Press, 2001.

Murase, Miyeko. *Bridge of Dreams: The Mary Griggs Burke Collection of Japanese Art*. New York: Metropolitan Museum of Art, 2000.

Nickel, Lukas, ed. *Return of the Buddha: The Qingzhou Discoveries*. London: Royal Academy of Arts, 2002.

Pak, Youngsook, and Roderick Whitfield. *Buddhist Sculpture*. Handbook of Korean Art. London: Laurence King Publishing, 2003.

Sullivan, Michael. *The Arts of China*. 5th ed., rev. & exp. Berkeley: Univ. of California Press, 2008.

Thorp, Robert L., and Richard Ellis Vinograd. *Chinese Art & Culture*. New York: Abrams, 2001.

Topsfield, Andrew, ed. *In the Realm of Gods and Kings: Arts of India*. London: Philip Wilson, 2004.

Tucker, Jonathan. *The Silk Road: Art and History*. Chicago: Art Media Resources, 2003.

Tregear, Mary. *Chinese Art*. Rev. ed. World of Art. New York: Thames & Hudson, 1997.

Vainker, S.J. *Chinese Pottery and Porcelain: From Prehistory to the Present*. New York: Braziller, 1991.

African and Oceanic Art and Art of the Americas, General

Anderson, Richard L., and Karen L. Field, eds. *Art in Small-Scale Societies: Contemporary Readings*. Upper Saddle River, NJ: Pearson/Prentice Hall, 1993.

Bacquart, Jean-Baptiste. *The Tribal Arts of Africa*. New York: Thames & Hudson, 1998.

Bassani, Ezio, ed. *Arts of Africa: 7000 Years of African Art*. Milan: Skira, 2005.

Benson, Elizabeth P. *Retratos: 2,000 Years of Latin American Portraits*. San Antonio, TX: San Antonio Museum of Art, 2004.

Berlo, Janet Catherine, and Lee Anne Wilson. *Arts of Africa, Oceania, and the Americas: Selected Readings*. Upper Saddle River, NJ: Prentice Hall, 1993.

Calloway, Colin G. *First Peoples: A Documentary Survey of American Indian History*. 3rd ed. Boston: Bedford/St. Martin's, 2008.

Coote, Jeremy, and Anthony Shelton, eds. *Anthropology, Art, and Aesthetics*. New York: Oxford Univ. Press, 1992.

Drewal, Henry, and John Pemberton III. *Yoruba: Nine Centuries of African Art and Thought*. New York: Center for African Art, 1989.

Evans, Susan Toby. *Ancient Mexico & Central America: Archaeology and Culture History*. 2nd ed. New York: Thames & Hudson, 2008.

———, and David L. Webster, eds. *Archaeology of Ancient Mexico and Central America: An Encyclopedia*. New York: Garland, 2001.

———, and Joanne Pillsbury, eds. *Palaces of the Ancient New World: A Symposium at Dumbarton Oaks, 10th and 11th October, 1998*. Washington, DC: Dumbarton Oaks Research Library and Collection, 2004.

Geoffroy-Schneiter, Bérénice. *Tribal Arts*. New York: Vendome Press, 2000.

Hiller, Susan, ed. & compiled. *The Myth of Primitivism: Perspectives on Art*. London: Routledge, 1991.

Mack, John, ed. *Africa, Arts and Cultures*. London: British Museum Press, 2000.

Mexico: Splendors of Thirty Centuries. New York: Metropolitan Museum of Art, 1990.

Nunley, John W., and Cara McCarty. *Masks: Faces of Culture*. New York: Abrams in assoc. with the Saint Louis Art Museum, 1999.

Perani, Judith, and Fred T. Smith. *The Visual Arts of Africa: Gender, Power, and Life Cycle Rituals*. Upper Saddle River, NJ: Pearson/Prentice Hall, 1998.

Phillips, Tom, ed. *Africa: The Art of a Continent*. New York: Prestel, 1995.

Price, Sally. *Primitive Art in Civilized Places*. 2nd ed. Chicago: Univ. of Chicago Press, 2001.

Rabineau, Phyllis. *Feather Arts: Beauty, Wealth, and Spirit from Five Continents*. Chicago: Field Museum of Natural History, 1979.

Schuster, Carl, and Edmund Carpenter. *Patterns that Connect: Social Symbolism in Ancient & Tribal Art*. New York: Abrams, 1996.

Scott, John F. *Latin American Art: Ancient to Modern*. Gainesville: Univ. Press of Florida, 1999.

Stepan, Peter. *Africa*. Trans. John Gabriel and Elizabeth Schwaiger. London: Prestel, 2001.

Visonà, Monica Blackmun, et al. *A History of Art in Africa*. 2nd ed. Upper Saddle River, NJ: Pearson/Prentice Hall, 2008.

Chapter 24 Art of South and Southeast Asia after 1200

Asher, Catherine B. *Architecture of Mughal India*. New York: Cambridge Univ. Press, 1992.

Beach, Milo Cleveland. *Mughal and Rajput Painting*. New York: Cambridge Univ. Press, 1992.

Guy, John, and Deborah Swallow, eds. *Arts of India, 1550–1900*. London: V&A Publications, 1990.

Khanna, Balraj, and Aziz Kurtha. *Art of Modern India*. London: Thames & Hudson, 1998.

Koch, Ebba. *Mughal Art and Imperial Ideology: Collected Essays*. New Delhi: Oxford Univ. Press, 2001.

Love Song of the Dark Lord: Jayadeva's Gitagovinda. Trans. Barbara Stoler Miller. New York: Columbia Univ. Press, 1977.

Michell, George. *Hindu Art and Architecture*. World of Art. London: Thames & Hudson, 2000.

Moynihan, Elizabeth B., ed. *The Moonlight Garden: New Discoveries at the Taj Mahal*. Asian Art & Culture. Washington, DC: Arthur M. Sackler Gallery, 2000.

Nou, Jean-Louis. *Taj Mahal*. Text by Amina Okada and M.C. Joshi. New York: Abbeville Press, 1993.

Pal, Pratapaditya. *Court Paintings of India, 16th–19th Centuries*. New York: Navin Kumar, 1983.

———. *The Peaceful Liberators: Jain Art from India*. New York: Thames & Hudson, 1994.

Rossi, Barbara. *From the Ocean of Painting: India's Popular Paintings, 1589 to the Present*. New York: Oxford Univ. Press, 1998.

Schimmel, Annemarie. *The Empire of the Great Mughals: History, Art and Culture*. Ed. Burzine K. Waghmar. Trans. Corinne Attwood. London: Reaktion Books, 2004.

Stronge, Susan. *Painting for the Mughal Emperor: The Art of the Book, 1560–1660*. London: V&A Publications, 2002.

Tillotson, G.H.R. *Mughal India*. Architectural Guides for Travelers. San Francisco: Chronicle Books, 1990.

———. *The Tradition of Indian Architecture: Continuity, Controversy, and Change since 1850*. New Haven: Yale Univ. Press, 1989.

Verma, Som Prakash. *Painting the Mughal Experience*. New York: Oxford Univ. Press, 2005.

Welch, Stuart Cary. *The Emperors' Album: Images of Mughal India*. New York: Metropolitan Museum of Art, 1987.

———. *India: Art and Culture 1300–1900*. New York: Metropolitan Museum of Art, 1985.

Chapter 25 Chinese and Korean Art after 1279

Andrews, Julia Frances, and Kuiyi Shen. *A Century in Crisis: Modernity and Tradition in the Art of Twentieth-Century China*. New York: Solomon R. Guggenheim Museum, 1998.

Barnhart, Richard M. *Painters of the Great Ming: The Imperial Court and the Zhe School*. Dallas: Dallas Museum of Art, 1993.

Barrass, Gordon S. *The Art of Calligraphy in Modern China*. London: British Museum Press, 2002.

Berger, Patricia Ann. *Empire of Emptiness: Buddhist Art and Political Authority in Qing China*. Honolulu: Univ. of Hawai'i Press, 2003.

Bickford, Maggie. *Ink Plum: The Making of a Chinese Scholar-Painting*. New York: Cambridge Univ. Press, 1996.

Billeter, Jean François. *The Chinese Art of Writing*. New York: Skira/Rizzoli, 1990.

Bush, Susan, and Hsio-yen Shih, eds. *Early Chinese Texts on Painting*. Cambridge, MA: Harvard Univ. Press, 1985.

Cahill, James. *The Distant Mountains: Chinese Painting in the Late Ming Dynasty, 1580–1644*. New York: Weatherhill, 1982.

———. *Hills Beyond a River: Chinese Painting of the Y'uan Dynasty, 1279–1368*. New York: Weatherhill, 1976.

———. *Parting at the Shore: Chinese Painting of the Early and Middle Ming Dynasty 1368–1580*. New York: Weatherhill, 1978.

Chaves, Jonathan (trans.). *The Chinese Painter as Poet*. New York: Art Media Resources, 2000.

Chung, Anita. *Drawing Boundaries: Architectural Images in Qing China*. Honolulu: Univ. of Hawai'i Press, 2004.

Clunas, Craig. *Pictures and Visuality in Early Modern China*. Princeton, NJ: Princeton Univ. Press, 1997.

Fang, Jing Pei. *Treasures of the Chinese Scholar: Form, Function, and Symbolism.* Ed. J. May Lee Barrett. New York: Weatherhill, 1997.

Fong, Wen C. *Between Two Cultures: Late-Nineteenth- and Twentieth-Century Chinese Paintings from the Robert H. Ellsworth Collection in the Metropolitan Museum of Art.* New York: Metropolitan Museum of Art, 2001.

Hearn, Maxwell K., and Judith G. Smith, eds. *Chinese Art: Modern Expressions.* New York: Dept. of Asian Art, Metropolitan Museum of Art, 2001.

Ho, Chuimei, and Bennet Bronson. *Splendors of China's Forbidden City: The Glorious Reign of Emperor Qianlong.* Chicago: Field Museum, 2004.

Ho, Wai-kam, ed. *The Century of Tung Ch'i-Ch'ang, 1555–1636.* 2 vols. Kansas City, MO: Nelson-Atkins Museum of Art, 1992.

Kim, Hongnam. *The Life of a Patron: Zhou Lianggong (1612–1672) and the Painters of Seventeenth-Century China.* New York: China Institute in America, 1996.

Knapp, Ronald G. *China's Vernacular Architecture: House Form and Culture.* Honolulu: Univ. of Hawai'i Press, 1989.

Lee, Sherman, and Wai-Kam Ho. *Chinese Art Under the Mongols: The Y'uan Dynasty, 1279–1368.* Cleveland: Cleveland Museum of Art, 1968.

Lim, Lucy, ed. *Wu Guanzhong: A Contemporary Chinese Artist.* San Francisco: Chinese Culture Foundation, 1989.

Moss, Paul. *Escape from the Dusty World: Chinese Paintings and Literati Works of Art.* London: Sydney L. Moss, 1999.

Ng, So Kam. *Brushstrokes: Styles and Techniques of Chinese Painting.* San Francisco: Asian Art Museum of San Francisco, 1993.

The Poetry [of] Ink: The Korean Literati Tradition, 1392–1910. Paris: Réunion des Musées Nationaux: Musée National des Arts Asiatiques Guimet, 2005.

Smith, Karen. *Nine Lives: The Birth of Avant-Garde Art in New China.* Zürich: Scalo, 2006.

Till, Barry. *The Manchu Era (1644–1912), Arts of China's Last Imperial Dynasty.* Victoria, BC: Art Gallery of Greater Victoria, 2004.

Vainker, S.J. *Chinese Pottery and Porcelain: From Prehistory to the Present.* London: British Museum Press, 1991.

Watson, William. *The Arts of China 900–1620.* Pelican History of Art. New Haven: Yale Univ. Press, 2000.

Weidner, Marsha Smith. *Views from Jade Terrace: Chinese Women Artists, 1300–1912.* Indianapolis, IN: Indianapolis Museum of Art, 1988.

Xinian, Fu, et al. *Chinese Architecture.* Ed. Nancy S. Steinhardt. New Haven: Yale Univ. Press, 2002.

Chapter 26 Japanese Art after 1333

Addiss, Stephen. *The Art of Zen: Painting and Calligraphy by Japanese Monks, 1600–1925.* New York: Abrams, 1989.

Berthier, François. *Reading Zen in the Rocks: The Japanese Dry Landscape Garden.* Trans. & essay Graham Parkes. Chicago: Univ. of Chicago Press, 2000.

Calza, Gian Carlo. *Ukiyo-e.* New York: Phaidon Press, 2005.

Graham, Patricia J. *Faith and Power in Japanese Buddhist Art, 1600–2005.* Honolulu: Univ. of Hawai'i Press, 2007.

———. *Tea of the Sages: The Art of Sencha.* Honolulu: Univ. of Hawai'i Press, 1998.

Guth, Christine. *Art of Edo Japan: The Artist and the City 1615–1868.* Perspectives. New York: Abrams, 1996.

Hickman, Money L. *Japan's Golden Age: Momoyama.* New Haven: Yale Univ. Press, 1996.

Kobayashi, Tadashi, and Lisa Rotondo-McCord. *An Enduring Vision: 17th to 20th Century Japanese Painting from the Gitter-Yelen Collection.* New Orleans: New Orleans Museum of Art, 2003.

Lillehoji, Elizabeth, ed. *Critical Perspectives on Classicism in Japanese Painting, 1600–1700.* Honolulu: Univ. of Hawai'i Press, 2004.

McKelway, Matthew P. *Traditions Unbound: Groundbreaking Painters of Eighteenth-Century Kyoto.* San Francisco: Asian Art Museum–Chong-Moon Lee Center, 2005.

Meech, Julia, and Jane Oliver. *Designed for Pleasure: The World of Edo Japan in Prints and Paintings, 1680–1860.* Seattle: Univ. of Washington Press in association with the Asia Society and Japanese Art Society of America, New York, 2008.

Miyajima, Shin'ichi and Sato Yasuhiro. *Japanese Ink Painting.* Ed. George Kuwayama. Los Angeles: Los Angeles County Museum of Art, 1985.

Munroe, Alexandra. *Japanese Art after 1945: Scream Against the Sky.* New York: Abrams, 1994.

Murase, Miyeko, ed. *Turning Point: Oribe and the Arts of Sixteenth-Century Japan.* New York: Metropolitan Museum of Art, 2003.

Newland, Amy Reigle, ed. *The Hotei Encyclopedia of Japanese Woodblock Prints.* 2 vols. Amsterdam: Hotei Publishing, 2005.

Ohki, Sadako. *Tea Culture of Japan.* New Haven: Yale Univ. Press, 2009.

Rousmaniere, Nicole, ed. *Crafting Beauty in Modern Japan: Celebrating Fifty Years of the Japan Traditional Art Crafts Exhibition.* Seattle: Univ. of Washington Press, 2007.

Screech, Timon. *The Lens Within the Heart: The Western Scientific Gaze and Popular Imagery in Later Edo Japan.* 2nd ed. Honolulu: Univ. of Hawai'i Press, 2002.

Singer, Robert T., and John T. Carpenter. *Edo, Art in Japan 1615–1868.* Washington, DC: National Gallery of Art, 1998.

Chapter 27 Art of the Americas after 1300

Bauer, Brian S. *Ancient Cuzco: Heartland of the Inca.* Joe R. and Teresa Lozano Long Series in Latin American and Latino Art and Culture. Austin: Univ. of Texas Press, 2004.

Berlo, Janet Catherine, and Ruth B. Phillips. *Native North American Art.* Oxford History of Art. Oxford: Oxford Univ. Press, 1998.

Bringhurst, Robert. *The Black Canoe: Bill Reid and the Spirit of Haida Gwaii.* Seattle: Univ. of Washington Press, l991.

Burger, Richard L., and Lucy C. Salazar, eds. *Machu Picchu: Unveiling the Mystery of the Incas.* New Haven: Yale Univ. Press, 2004.

Coe, Michael D. and Rex Koontz. *Mexico: From the Olmecs to the Aztecs.* 5th ed. New York: Thames & Hudson, 2005.

Fields, Virginia M., and Victor Zamudio-Taylor. *The Road to Aztlan: Art from a Mythic Homeland.* Los Angeles: Los Angeles County Museum of Art, 2001.

Griffin-Pierce, Trudy. *Earth is my Mother, Sky is my Father: Space, Time, and Astronomy in Navajo Sandpainting.* Albuquerque: Univ. of New Mexico Press, 1992.

Jonaitis, Aldona. *Art of the Northwest Coast.* Seattle: Univ. of Washington Press, 2006.

Kaufman, Alice, and Christopher Selser. *The Navajo Weaving Tradition: 1650 to the Present.* New York: Dutton, 1985.

Macnair, Peter L., Robert Joseph, and Bruce Grenville. *Down from the Shimmering Sky: Masks of the Northwest Coast.* Vancouver: Douglas & McIntyre, 1998.

Matos Moctezuma, Eduardo, and Felipe R. Solís Olguín. *Aztecs.* London: Royal Academy of Arts, 2002.

Matthews, Washington. "The Night Chant: A Navaho Ceremony." In *Memoirs of the American Museum of Natural History,* vol. 6. New York, 1902.

Moseley, Michael E. *The Incas and Their Ancestors: The Archaeology of Peru.* Rev. ed. London: Thames & Hudson, 2001.

Nabokov, Peter, and Robert Easton. *Native American Architecture.* New York: Oxford Univ. Press, 1989.

Pasztory, Esther. *Aztec Art.* Norman: Univ. of Oklahoma Press, 2000.

Rushing III, W. Jackson, ed. *Native American Art in the Twentieth Century: Makers, Meanings, Histories.* New York: Routledge, 1999.

Shaw, George Everett. *Art of the Ancestors: Antique North American Indian Art.* Aspen, CO: Aspen Art Museum, 2004.

Taylor, Colin F. *Buckskin & Buffalo: The Artistry of the Plains Indians.* New York: Rizzoli, 1998.

Townsend, Richard F., ed. *The Aztecs.* 2nd rev. ed. Ancient Peoples and Places. London: Thames & Hudson, 2000.

Trimble, Stephen. *Talking with the Clay: The Art of Pueblo Pottery in the 21st Century.* 20th anniversary rev ed. Santa Fe, NM: School for Advanced Research Press, 2007.

Wood, Nancy C. *Taos Pueblo.* New York: Knopf, 1989.

Chapter 28 Art of Pacific Cultures

Caruana, Wally. *Aboriginal Art.* 2nd ed. World of Art. New York: Thames & Hudson, 2003.

Craig, Barry, Bernie Kernot, and Christopher Anderson, eds. *Art and Performance in Oceania.* Honolulu: Univ. of Hawai'i Press, 1999.

D'Alleva, Anne. *Arts of the Pacific Islands.* Perspectives. New York: Abrams, 1998.

Herle, Anita, et al. *Pacific Art: Persistence, Change, and Meaning.* Honolulu: Univ. of Hawai'i Press, 2002.

Kaeppler, Adrienne Lois, Christian Kaufmann, and Douglas Newton. *Oceanic Art.* Trans. Nora Scott and Sabine Bouladon. New York: Abrams, 1997.

Kirch, Patrick Vinton. *The Lapita Peoples: Ancestors of the Oceanic World.* The Peoples of South-East Asia and the Pacific. Cambridge, MA: Blackwell, 1997.

Kjellgren, Eric. *Splendid Isolation: Art of Easter Island.* New York: Metropolitan Museum of Art, 2001.

———, and Carol Ivory. *Adorning the World: Art of the Marquesas Islands.* New Haven: Yale Univ. Press in assoc. with the Metropolitan Museum of Art, 2005.

Küchler, Susanne, and Graeme Were. *Pacific Pattern.* London: Thames & Hudson, 2005.

Lilley, Ian, ed. *Archaeology of Oceania: Australia and the Pacific Islands.* Malden, MA: Blackwell, 2006.

McCulloch, Susan. *Contemporary Aboriginal Art: A Guide to the Rebirth of an Ancient Culture.* Rev. ed. Crows Nest, NSW, Australia: Allen & Unwin, 2001.

Moore, Albert C. *Arts in the Religions of the Pacific: Symbols of Life.* Religion and the Arts Series. New York: Pinter, 1995.

Morphy, Howard. *Aboriginal Art.* London: Phaidon Press, 1998.

Morwood, M.J. *Visions from the Past: The Archaeology of Australian Aboriginal Art.* Washington, DC: Smithsonian Institution Press, 2002.

Neich, Roger, and Mick Pendergrast. *Traditional Tapa Textiles of the Pacific.* London: Thames & Hudson, 1997.

Newton, Douglas, et al. *Arts of the South Seas: Island Southeast Asia, Melanesia, Polynesia, Micronesia; The Collections of the Musée Barbier-Mueller.* Trans. David Radzinowicz Howell. New York: Prestel, 1999.

Rainbird, Paul. *The Archaeology of Micronesia.* Cambridge World Archaeology. New York: Cambridge Univ. Press, 2004.

Smidt, Dirk, ed. *Asmat Art: Woodcarvings of Southwest New Guinea.* New York: George Braziller in assoc. with Rijksmuseum voor Volkenkunde, Leiden, 1993.

Starzecka, D. C., ed. *Maori Art and Culture.* London: British Museum Press, 1996.

Taylor, Luke. *Seeing the Inside: Bark Painting in Western Arnhem Land.* Oxford Studies in Social and Cultural Anthropology. New York: Oxford Univ. Press, 1996.

Thomas, Nicholas. *Oceanic Art.* World of Art. New York: Thames & Hudson, 1995.

———, Anna Cole, and Bronwen Douglas, eds. *Tattoo: Bodies, Art, and Exchange in the Pacific and the West.* Durham, NC: Duke Univ. Press, 2005.

Chapter 29 Art of Africa in the Modern Era

Anatsui, El. *El Anatsui Gawu.* Llandudno, Wales, UK: Oriel Mostyn Gallery, 2003.

Astonishment and Power. Washington, DC: National Museum of African Art, Smithsonian Institution Press, 1993.

Beckwith, Carol, and Angela Fisher. *African Ceremonies.* 2 vols. New York: Abrams, 1999.

Binkley, David A. "Avatar of Power: Southern Kuba Masquerade Figures in a Funerary Context." *Africa—Journal of the International African Institute* 57/1 (1987): 75–97.

Cameron, Elisabeth L. *Art of the Lega.* Los Angeles: UCLA Fowler Museum of Cultural History, 2001.

Cole, Herbert M., ed. *I Am Not Myself: The Art of African Masquerade.* Los Angeles: Fowler Museum of Cultural History, Univ. of California, 1985.

———. *Icons: Ideals and Power in the Art of Africa.* Washington, DC: National Museum of African Art, Smithsonian Institution Press, 1989.

A Fiction of Authenticity: Contemporary Africa Abroad. St. Louis, MO: Contemporary Art Museum St. Louis, 2003.

Fogle, Douglas, and Olukemi Ilesanmi. *Julie Mehretu: Drawing into Painting.* Minneapolis, MN: Walker Art Center, 2003.

Gillow, John. *African Textiles.* San Francisco: Chronicle Books, 2003.

Graham, Gilbert. *Dogon Sculpture: Symbols of a Mythical Universe.* Brookville, NY: Hillwood Art Museum, Long Island Univ., C. W. Post Campus, 1997.

Hess, Janet Berry. *Art and Architecture in Postcolonial Africa.* Jefferson, NC: McFarland, 2006.

Jordán, Manuel, ed. *Chokwe! Art and Initiation Among the Chokwe and Related Peoples.* Munich: Prestel, 1998.

Kasfir, Sidney Littlefield. *Contemporary African Art.* World of Art. London: Thames & Hudson, 2000.

Morris, James, and Suzanne Preston Blier. *Butabu: Adobe Architecture of West Africa.* New York: Princeton Architectural Press, 2004.

Oguibe, Olu, and Okwui Enwezor. *Reading the Contemporary: African Art from Theory to the Marketplace.* Cambridge, MA: MIT Press, 1999.

Pemberton III, John, ed. *Insight and Artistry in African Divination.* Washington, DC: Smithsonian Institution Press, 2000.

Perrois, Louis, and Marta Sierra Delage. *The Art of Equatorial Guinea: The Fang Tribes.* New York: Rizzoli, 1990.

Picton, John, et al. *El Anatsui: A Sculpted History of Africa.* London: Saffron Books in conjunction with the October Gallery, 1998.

Roberts, Mary Nooter, and Allen F. Roberts, eds. *Memory: Luba Art and the Making of History.* New York: Museum for African Art, 1996.

Roy, Christopher D. *Art of the Upper Volta Rivers.* Meudon, France: Chaffin, 1987.

Stepan, Peter. *Spirits Speak: A Celebration of African Masks.* Munich: Prestel, 2005.

Van Damme, Annemieke. *Spectacular Display: The Art of Nkanu Initiation Rituals.* Washington, DC: National Museum of African Art, Smithsonian Institution Press, 2001.

Vogel, Susan Mullin. *Baule: African Art, Western Eyes.* New Haven: Yale Univ. Press, 1997.

Credits

Index

Figures in *italics* refer to illustrations and captions